Perceiving the Arts

Fifth Edition

Perceiving the Arts

An Introduction to the Humanities

Dennis J. Sporre

PRENTICE HALL, Upper Saddle River, New Jersey 07458

Library of Congress Cataloging-in-Publication Data

Sporre, Dennis J.
    Perceiving the arts: an introduction to the humanities / Dennis
J. Sporre. — 5th ed.
        p.   cm.
    Includes bibliographical references and index.
    ISBN 0–13–230236–5
    1. Arts.   2. Perception.   I. Title.
NX620.S68   1997
700′.1—dc20   95–16651
                                                    CIP

Acquisitions editor: Bud Therien
Editorial/production supervision
    and interior design: Jenny Moss
Photo research: Page Poore
Photo editor: Lori Morris-Nantz
Buyer: Bob Anderson
Editorial assistant: Lee Mamunes

This book was set in 10½/12 Bembo by The
Composing Room of Michigan, Inc., and
was printed and bound by RR Donnelley
& Sons Company. The cover was printed by
Phoenix Color Corp.

Printed in the United States of America

10   9   8   7   6   5   4   3   2   1

ISBN 0-13-230236-5

Prentice-Hall International (UK) Limited, *London*
Prentice-Hall of Australia Pty. Limited, *Sydney*
Prentice-Hall Canada Inc., *Toronto*
Prentice-Hall Hispanoamericana, S.A., *Mexico*
Prentice-Hall of India Private Limited, *New Delhi*
Prentice-Hall of Japan, Inc., *Tokyo*
Simon & Schuster Asia Pte. Ltd., *Singapore*
Editora Prentice-Hall do Brasil, Ltda., *Rio de Janeiro*

For my wife Hilda

Contents

The Environmental Arts

The Language Arts

Preface

This book first appeared in 1978. Since then, it has undergone a variety of reprints and new editions, each an effort to improve the substance of the material and to respond to its users' requests. This fifth edition reflects the first time I have undertaken a cover-to-cover review of text and content. Those intimately familiar with the book will see in this edition a leaner and more transparent style. The organization and approach remain the same, but some illustrations have changed in order to reflect not only clarity but cultural diversity. This is a compendium of definitions, not a cultural history. However, it is important that the illustrations of the definitions introduce students to the vast array of art from around the world and from within the rich fabric of American culture. African, African American, Native American, and East Asian cultures are all represented.

Fundamentally, *Perceiving the Arts* has a very specific and limited purpose: to provide an introductory, technical, and respondent-related reference to the arts and literature. Its audience comprises individuals who have little or no knowledge of the arts, and it is designed to give those readers touchstones concerning what to look and listen for in works of art and literature. Such a purpose, attempted in such a short text, is challenging because most artistic terminology and concepts are complex. Many characteristics of the arts change (sometimes subtly and sometimes profoundly) as historical periods and styles change. Further, most artists do not paint, sculpt, compose, or write to neat, fixed formulas. For example, widely used terms like *symphony* have many subtle connotations and can be defined accurately only within specific historical contexts. Nonetheless, our understanding begins with generalities, and the treatment of definitions and concepts in this text remains at that basic and general level. When a course requires more detailed and sophisticated understanding than the basic definitions provided here, an instructor can easily add those layers.

The arts may be approached in a variety of ways. One of those deals with the questions of what we can see and hear in works of art and what we can read in literature. *Perceiving the Arts* takes that approach and relates the arts to the perceptual process. To do that, we adapt Harry Broudy's formulation of aesthetic response. That is, we can ask four questions about an art, an artwork, or a work of literature: (1) What is it? (a formal response); (2) How is it put together? (a technical response); (3) How does it appeal to the senses? (an experiential response); and (4) What does it mean? (a contextual and personal response). These questions constitute a consistent and workable means and comfortable springboard for getting into the arts at a basic level. However, like any categorical device, this one is not foolproof. People don't always agree on definitions of terms and concepts. Also, choices of what to include and exclude, and how best to illustrate, remain arbitrary.

Getting the most from an experience with the arts depends to a large degree on our skills of perception. Knowing what to see and what to hear in a poem, painting, play, building, or musical composition is one step toward developing discriminating perception and toward making effective steps into getting the most from a relationship with the arts. Introducing the aesthetic experience through terminology may be arguable, but the approach gains credence from the College Board statement on "Academic Preparation for College" where use of "the appropriate vocabulary" is emphasized as fundamental. Vocabulary isolates for us characteristics of what to see and hear in individual works of art and helps us focus our perceptions and responses. Knowing the difference between polyphony and homophony, between a suite and a concerto, between prints and paintings, and between fiction and poetry is as important as knowing the difference between baroque and romantic, iconoclasm and cubism.

The arts are accessible to everyone. This text illustrates how much can be approached using the perceptual skills we have been developing since childhood. However, this step is only the beginning. I hope the understanding and confidence readers develop will make them want to make study and involvement with the arts a lifetime venture.

This book originated as a text for an interdisciplinary course in aesthetic perception. The text was designed as an information sourcebook and should be flexible enough to serve any course that examines more than one artistic discipline. Its information is basic and more easily presented in a text than in a lecture. Those whose background is expansive can read it rapidly, pausing to fill in the holes in their background. Students who have no or little experience with the arts can spend the necessary time memorizing. Thus classroom time can be utilized on expanded illustration, discussion, analysis, and experience of actual works. Readers' personal philosophy about the arts and literature should not be affected by this work. For example, when theories, philosophies, or definitions differ, we provide an overview. We might compare this text to a dictionary in a writing course.

The interviews in Chapter 2 introduce a human element into this compendium of terms. Understanding that experiencing art is experiencing another human being is critical. The interviews provide, in an artist's own words, some of the problems, concerns, and processes that the rest of the chapters try to define. Further, the artists interviewed in Chapter 2 are our contemporaries. Comments by historical giants like Beethoven and Mozart are available elsewhere. However, most of our art in the late twentieth century is created by men and women who have not yet reached the status of giants. We need to hear their story and understand their perceptions and concerns.

The photographs in the chapter on landscape architecture are the property of Donald Girouard, and I am extremely grateful to him, Ellis Grove, and Warren Smith for their contributions to this text. Also, I am fundamentally indebted to the editors at Prentice Hall who through the years have been so generous with their assistance and insights. Finally, I am grateful to my wife, Hilda, to whom this book is dedicated, for her patience, editorial and critical assistance, and love.

D. J. S.

What Are the Arts and How Do We Respond to Them?

We live in buildings and listen to music constantly. We hang pictures on our walls and react like personal friends to characters in television, film, and live dramas. We escape to parks, engross ourselves in novels, wonder about a statue in front of a public building, and dance the night away. All of these situations involve forms of art in which we engage and are engaged every day. Curiously, as close to us as they are, in many ways they remain mysterious. What are they? How are they put together? How do they stimulate us? What do they mean? In eleven relatively short chapters, we will attempt to answer those and other questions about the arts. We begin with the questions What *are* the arts? and How do we respond to them?

Humans are a creative species. Whether in science, politics, business, technology, or the arts, we depend on our creativity almost as much as anything else to meet the demands of daily life. Any story about the arts is a story about us: our perceptions of the world as we have come to see and respond to it and the ways we have communicated our understandings to each other since the Ice Age, more than 35,000

years ago (Fig. 1.1). At that time, we were already fully human. Since then, we have learned a great deal about our world and how it functions, and we have changed our patterns of existence. However, the fundamental characteristics that make us human—that is, our ability to intuit and to symbolize—have not changed. Art—the major remaining evidence of our earliest times—reflects these unchanging human characteristics in terms that are inescapable.

Our study will focus on vocabulary and perception, and we begin with an overview about art itself and its place in our world. This chapter provides a foundation. It is more conceptual than the remainder of the book, and the following questions can be used as a guide for reading this material:

- What is meant by the term *humanities?* How do the humanities differ from other ways of knowing?
- What is meant by the statement that the arts are *processes*, *products*, and *experiences?*
- Why does a definition of a work of art imply nonrestrictiveness, human enterprise, a medium of expression, and communication?

Figure 1.1 General view of cave chamber at Lascaux, France, from the early Stone Age (c. 15,000 B.C.). Archiv fur Kunst und Geschichte, Berlin.

- What is a *symbol* and in what ways can it communicate?
- What are the major functions of art?
- How is it possible for a work of art to fulfill more than one function?
- How may religious ritual qualify as art?

THE HUMANITIES AND THE ARTS

The humanities, as opposed, for example, to the sciences, can very broadly be defined as those aspects of culture that look into the human spirit. But despite our desire to categorize, there really are few clear boundaries between the humanities and the sciences. The basic difference lies in the approach that separates investigation of the natural universe, technology, and social science from the sweeping search of the arts for human reality and truth.

Within the educational system, the humanities have traditionally included the fine arts, literature, philosophy, and, sometimes, history. These subjects are all oriented toward exploring what it is to be human, what human beings think and feel, what motivates their actions and shapes their thoughts. Many of the answers lie in the millions of artworks all round the globe, from the earliest sculpted fertility figures to the video art of the 1990s. These artifacts and images are themselves expressions of the humanities, not merely illustrations of past or present ways of life.

Artistic styles, schools, and conventions are the stuff of art history. But change in the arts differs from change in the sciences in one significant way: New technology usually displaces the old; new scientific theory explodes the old; but new art does not invalidate earlier human expression. Obviously, not all artistic styles survive, but the art of Picasso cannot make the art of Rembrandt an idle curiosity of history the way the theories of Einstein did the theories of Newton.

Works of art also remain, in a curious way, always in the present. We react *now* to the sound of a symphony or to the color and composition of a painting. No doubt an historical perspective on the composer or painter and a knowledge of the circumstances in which the art was created enhance understanding and appreciation. But for most of us, today's reaction is most important.

The arts can be approached with all the subtlety we normally apply to human relationships. We learn very young that people cannot simply be categorized as "good" or "bad," as "friends," "acquaintances," or "enemies." We relate in complex ways. Some friendships are pleasant but superficial, some people are easy to work with, and others (but few) are lifelong companions. Similarly, when we have gone beyond textbook categories and learned this sort of sensitivity, we find that art, like friendship, has a major place in our growth and quality of life.

WHAT IS ART?

In a broad sense, the arts are *processes, products,* and *experiences* that communicate aspects of human living in a variety of ways, many of which do not use words. *Processes* are the creative actions, thoughts, materials, and techniques artists combine to create *products*—that is, the artworks. *Experiences* are the human interactions and responses that occur when people encounter the vision of the artist in the artwork. These are a few of the characteristics that identify the arts—as opposed to science, technology, and social science—as vantage points we use to understand our attitudes, actions, and beliefs.

But what is art? Scholars, philosophers, and aestheticians have attempted to answer this question for centuries without yielding many adequate results. The late pop artist Andy Warhol reportedly said, "Art is anything you can get away with" (Fig. 1.2). Perhaps we should be a little less cynical, and a little more specific. Instead of asking "What is art?" let us ask "What is a work of art?" A work of art is one person's vision of human reality (emotions, ideas, values, religions, political beliefs, etc.),

which is expressed in a particular medium and shared with others. Now we can explore the terms of this definition.

Nonrestrictiveness

First, the definition is sufficiently nonrestrictive: An artwork is anything that attempts to communicate a vision of human reality through a means traditionally associated with the arts—for example, drawing, painting, printmaking, sculpture, as well as works of music, dance, literature, film, architecture, and theatre. If the originator *intends* it as a work of art, it is one. Whether it is good or bad, sophisticated or naive, profound or inconsequential, matters little. A child's drawing that expresses some feeling about mother, father, and home is as much an artwork as Michelangelo's Sistine Chapel frescoes. The music of the Grateful Dead and that by Mozart both qualify as artworks under our definition, even though the *qualities* we might ascribe to these artworks probably would be different. (We discuss *value judgments* later in this chapter.)

Human Enterprise

The second implication of our definition is that a work of art is a human enterprise: Whenever we experience a work of art, we are coming into contact with another human being. We experience human contact in works of art because artworks are intended to engage us and to initiate a desire to respond. In the theatre, for example, we are exposed to a variety of visual and aural stimuli that attempt to make us feel, think, or react in harmony with the goals of the artists.

Medium of Expression

Among the problems people may have with an artwork is that of its medium. Although we can readily accept the traditional media—for example, painting, traditional sculpture, music using traditional instruments, theatre using a script and performed in an auditorium, and so

Figure 1.2 Andy Warhol, *Green Coca-Cola Bottles* (1962). Oil on canvas, 6'10" × 4'9". Collection of Whitney Museum of Art, New York. Purchase, with funds from the Friends of the Whitney Museum of American Art.

on—sometimes when a medium of expression does not conform to our expectations or experiences, we might decide that the work is not art. For example, Figures 1.3A and B show one gigantic installation in two parts of blue and yellow umbrellas in Japan and the United States, respectively, created (and entirely financed) by the artists Christo and Jeanne-Claude. For them, this temporary work of art is an artwork. For other people, it most definitely was not. Even though the medium was unconventional and the work transitory, our definition would allow the artwork because the *intent* of the work was clearly artistic.

Communication

Artworks involve communication and sharing. The common factor in all artwork is the humanizing experience; Artists need other people with whom they can share their perception of human reality. When artworks and humans interact, many possibilities exist. Interaction may

Figure 1.3 A and B Christo and Jeanne-Claude, *The Umbrellas, Japan-USA (1984–91).* (A) Valley north of Los Angeles, California, 1,760 yellow umbrellas; (B) Valley in prefecture of Ibaraki, Japan, 1,340 blue umbrellas. Combined length: 30 miles. © Christo, 1991. Photographs: Wolfgang Volz.

be casual and fleeting, as in the first meeting of two people, when one or both are not at all interested in each other. Similarly, an artist may not have much to say, or may not say it very well. For example, a poorly written or produced play probably will not excite an audience. Similarly, if an audience member is self-absorbed, distracted, has rigid preconceptions not met by the production, or is so preoccupied by what may have occurred outside the theatre that he or she finds it impossible to perceive what the production offers, then the artistic experience also fizzles. On the other hand, all conditions

may be optimum, and a profoundly exciting and meaningful experience may occur: The play may treat a significant subject in a unique manner, the acting, directing, and design may be excellent, and the audience may be receptive. Or the interaction may fall somewhere between these two extremes. In any case, the experience is a human one, and one that is fundamental to art.

In discussing art as communication, we need to note one important term, and that is *symbol*. Symbols are things that *represent* something else. They often use a material object to suggest something less tangible or less obvious: a wedding ring, for example. Symbols differ from *signs,* which suggest a fact or condition. Signs are what they denote. Symbols carry deeper, wider, and richer meanings. Look at Figure 1.4. What do you see? You might identify this figure as a sign, which looks like a plus sign in arithmetic. But the figure might be a Greek cross, in which case it becomes a symbol because it suggests many images, meanings, and implications. Artworks use a variety of symbols to convey meaning. By using symbols, artworks can relay meanings that go well beyond the surface of the work and offer glimpses of human reality that cannot be sufficiently described in any other manner. Symbols make artworks into doorways through which we pass in order to experience, in limited time and space, more of the human condition.

The Functions of Art

Art can function in many ways: as enjoyment, political and social weapon, therapy, and artifact. One function is no more important than the others. Nor are they mutually exclusive; one artwork may fill many functions. Nor are the four functions just mentioned the only ones. Rather, they serve as indicators of how art has functioned in the past and can function in the present. Like the types and styles of art that have occurred through history, these four functions and others are options for artists and

Figure 1.4 Greek cross?

depend on what artists wish to do with their artworks.

Enjoyment

Plays, paintings, and concerts can provide escape from everyday cares, treat us to a pleasant time, and engage us in social occasions. Works of art that provide enjoyment may perform other functions as well. The same artworks we enjoy may also create insights into human experience. We can also glimpse the conditions of other cultures, and we can find healing therapy in enjoyment.

An artwork in which one individual finds only enjoyment may function as a profound social and personal comment to another. A Mozart symphony, for example, may relax us and allow us to escape our cares. It may also comment on the life of the composer and/or the conditions of eighteenth-century Austria. Grant Wood's *American Gothic* (Fig. 1.5) may amuse us, and/or provide a detailed commentary about nineteenth-century America, and/or move us deeply. The result depends on the artist, the artwork, and us.

Political and Social Commentary

Art used to bring about political change or to modify the behavior of large groups of people has political or social functions. In ancient Rome, for example, the authorities used music and theatre to keep masses of unemployed people occupied in order to quell urban unrest. At the same time, Roman playwrights used plays to attack incompetent or corrupt officials. The Greek playwright Aristophanes used comedy in such plays as *The Birds* to attack the political ideas of the leaders of ancient Athenian society. In *Lysistrata,* he attacks war by creating a story in which all the women of Athens go on a sex strike until Athens is rid of war and warmongers.

In nineteenth-century Norway, Henrik Ibsen used *An Enemy of the People* as a platform for airing the issue of whether a government

Figure 1.5 Grant Wood, American (1891–1942), *American Gothic* (1930). Oil on beaver board, 30″ × 25″. Friends of American Art Collection. Photograph © 1990. The Art Institute of Chicago. All rights reserved.

should ignore pollution in order to maintain economic well-being. In the United States in the 1990s, many artworks act as vehicles to advance social and political causes, or to sensitize viewers, listeners, or readers to particular cultural situations like racial prejudice and AIDS.

Therapy

In a therapeutic function, creating and experiencing works of art may provide therapy for individuals with a variety of illnesses, both physical and mental. Role playing, for example, is used frequently as a counseling tool in treating dysfunctional family situations. In this context, often called psychodrama, mentally ill patients act out their personal circumstances in order to find and cure the cause of their illness. The focus of this use of art as therapy is the individual. However, art in a much broader context acts as a healing agent for society's general illnesses as well. In hopes of saving us from disaster, artists use artworks to illustrate the failings and excesses of society. In another vein, the laughter caused by comedy releases endorphins, chemicals produced by the brain, which strengthen the immune system.

Artifact

Art also functions as an *artifact:* A product of a particular time and place, an artwork represents the ideas and technology of that specific time and place. Artworks often provide not only striking examples but occasionally the only tangible records of some peoples. Artifacts, like paintings, sculptures, poems, plays, and buildings, enhance our insights into many cultures, including our own. Consider, for example, the many revelations we find in a sophisticated work like the Igbo-Ukwu roped pot on a stand (Fig. 1.6). This ritual water pot from the village of Igbo-Ukwu in eastern Nigeria was cast using the *cire perdue* or "lost wax" process and is amazing in its virtuosity. It

Figure 1.6 Roped pot on a stand, from Igbo-Ukwu (ninth or tenth century). Leaded bronze, height 12¹/₂″. The National Museum, Lagos.

tells us much about the vision and technical accomplishment of this ninth- and tenth-century African society.

The Igbo-Ukwu pot suggests that when we examine art in the context of cultural artifact, one of the issues we face is the use of artworks in religious ritual. We could consider ritual as a separate function of art. However, we may not think of religious ritual as art at all, but in the context we have adopted for this text, ritual often meets our definition of human communication using an artistic medium. Music, for example, when part of a religious ceremony, meets the definition, and theatre—if seen as an occasion planned and intended for presentation—would include religious rituals as well as events that take place in theatres. Often, as a survey of art history would confirm, we cannot discern when ritual stops and secular production starts. For example, Ancient Greek tragedy seems clearly to have evolved from and maintained ritualistic practices. When ritual, planned and intended for presentation, uses traditionally artistic media like music, dance, and theatre, we can legitimately study ritual as art, and see it also as an artifact of its particular culture.

What Is Art Criticism?

One of the questions we all seem to ask about an artwork is, "Is it any good?" Whether rock music, a film, a play, a painting, or a classical symphony, judgments about the quality of a work often vary from one extreme to the other, ranging from "I liked it" and "interesting," to specific reasons why the artwork is thought to be effective or ineffective.

Because the word *criticism* implies many things to many people, we must first agree what it means—or what it does not. Criticism is not necessarily saying negative things about a work of art. All too often we think of critics as people who write or say essentially negative things, giving their opinions on the value of a play, a concert, or an exhibition. (We will learn more on that subject in Chapter 2.) Personal judgment may result from criticism, but criticism implies more than passing judgment.

Criticism should be a detailed process of analysis to gain understanding and appreciation. Identifying the formal elements of an artwork—learning what to look for or listen to—is the first step. We describe an artwork by examining its many facets and then try to understand how they work together to create meaning or experience. We then try to state what that meaning or experience is. Only when the process is complete should the critic offer judgment.

The critic, however, also brings a set of standards developed essentially from personal experience. Applying these standards makes value judgment a tricky task. Our *knowledge* of an art form can be shallow. Our *perceptual skills* may be faulty, the range of our *experiences* may be limited. The application of standards may be especially difficult if we try to judge an artwork as good or bad based on preestablished criteria: If someone believes a plot is the most important element in a film or a play, then any film or play that does not depend heavily on a plot may be judged as faulty, despite other qualities it presents. Preestablished criteria often deny critical acclaim to new or experimental approaches in the arts.

History is full of examples of new artistic attempts that received terrible receptions from so-called experts, whose ideas of what an artwork ought to be could not allow for experimentation or departures from accepted practice. In 1912, when Vaslav Nijinsky choreographed the ballet *Rite of Spring* to music by Igor Stravinsky, the unconventional music and choreography actually caused a riot: Audiences and critics could not tolerate that the ballet did not conform to accepted musical and ballet standards. Today, both the music and the choreography are considered masterpieces. Similarly, Samuel Beckett's *Waiting for Godot* (1953) (Fig. 1.7) does not have a plot, characters, or thoughts that are expressed in the conventional manner of the late nineteenth century. In *Godot* two tramps wait beside the road by a withered tree for the arrival of someone named Godot. The tramps tell stories to each other, argue, eat some food, and are interrupted by a character named Pozzo leading a slave, Lucky, by a rope. After a brief conversation, Lucky and Pozzo leave. At the end of the first act, a boy enters to announce that Godot will not come today. In Act 2, much the same sequence of events occurs. Then, Lucky leads in a blind Pozzo. The tree has sprouted a few leaves. The play ends as the young boy returns to indicate Godot will not arrive that day either. If your standards require a successful play to have a carefully fash-

Figure 1.7 Samuel Beckett, *Waiting for Godot*, Utah Shakespearean Festival (1990). Director: Tom Marlens.

ioned plot wrapped around fully developed characters and a clear message, then *Waiting for Godot* cannot possibly be a good play. Some people agree with such an assertion; others disagree vehemently. What, then, are we to conclude? What if my criteria do not match yours? What if two experts disagree on the quality of a movie? Does that make any difference to our experience of it?

Value judgments are intensely personal, but some opinions are more informed than others and represent more authoritative judgment. However, sometimes even knowledgeable people disagree. Disagreements about quality, however, can enhance our experience of a work of art when they lead us to think about why the differences exist. In this way, we gain a deeper understanding of the artwork. Nonetheless, criticism can be exercised without involving any judgment. We can thoroughly dissect any

work of art and describe what it comprises—for example, we can describe and analyze line, color, melody, harmony, texture, plot, character, and/or message. We can observe how all of these factors affect people and their responses. We can spend a significant amount of time doing this and never pass a value judgment at all.

Does this discussion mean all artworks are equal in value? Not at all. It means that in order to understand what criticism involves, we must separate descriptive analysis, which can be satisfying in and of itself, from the act of passing value judgments. We may not like the work we have analyzed, but we may have understood something we did not understand before. Passing judgment may play no role whatsoever in our understanding of an artwork. But we are still involved in *criticism*.

As an exercise in understanding, criticism is

necessary. We must investigate and describe. We must experience the need to know enough about the process, product, and experience of art if we are to have perceptions to share.

Now that we have examined briefly what criticism is and why we might do it, what criteria or approaches can we use?

Types of Criticism

In general, there are two types of criticism. If we examine a single artwork by itself, it is called *formal criticism*. If we examine the same work in the context of the events surrounding it or, perhaps, the circumstances of its creation, it is called *contextual criticism*.

Formal Criticism

In formal criticism, we are interested primarily in the artwork itself, applying no external conditions or information. We analyze the artwork just as we find it: If it is a painting, we look only within the frame; if it is a play, we analyze only what we see and hear. Formal criticism approaches the artwork as an entity within itself. As an example, consider this brief analysis of Molière's comedy *Tartuffe* (1664) (Fig. 1.8):

> Orgon, a rich bourgeois, has allowed a religious con man, Tartuffe, to gain complete control over him. Tartuffe has moved into Orgon's house, and tries to seduce Orgon's wife at the same time he is planning to marry Orgon's daughter. Tartuffe is unmasked, and Orgon orders him out. Tartuffe seeks his revenge by claiming title to Orgon's house and blackmailing him with some secret papers. At the very last instant, Tartuffe's plans are foiled by the intervention of the king, and the play ends happily.

We have just described a story. Were we to go one step further and analyze the plot, we

Figure 1.8 Jean-Baptiste Molière, *Tartuffe*. University of Arizona Theatre (1990). Director: Charles O'Connor.

would look, among other things, for points at which *crises* occur and cause important decisions to be made by the characters; we would also want to know how those decisions moved the play from one point to the next. In addition, we would try to locate the extreme crisis, the *climax*. Meanwhile, we would discover auxiliary parts of plot such as *reversals*—for example, when Tartuffe is discovered and the characters become aware of the true situation. Depending on how detailed our criticism were to become, we could work our way through each and every aspect of the plot. We might then devote some time to describing and analyzing the driving force—the *character*—of each person in the play and how the characters relate to each other. Has Molière created fully developed characters? Are they types or do they seem to behave more or less like real individuals? In examining the *thematic* elements of the play, we would no doubt conclude the play deals with religious hypocrisy and that Molière had a particular point of view on that subject.

In this formal approach, information about the playwright, previous performances, historic relationships, and so on, is irrelevant. Thus the formal approach helps us analyze how an artwork operates and helps us decide why the artwork produces the responses it does. We can apply this form of criticism to any work of art and come away with a variety of conclusions. Of course, knowledge about how artworks are put together, what they are, and how they stimulate the senses enhances the critical process. Knowing the basic elements that comprise formal and technical elements of the artwork (which are the subjects of the succeeding chapters of this book) gives us a ready outline on which to begin a formal analysis.

Contextual Criticism

The other general approach, contextual criticism, seeks meaning by adding to formal criticism an examination of related information outside the artwork, such as facts about the artist's life, his or her culture, social and political conditions and philosophies, public and critical responses to the work, and so on. These can all be researched and applied to the work in order to enhance perception and understanding. Contextual criticism views the artwork as an artifact generated from particular contextual needs, conditions, and/or attitudes. If we carry our criticism of *Tartuffe* in this direction, we would note that certain historical events help clarify the play. For example, the object of Molière's attention probably was the Company of the Holy Sacrament, a secret, conspiratorial, and influential religious society in France at the time. Like many fanatical religious sects—including those of our own time—the society sought to enforce its own view of morality by spying on the lives of others and seeking out heresies—in this case, in the Roman Catholic church. Its followers were religious fanatics, and they had considerable impact on the lives of the citizenry at large. If we were to follow this path of criticism, we would pursue any and all contextual matters that might illuminate or clarify what happens in the play. Contextual criticism may also employ the same kind of internal examination followed in the formal approach.

Making Judgments

Now that we have defined criticism and noted two approaches we might take in pursuit of understanding and enjoying a work of art, we can move on to the final step: making value judgments.

There are several approaches to the act of judgment. Two characteristics, however, apply to all artworks: Artworks are *crafted* and they *communicate* something to us about our experiences as humans. Making a judgment about the quality of an artwork should address each of these characteristics.

Craftsmanship

Is the work well made? To make this judgment, we first need some understanding of the medium in which the artist works. For example, if the artist proposes to give us a realistic vision of a tree, does the artist's handling of the paint yield a tree that looks like a tree? If craftsmanship depended only on the ability to portray objects realistically, judgment would be quite simple. However, we must remember that judgments about the craftsmanship of an artwork require some knowledge about the techniques and styles of its medium. Although we may not yet be ready to make judgments about all of the aspects of craftsmanship in any art form, we can apply what we know. Good craftsmanship means the impact of the work will have clarity and not be confusing. It also means the work will hold our interest (given basic understanding and attention on our part). If the artwork does not appear coherent or interesting, we may wish to examine whether the fault lies in the artwork or in ourselves before rendering judgment. Beyond that, we are left to learn the lessons that the rest of this book seeks to teach. Each chapter will give us more tools to evaluate the craftsmanship of a work of art.

Communication

Evaluating what an artwork is trying to say offers more immediate opportunity for judgment and less need for expertise. Johann Wolfgang von Goethe, the nineteenth-century poet, novelist, and playwright, set out a basic, commonsense approach to communication. Because Goethe's approach provides an organized means for discovering an artwork's communication by progressing from analytical to judgmental functions, it is a helpful way to end our discussion on criticism. Goethe suggests that we approach the critical process by asking three questions: What is the artist trying to say? Does he or she succeed? Was the artwork worth the effort? These three questions focus on the artist's communication by making us identify first what was being attempted, and then on the artist's success in that attempt. The third question, whether or not the project was worth the effort, raises other issues, such as uniqueness or profundity. This question asks us to decide if the communication offered important or unique perceptions (as opposed to the trivial or inane). A well-crafted work of art that merely restates obvious insights about the human condition lacks quality in its communicative component. One that offers profound and unique insights exhibits quality.

We should be wiser, I believe, to think of the arts more as we think of people. We learn, most of us, at a very early age that an adequate adjustment to the world cannot be made from social responses that simply divide the "good people" from the "bad people." We have learned to be skeptical even of such categories as "the people I like" and "the people I don't like." If we do maintain such divisions, we find individuals constantly moving from one group to the other. Eventually we find human differences too subtle for easy classification, and the web of our relationships becomes too complex for analysis. We try to move toward more and more sensitive discrimination, so that there are those we can learn from, those we can work with, those good for an evening of light talk, those we can depend on for a little affection, and so on—with perhaps those very few with whom we can sustain a deepening relationship for an entire lifetime. When we have learned this same sensitivity and adjustment to works of art—when we have gone beyond the easy categories of the textbooks and have learned to regard our art relationships as part of our own growth—then we shall have achieved a dimension in living that is as deep and as irreplaceable as friendship.

LIVING WITH THE ARTS

Because of unfamiliarity, many individuals are uncomfortable approaching the arts and literature. That unfamiliarity, perhaps, has been fostered by individuals, both within the disciplines and without, who try to make involvement in the arts and literature elitist, and art galleries, museums, concert halls, theatres, and opera houses open only to the knowledgeable and the sophisticated. Nothing could be further from actuality. As we suggest by the title of this section, the arts are elements of life with which we can and must deal and to which we must respond every day. We live with the arts because the principles of *aesthetics* permeate our existence. Specifically, the aesthetic experience is a way of knowing and communicating in and of itself, separate from other ways of knowing and communicating. It forms a significant part of our existence.

The arts play important roles in making the world around us a more interesting and habitable place. Artistic ideas join with *conventions* to make everyday objects attractive and pleasurable to use. The term *convention* is one we use repeatedly in this text. A convention is a set of rules or mutually accepted conditions. For example, that all of our electrical appliances have a standard male connector that we can be relatively assured fits every wall socket in every building in the United States is a convention. It is a practical convention to which those who have traveled abroad can testify. A more relevant example of a convention might be the keyboard and tuning of a piano. In any case, from these two examples we can clearly imagine the role that conventions play in our lives.

Figure 1.9, a scale drawing of an eighteenth-century highboy, illustrates how art and con-

Figure 1.9 Scale drawing of an eighteenth-century highboy.

vention combine in everyday items. The high chest was conceived to fill a practical purpose—to provide for storage of household objects in an easily accessible, yet hidden, place. However, while designing an object to accommodate that practical need, the cabinetmakers felt the additional need to provide an interesting and attractive object. Our total experience of this piece of furniture can be enlightening and challenging if we perceive it with discrimination and imagination.

First of all, the design is controlled by a convention that dictates a consistent height for tables and desks. So the lower portion of the chest, from point A to point B, designs space within a height that will harmonize with other furniture in the room. If we look carefully, we also can see that the parts of the chest are designed with a sophisticated and interesting series of proportional and progressive relationships. The distance from A to B is twice the distance from A to D and is equal to the distance from B to C. The distances from A to F and C to E bear no recognizable relationship to the previous dimensions but are, however, equal to each other and to the distances from G to H, H to I, and I to J. In addition, the size of the drawers in the upper chest decreases at an even and proportional rate from bottom to top.

A further example might be the Volkswagen shown in Figure 1.10. Here repetition of form reflects a concern for unity, one of the fundamental characteristics of art. The design of the early Volkswagen used strong repetition of the oval. We need only to look at the rear of the Bug to see variation on this theme as applied in the window, motor-compartment hood, taillights, fenders, and bumper. Later models of the Volkswagen differ from this version and reflect

the intrusion of conventions, again, into the world of design. As safety standards called for larger bumpers, the oval design of the motor-compartment hood was flattened so a larger bumper could clear it. The rear window was enlarged and squared to accommodate the need for increased rear vision. The intrusion of these conventions changed the design of the Beetle by breaking down the strong unity of the original composition.

Finally, as Edwin J. Delattre states when he compares the purpose for studying technical subjects to the purpose for studying the humanities or the arts, "When a person studies the mechanics of internal combustion engines the intended result is that he should be better able to understand, design, build, or repair such engines, and sometimes he should be better able to find employment because of his skills, and thus better his life. . . . When a person studies the humanities [the arts] the intended result is that he should be better able to understand, design, build, or repair a life—for living is a vocation we have in common despite our differences.

"The humanities provide us with opportunities to become more capable in thought, judgment, communication, appreciation, and action." Delattre goes on to say that these pro-

Figure 1.10 Volkswagen Beetle (1953). Courtesy of Volkswagen of America.

visions enable us to think more rigorously and to imagine more abundantly. "These activities free us to possibilities that are new, at least to us, and they unbind us from portions of our ignorance about living well . . . Without exposure to the cultural . . . traditions that are our heritage, we are excluded from a common world that crosses generations."* The poet Archibald MacLeish is more succinct: "Without the Arts, how can the university teach the Truth?"

The information in this text helps us understand the elements that comprise works of art, which we can respond to and which make our experiences more rewarding.

AESTHETIC PERCEPTION AND RESPONSE

In this chapter we have examined the nature of the arts and a bit of their relationship to life. The question of how we go about approaching them, or how we study them, is another challenge. A myriad of methods is available, and so it remains to choose one and carry on from there. The purpose of this book is to provide a concentrated reference that covers all the arts. We assume those who are interested in such a work have had only limited exposure to the arts. So we have chosen a method of study that can act as a springboard into the arts and literature, as a point of departure from the realm of the familiar into the unknown. Inasmuch as we live in a world of facts and figures, weights and measures, it seems logical to begin our study by dealing with some concrete characteristics. In other words, from mostly an intellectual point of view, what can we see and what can we hear in the arts and literature?

*Edwin J. Delattre, "The Humanities Can Irrigate Deserts," *The Chronicle of Higher Education,* October 11, 1977, p. 32.

To put that question in different terms, how can we sharpen our aesthetic perception?

- First of all, we must identify those items that can be seen and heard in works of art and literature.
- Second, we must learn—just as we learn a foreign language—some of the terminology relating to those items.
- Third, we must understand why and how what we perceive relates to our response.

It is, after all, our response to an artwork that interests us. We can *perceive* an object. We *choose* to *respond* to it in aesthetic terms.

We need to employ a consistent method as we pass from one art discipline to another. We will ask three questions: (1) What is it? (2) How is it put together? (3) How does it stimulate our senses? We will study these questions in each of the art disciplines. As we will see, these are also the basic questions we can ask about individual artworks.

When we respond to the question *What is it?* we make a *formal* response. We recognize we are perceiving the two-dimensional space of a picture, the three-dimensional space of a sculpture or a piece of architecture, or perhaps time in sound, or time and space in dance. We also recognize the form of the item—for example, a still life, a human figure, a tragedy, a ballet, a concerto, a narrative film, a park, or a residence. The term *form* is a broad one: There are *art forms, forms* of arts, and *forms* in art.

When we respond to the question *How is it put together?* we respond to the technical elements of the artwork. We recognize and respond to, for instance, the fact that the picture has been done in oil, made by a printmaking technique, or created as a watercolor. We also recognize and respond to the elements that constitute the work, the items of composition—line, form or shape, mass, color, repetition, harmony—and the unity that results from all of these. What devices have been employed, and how does each part relate to the others to make a whole? A concerto is composed of melody, harmony, timbre, tone, and more; a tragedy utilizes language, mise-en-scène, exposition, complication, denouement; a ballet has formalized movement, mise-en-scène, line, idea content, and so on.

Moving to the third question, we examine *how the work stimulates our senses*—and why. In other words, how do the particular formal and technical arrangements (whether conscious or unconscious on the part of the artist) elicit a sense response from us? Here we deal with physical and mental properties. For example, our response to sculpture can be physical. We can touch a piece of sculpture and sense its smoothness or its hardness. In contrast, we experience sense responses that are essentially mental. For example, upright triangles give us a sense of solidity. When we perceive the colors green and blue we call them "cool"; reds and yellows are "warm" colors. Pictures that are predominantly horizontal or composed of broad curves are said to be "soft" or placid. Angular, diagonal, or short, broken lines stimulate a sense of movement. Music that utilizes undulating melodic contours can be "smooth"; music that is highly consonant can be "warm" or "rich." These and other sense responses tend to be universal; most individuals respond in similar fashion to them.

We also can ask a fourth question about a work of art: *What does the work mean?* We may answer that question in strictly personal terms, for example, a painting may remind us of some personal experience. However, we cannot dismiss the question *What does it mean?* as a reference to purely personal experience. Meaning in a work of art implies a certain level of communication from artist to respondent. A work of art, including literature,* *is a way of looking*

*From here on, *art* and *artwork* can be assumed to include literary works as well.

at the universe that is manifested in a particular medium and shared with others. So the ultimate response, meaning, and experience of an artwork goes beyond opinion to encompass an attempt to understand what the communicator may have had in mind. It is not sufficient, for example, merely to regard the disproportionate forms of a Mannerist painting as "strange." *Meaning* implies an understanding of the discomforting circumstances of religion and society that existed during that period. When we understand that, we may understand *why* the paintings of that period appear as they do. We may also sympathize with the agonies of individuals trying to cope with their universe. As a result, the "strangeness" of the artwork may come to mean something entirely different to us personally. Sometimes meaning in an artwork can be enhanced by understanding cultural or historical contexts, including biography. Sometimes artworks spring from purely aesthetic necessity. Sometimes it is difficult to know which case applies or whether both cases apply.

In this book, we delve into only the first three questions (What is it? How is it put together? How does it stimulate our senses?) because the fourth involves a great deal more information than our space allows.

STYLE IN THE ARTS

A work of art or an art form is a way of looking at the universe that is manifested in a particular medium and shared with others. That summation indicates briefly what the aesthetic experience is about. The manner in which artists express themselves constitutes their style. Style is tantamount to the personality of an artwork. However, applying its connotations to a body of artworks calls for breadth and depth of knowledge. Style is that body of characteristics that identifies an artwork with an individual, a historical period, a school of artists, or a nation. Applying the term means assimilating materials and drawing conclusions.

Therefore, determining the style of any artwork requires analysis of how the artist has arranged the characteristics applicable to his or her medium. If the usage is similar to others, we might conclude they exemplify the same style. For example, Bach and Handel typify the *baroque* style in music; Haydn and Mozart, the *classical*. Listening to works by these composers quickly leads to the conclusion that the ornate melodic developments of Bach are like those of Handel, and quite different from the precise concern for structure and clearly articulated motifs of Mozart and Haydn. The precision and symmetry of the Parthenon compared with the ornate opulence of the Palace of Versailles suggest that in line and form the archi-

tects of these buildings treated their medium differently. Yet the design of the Parthenon is very much a visual companion, stylistically, of Mozart and Haydn; Versailles reflects an approach to design similar to that of Bach and Handel.

We can take our examination one step further and play a game of stylistic analysis with four paintings. The first three of these paintings were done by three different artists; the fourth, by one of those three. By stylistic analysis we will determine the painter of the fourth painting. Inasmuch as we have not yet dealt with definitions in composition, our analysis will be as nontechnical as possible. We use three characteristics only: *line, palette,* and *brush stroke.*

The first painting (Fig. 1.11) is Corot's

Figure 1.11 Jean-Baptiste-Camille Corot, French (1796–1875), *A View Near Volterra* (1838). Canvas, 27³/₈″ × 37¹/₂″. National Gallery of Art, Washington, D.C. Chester Dale Collection. (See also color insert Plate 6.)

A View Near Volterra. We can see that Corot has used curvilinear line primarily, and that line (which creates the edges of the forms or shapes in the painting) is somewhat softened. That is, many of the forms—the rocks, trees, clouds, and so on—do not have crisp, clear edges. Color areas tend to blend with each other, giving the painting a softened, somewhat fuzzy or out-of-focus appearance. That comfortable effect is heightened by Corot's use of *palette.* Palette, as we note later, encompasses the total use of color and contrast, and because our illustrations are black and white we can deal with only one aspect of palette: *value contrast.* As with his use of line, Corot maintains a subtle value contrast—that is, a subtle relationship of blacks to whites. His movement from light to dark is gradual, and he avoids stark contrasts. He employs a full range of black, grays, and whites, but does so without calling attention to their positioning. His *brush stroke* is somewhat apparent: If we look carefully, we can see brush marks, individual strokes where paint has been applied. Even though the objects in the painting are lifelike, Corot has not made any pretensions about the fact that his picture has been painted. We can tell the foliage was executed by stippling (by dabbing the brush to the canvas as you would dot an "i" with a pencil). Likewise, we can see marks made by the brush throughout the painting. The overall effect of the painting is one of realism, but we can see in every area the spontaneity with which it was executed.

The second painting (Fig. 1.12) is Picasso's *Guernica.* We hardly need be an expert to tell that this painting is by a different painter—or certainly in a different style than the previous one. Picasso has joined curved lines and straight lines, placing them in such relationships that they create movement and dissonance. The edges of color areas and forms are sharp and distinct; nothing here is soft or fuzzy. Likewise, the value contrasts are stark and extreme. Areas of the highest value—that is, white—are forced against areas of the lowest value—black. In fact, the range of tonalities is far less broad than in the previous work. The mid or medium (gray) tones are there, but they play a minor role in the effect of the palette. Our examination of palette does not suffer here because the work is executed only in blacks, whites, and grays. The

Figure 1.12 Pablo Picasso, *Guernica* (mural) (1937, May–early June). Oil on canvas, 11′5¹⁄₂″ × 25′8″. Museo del Prado.

starkness of the work is also reinforced by brush stroke, which is noteworthy in its near *absence* of effect. Tonal areas are flat, and few traces of brush exist.

The third painting (Fig. 1.13) is van Gogh's *The Starry Night*. Use of line is highly active although uniformly curvilinear. Forms and color areas have both hard and soft edges, and van Gogh, like Picasso, uses outlining to strengthen his images and reduce their reality. The overall effect of line is a sweeping and undulating movement, highly dynamic and yet far removed from the starkness of the Picasso. In contrast, van Gogh's curvilinearity and softened edges are quite different in effect from the relaxed quality of the Corot. Van Gogh's value contrasts are very broad, but moderate. He ranges from darks through medium grays to white, all virtually equal in importance. Even

when movement from one area to another is across a hard edge to a highly contrasting value, the result is moderate: not soft, not stark. It is, however, brush stroke that gives the painting its unique personality. We can see thousands of individual brush marks where the artist applied paint to canvas. The nervous, almost frenetic use of brush stroke makes the painting come alive.

Now that we have examined three paintings in different styles and by different artists, can you determine which of the three painted Figure 1.14? First, examine the use of line. Form and color edges are hard. Outlining is used. Curved and straight lines are *juxtaposed* against each other. The effect is active and stark. By comparison, use of line is not like Corot, a bit like van Gogh, and very much like Picasso. Next, examine palette. Darks, grays, and whites

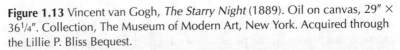

Figure 1.13 Vincent van Gogh, *The Starry Night* (1889). Oil on canvas, 29″ × 36¼″. Collection, The Museum of Modern Art, New York. Acquired through the Lillie P. Bliss Bequest.

Figure 1.14 Exercise painting. See color insert Plate 5 for identification.

are used broadly. However, the principal utilization is of strong contrast—the darkest darks against the whitest whites. This is not like Corot, a bit like van Gogh, and most like Picasso. Finally, brush stroke is generally unobtrusive. Tonal areas mostly are flat. This is definitely not a van Gogh and probably not a Corot. Three votes out of three go to Picasso, and the style is so distinctive you probably had

no difficulty deciding, even without the analysis. However, could you have been so certain if asked whether Picasso painted Figure 1.15? A work by another cubist painter would pose even greater difficulty. So some differences in style are obvious; some are unclear. Distinguishing the work of one artist from another who designs in a similar fashion becomes even more challenging. However, the analytical

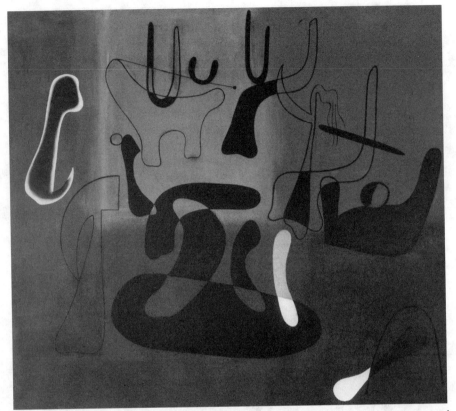

Figure 1.15 Joan Miró, *Painting* (1933). Oil on canvas, 68¹/₂″ × 77¹/₄″. The Museum of Modern Art, New York. Loula D. Lasker Bequest (by exchange). Photograph © 1995 The Museum of Modern Art, New York. (See also color insert Plate 3.)

process we just completed is indicative of how we can approach artworks to determine *how* they exemplify a given style, or what style they reflect.

We recognize differences in style sometimes without thinking much about it. Our experience or formal training need not be extensive to recognize the buildings in Figure 1.16 and 1.18 reflect different cultural circumstances. The Russian Orthodox Church in Figure 1.16

Figure 1.16 The Church of Nikolai Khamovnik (1679–1682). Moscow, Russia. (See also color insert Plate 1.)

Figure 1.17 Detail, front portal, The Church of Nikolai Khamovnik (1679–1682). Moscow, Russia.

(see also color insert Plate 1) is distinguishable by its characteristic domes and by the icons that decorate its walls (Fig. 1.17). In the same sense, the tomb in Figure 1.18 is typically Moslem, identifiable by its arch.

The decorative embellishment (Fig. 1.19), in contrast to the icons of the Orthodox church, reflects the prohibition of the Islamic faith of depicting human form in architectural decoration.

23

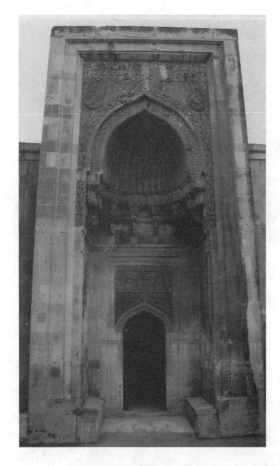

Figure 1.18 Tomb of the Shirvanshah (fifteenth century A.D.). Baku, Azerbaijan.

Figure 1.19 Detail, entrance portal, Tomb of the Shirvanshah (fifteenth century A.D.). Baku, Azerbaijan.

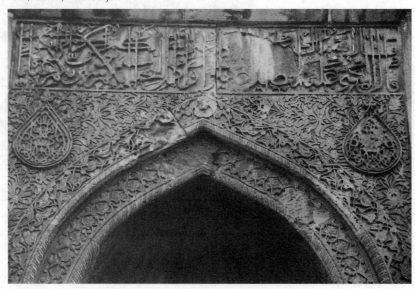

2

The Human Process

Every work of art has a person behind it. Part of our involvement in and response to artworks immerses us in a relationship with the ideas and choices of the person who made the work. We don't necessarily need to know anything about the person who made the art in order to respond to it, but our enjoyment of the experience can be enhanced when we realize that this person—the artist—went through processes, anguishes, and decisions in order to give birth to the work. In this chapter three artists and a critic discuss some of the issues involved in their personal approaches. These four individuals are not famous, but they are successful and reasonably well known among their peers. They give us a glimpse of the human side of a work of art.

First, a critic discusses his role in the aesthetic process. He gives some controversial opinions on what skills and background a critic needs, and how he approaches the same performance relative to his differing readership. He expands on his relationship to art, to artists, to the role of art, and to the public, and finally gives his opinion of what the arts need to do to fulfill *their* role in society.

Next, a painter describes the elusive quality of development and achievement. He wonders about the nature of growth as an artist, the need to survive, and the relation between the two. Within that relationship of growth and survival, a delicate balance sometimes exists between communicating what the artist feels and what he knows will sell. There also exists a problem of wishing to speak in visual language to a mass audience who cannot speak or understand that language. Yet the need to communicate persists. Finally, the painter discusses how an artwork is developed, what makes an appropriate subject, and how the medium in which he works relates to the final product.

A musician discusses the framework of balance among the various artists who contribute to a musical presentation, the composer, the conductor, the players. Like the painter's, the musician's work is the result of a developmental process. However, creation of a score and interpretation and performance of it require different talents and procedures. Yet music needs to be communicated, and the audience as a whole plays a role in that process for the musician. In addition, because music occupies time only, the art itself places certain constraints on the artist—what he can or cannot communicate and what goals he may set for himself.

Finally, a theatre director faces some of the same problems the musician does: Usually, he must use other performers and his own creativity to shape a work not of his own creation. The director, in my interview with him, speculates on his role as a collaborator, yet leader. The factor of human-to-human response in the live theatre brings the audience into a more forceful role in the communicative process, and direct control of audience response becomes a part of the director's concern.

THE CRITIC AND CRITICISM

Interview with Philip Radcliffe

Educated at the University of Sheffield and Cambridge University in England, Philip Radcliffe has been Head of Communications at the University of Manchester, England, and a critic of music and theatre for the Sunday Times *and the* Daily Mail, *two of the national newspapers in England. He also has written for the* London Times Literary Supplement *and the* Manchester Guardian.

What do you feel are the particular tools or skills that are requisite to functioning as an arts critic? I think the problem is, as you get into the professional work as a critic, it's all too easy to be a critic of anything at any time at the drop of a hat. You do develop the professional skills, almost, of hack journalism. I think that is fairly inevitable. You just have to keep them under control. The skills required I find very difficult to identify because basically my view is that it just so happens that one is fortunate enough to be paid to do this work. I still consider myself

very fortunate that people will pay me to go to the theatre to express an opinion, or go to a concert to express an opinion, and provide me, free of charge, the very best tickets. In addition, they actually pay me for doing so. It really is remarkable. The skills clearly have to be largely professional journalistic skills, in the sense that you have to be able to work within the disciplines of time: You may have to write a notice within a half-hour of leaving the event. You have to be able and prepared to work within the disciplines of space; the newspaper only allows you so much space, and you have to work within it. You have to be prepared to work within the disciplines of style: You must have a clear idea of the audience for which you are writing, depending on the newspaper for which you are writing. You have to be able professionally to combine these skills with a critical faculty, which is very indefinable, and an experience which produces judgment values which may be taken to be reasonable. So you are basing your judgment on something or other—probably a wide experience of having seen good performances and bad performances before. You have to have the facility to express yourself, to communicate your interest, enthusiasm, disappointment, or whatever, to the reader. So it is very much a combination of skills and interests which take some time, I think, to come together.

Is there a difference between a newspaper critic and one who writes for a scholarly journal that only comes out quarterly, for example? My own experience of this is immediate, in the sense I might well be covering the same event for two quite different newspapers, the *Daily Mail* and the *Sunday Times.* There you are working within different time scales, different wordage, and to a different readership. Therefore, it is different. In one case I am writing for a popular newspaper, and writing for an audience who well may not be particularly interested in the first place in a symphony concert, who may never go near a concert hall. But what I want to do is to write a piece which they can read with interest and understanding, and perhaps sense the enjoyment and enthusiasm of the event. I have a kind of missionary zeal, I must confess, that I hope that maybe they might be encouraged to put their nose inside a concert hall for the first time ever, and maybe find a new level of pleasure. The notice has to be written within a very short word span and within a very short time scale. With the *Sunday Times* one is writing in a different medium altogether, in the sense that one is writing for a quality newspaper with a very high educational level in its readership. The review appears in the actual arts-review section of the paper, which is separate from the business section and general news section of the magazine. The person who is reading you there is likely to be much better informed and has chosen in the first place to read the *Sunday Times;* that classifies him to an extent. That person has chosen to read the arts-review section and within that section has chosen to read your criticism. Therefore, it is a much more specialized audience. You have more time to write because the deadline is further away, and you generally get more space to write what you want to write. I think one of the main considerations is that nothing is ever complete and nothing is ever totally satisfactory. So the constraints of space and time often lead you to be unable to say the things you would like to say, maybe even to mention people you feel deserve to be mentioned, and similarly may lead you to say things which on further reflection you might not have said. Such reviewing is very much a product of the moment.

Your experience has been in the performing arts. Do you see a difference between your approach or task and that of a critic of the visual arts? I'm tempted to say yes, perhaps because I have not really had the experience of covering the visual arts. Therefore, something you

haven't done you tend to think of as different. I suspect it may not be that much different, although there again, what you need to have is knowledge gained by experience. I spend a lot of time looking at paintings as a personal pleasure in various parts of the world, and so I might be able to have a go at some visual-arts criticism, I suppose. However, nobody has ever asked me to do it. I think that what I would say which may be helpful is that there is a vast difference, I find, between writing criticism of music and writing criticism of theatre. Music is much more difficult to describe to a reader. To communicate sound through words is not that easy. With a play you start with a common language: You describe a story as well as a performance. Also, in the music field, almost by definition the level of performance is in a sense much less variable than the level of performance in the theatre. Most often one is listening to music that is well-established "classical music." Of course, one hears new works and has to assess those, but by and large one hears a standard repertoire and one hears constantly performers of international repute. Therefore, the demands on the music critic are much more keenly felt than the demands on the theatre critic.

Do you see any kind of special purpose behind the role of the arts critic? I personally think that it is very important for a critic to keep in perspective his own position in the total context of the performing arts—or the visual arts, for that matter. There is a quotation which says, "One man in the arena is worth one hundred critics," and I would certainly go along with that. I think every critic should have that hanging over his or her desk. It's too easy to exaggerate your own importance as a critic. You have a lot of opportunities because, since you are writing for a newspaper often with a large readership, you are given a very privileged position to express what, after all, is only your opinion. Therefore, I think you want to be sure that at the very least you are being fair to the artist. That's the way I would like to be known. I think sometimes the critic can be constructively critical so that the artists themselves would find some enlightenment there, and may be able to build that into subsequent performances. That would be very encouraging. One should be critical and constructive. It is too easy, and too often done throughout the world, for newspaper critics to be destructive and smart. Often, it seems to me, editors even demand it in the sense that the critic who is destructive and smart is often highly readable or highly amusing. It is easy to score off somebody else. It boosts circulation, and newspapers like to boost circulation, of course. I think, therefore, it is up to the individual critic to decide how far he wants to go along that line. My own view would be that I would not want to work in that situation. Indeed, I would go so far as to say that sometimes today I would choose not to write—indeed, I do choose not to write, occasionally—some totally destructive notices because it seems to me it is not doing any good to anybody, and is really wasting precious space in my newspapers. If I am writing in the newspaper, there are a dozen other critics in other parts of the world who are not able to get anything into the newspaper that particular week. So I think one should use judgment and one should try to be fair. I would always like to be able to face up to the people I criticize and defend, if necessary, my view and hopefully get their agreement that it was reasonable at the time.

Do you interact socially with artists, or do you feel a need to remain separate from them, personally, in order to be objective? Well, I think a bit of both in my own case. I live a normal, rounded life, I would like to think, because I do spend a lot of my time in this sense working in theatres and concert halls and what not. Inevitably, of course, I see a lot of artists and musicians, and talk with them. I think this

builds up a general background of knowingness. I think, also, that any critic worth his salt really hopes that the people he is sitting in judgment upon not exactly value his opinion, but at least trust his opinion. I think that you need to have, for your own self-preservation, a credibility. Therefore, it's important to know as much as you can about the topic, even though you are judging a particular performance on a particular night and no more than that.

You spoke earlier of missionary zeal. Do you ever feel in conflict with yourself in your role of a critic as opposed to an apologist for the arts? My missionary zeal relates to the context of one particular paper—that is, the context of writing for a paper with a general readership rather than a readership you know is already committed to an interest in the arts. That zeal would not lead me to give false judgment on any performance or event. I would express my opinion and would not change that opinion simply because it did not convince people that they ought to go to see it. That would be counterproductive, and would spoil the missionary zeal when I really wanted to exploit it. I think my concern is really to better the arts and to make a contribution to the furtherance of the arts. One of the exciting things, really, would be the thought that one just might communicate to somebody who hasn't had that experience the possibilities held for them in terms of lasting pleasure in such things as paintings, music, and theatre. I think if a critic can do that while at the same time being constructively critical of what's happening, then I think that is a reasonable way to spend part of one's time.

From your point of view, what do the arts need to do to fulfill their role in society? I find this very difficult because in the end the public is going to make up their own minds. I think what worries me to an extent, and links it to my missionary-zeal feeling, is that the arts are not so easily communicated in terms of the use of television. When you think about it, it is very rare for people to see through such a medium as television—although it is ideal for the job— the work of the artist or the workings of a musician. What I am trying to say, really, is that I would like to see the arts made more accessible to a wider public, because I suspect that as long as the arts seem to be a kind of elitist, intellectual preserve there are a lot of people who are missing a lot of pleasure. Anything the arts can do—I don't know what the answer is, really— to disassociate themselves from this mystique that they are terribly special things for terribly special people, the better. How you do it I don't know. Sometimes I think it works by, if you like, cheating slightly. Certainly, at home I know we had a very popular exhibition at an art gallery; it was an exhibition of Hollywood costumes from the movie houses in Hollywood, costumes worn in various movies by distinguished actors. That attracted people into the museum, into the art gallery, for the first time; many people had never been there before. If by chance a few of those, then, see enough while they're there to want to come again and look at the other things in the art gallery, then that's good. I think that's an idea: That one offers a temptation for people to come in who otherwise wouldn't come in. In any case I would like to see this mystique broken down.

THE PAINTER

Interview with Richard Mayhew

Richard Mayhew is a painter who delights in multimedia. He has received, among other awards, a John Hay Whitney Fellowship, an Ingram Merril Foundation Grant, a Ford Foundation Purchase Award, a Tiffany Foundation Grant, and the Benjamin Altman Award of the National Academy of Design in 1970.

His list of exhibitions includes the American Academy of Arts and Letters, Brooklyn Museum, Chicago Institute, Gallery of Modern Art, Museum of Modern Art, and the Whitney Museum.

He has taught art at Pratt Institute, Smith College, Hunter College, and Pennsylvania State University.

What do you strive to achieve and what do you feel you accomplish in your art? When I started as an artist, there was a need to create, which now I can evaluate on the basis of a need for survival. As the years went by there was more dependence on the area of multimedia as I got involved with theatre and music. The various challenges through the years continued to build; in the beginning it was just a matter of mirroring or reflecting objects and the challenge of mastering technique. In the course of time it kept building, because new challenges kept coming up, such as the use of color, the understanding of space, and the science of the art itself. There is a continuation through the years; nothing was ever solved, because it kept building with new challenges developing.

Do you feel that there is a conscious effort on your part to communicate something to a respondent? Again, this is a question debated in conversation with other artists. Is one painting for an audience or painting for himself? I guess many artists paint for an audience out of survival, in terms of protecting their creative existence, because it is very difficult to survive as an artist, composer, or whatever. There isn't a subsidy for that kind of function in our society. So there are many artists who compromise their values on the basis of catering to a particular public which is not necessarily reflective of their image or impression, and so there is a prostitution of their art somewhere along the way in doing that. I haven't compromised my particular values because there is a dedication to a constant challenge of science in the art. In the course of this how does one communicate with the public? I found myself being involved with a lot of art programs within the various communities in making the community aware of the arts. There is a problem in that the public is not educated to the degree to comprehend what the artists are doing. There is difficulty there. There is a need to communicate, and there is certainly a joy if someone understands and appreciates what one does. But to directly appeal to a particular public is difficult because what you are doing is unique, and if you compromise for a dictation of, let us say, the art market or a general public, you stagnate in development.

But how important is it to you that a respondent receive whatever message you may feel, as an individual artist, you have put into a work? There is a certain satisfaction that the artist is making a contribution in his society. Now, again, there is the commitment to what one is doing and the feeling that one has an influence in subliminal contributions to persons' development. If you are a dedicated artist there is a profound element in your work which is very strong, and anyone exposed to it is influenced by it. There are those who are very deliberate in their control over it, using subject matter and the manipulation of the science to control the viewer where there is a popular subject matter, also manipulating them in control of the geometry or physics of the composition.

In your own personal work do you find any particular ways in which ideas come to you for a particular work? Everything being visualized, that one sees or comes in contact with, is potential subject matter. So it is impossible ever to paint all the things you want to paint, to meet all the challenges you would like to meet; there is never enough time; life is just too short to do it, especially if there is complete dedication to it. It is constantly elusive: It's like in a dream, trying to hold on to a doorknob, and you can't quite get the grip of it, and it always keeps changing and moving. When you do open the door there is another one beyond it that you have to open.

Once you decide on a subject or a treatment, do you conceive of the total painting before you begin, or is it a developmental thing as you work? In the early stages I was working directly from subject matter as a landscape painter; I was apprenticed, very young, to an illustrator and Hudson Valley painter. At the time I didn't realize the value of it. When I started painting, the fascination of the medium came from picking up color from blobs on a palette and transferring it over to the canvas. Pictures came out of the end of the brush. It was unbelievable fascination—magic. One does not have control over it. No matter how well you plan that image, it evolves and changes because of an intuitive extension which you cannot predetermine. Many writers talk about the world beyond, that marvel of consciousness that they have planned, that keeps changing.

THE MUSICIAN

Interview with Robert Hull

Robert Hull has had a long and successful career as conductor, performer, composer, and teacher. He earned bachelor's and master's degrees from Eastman School of Music and a Ph.D. degree from Cornell University. He has been director and conductor of the Fort Worth Symphony Orchestra and conductor of the Fort Worth Ballet Company, as well as guest conductor of many orchestras around the country, including the Rochester Philharmonic, Buffalo Philharmonic, and Phoenix, Flagstaff, and Tucson symphony orchestras. Listed in Who's Who in America, *Dr. Hull also has been Dean of Fine Arts at Texas Christian University and the University of Arizona. He has made recordings in New York City for the Concert Hall Society and the Handel Society and in Los Angeles for Columbia Records.*

What do you feel are the relationships among the composer, conductor, and individual musician relative to the creation and interpretation of a musical work? Let me respond as I envision what the conductor's (or interpreter's) relationship should be to the composer when he is conducting an orchestral work. I think it is incumbent upon the conductor to know as much as possible about the composer and his music, the circumstances of its creation, first performance, things of that nature, before he even begins to study the work intensively. It is important, therefore, for him to transmit that kind of knowledge to the musicians of the orchestra, so it, in turn, can with him transmit coherent and cohesive interpretation for the benefit of the audience. I think the relationship we have to remember is that the creative artist is the composer, and the conductor and individual musician in a sense exist to serve him. Without him, in other words, there would be no performance. So I would rate in order of importance, first the composer, possibly second the individual musician, and third the conductor, even though I happen to prefer conducting as a method of performance rather than violin or viola playing, which I also have done.

As a composer, what events or occurrences trigger your conceptualization of a work? I can't really claim to be a composer, although for a period of about ten years earlier in my life I spent some time in compositional activities. Almost anything could trigger the conceptualization of a work, although most of the time my ideas came from some kind of philosophic or inner urge, rather than being triggered by some outside or natural occurrence—for example, a dream sequence, thinking about relationships between people, or idealizing a perfect performance of a work which you would like to create. These are some of the ways it happens. Of course, it happens another way: An idea occurs to you, a portion of the tune or a fragment of a tune occurs to you, as far as I'm concerned,

for no particular reason. You examine that; you try it out; you work with it; you stretch it; you pound it; you turn it upside down, forwards and backwards, and decide you have something you can work with. From there, depending on the kind of material you have and the idea, you let it grow into what you hope will be some kind of final form.

Do you conceptualize a work in its entirety, or does it grow as you work on it? Well, I think I inadvertently answered this earlier. For the most part, at least with me, the conception begins with a small germ and, usually, grows organically from that point until it is a completed work. I don't think it is possible in a temporal art form such as music to conceive a thing in its entirety unless it is a very small song form.

As a conductor or performer, how do you go about your preparation for a concert? As a performer, meaning a violinist or violist, of course, I spend a considerable number of hours in various slow and painful practices just to make sure that I have solved all the technical problems and that whatever technique I have is at the command of the interpretive artist. Obviously, before I engage in that kind of practice I play through the work several times at near concert speed to see whether it serves the purpose, whether I can cope with it. Obviously, also in the matter of preparation, I must go back to make sure I understand the work, how it fits into the scheme of things in its era, in its composer's life, whether or not he had any extramusical motives for composing it, or any extramusical ideas that he wanted to convey through the composition. Once I have ascertained all this, and once I have been able to make the work one of my own (meaning I feel comfortable with it, I believe in it, and I want to share it with somebody else), then I set about the very painful technical development of the means to interpret it properly. As far as the conductor is concerned, I do somewhat the same process, but my preparation here, of course, is a matter not necessarily of making music but of studying the score, making sure I understand all of its harmonic, contrapuntal, and melodic implications, and where the countermelodies are at every stage of the game. I must know where I want my rubatos, what it is that is being expressed, and how I am going to react to it as a conductor. I have to be aware, of course, of what all the instruments are doing every step of the way, and yet I have to prepare an overall concept of how I want them balanced one against the other. You do that in terms of your understanding in terms of the style of the period in which the composer was doing his work. You also try to understand, in terms of the capability of your performing organization, whether or not the work fits it, whether or not the organization will be able to give a reasonable accounting of itself when it plays the work, and therefore whether you are able to give a reasonably accurate and a reasonably faithful interpretation to the audience. This requires many hours of painful study and slow study, and for the most part it should be quiet study. From time to time, if there is a recording in existence of the work I am preparing and if the interpretation of the recording is relatively close to my conceptualization of the work, I may listen to the recording a few times, just so it will help me hear the work, visualize it, as it were, so that it makes it a little easier for me to keep the whole thing in mind, and a little easier to memorize it.

Is it important to you that the audience respond in a particular manner to your artwork? This is a difficult one to answer. At the moment I am not performing publicly or conducting publicly enough to recall with any degree of certainty exactly how I react each time I do a performance. I must say that for the most part I believe I know when I have done something well, and that therefore the audience's immediate reaction may not be that important to me.

But I share with all artists and with all people a desire sometime to get my message across and, if you will, to please. In that respect it is important, and particularly the communicative artist, the performing artist, must know that some of his ideas are reaching the public. Therefore, it is terribly important that at least we get some reaction; I believe it is more important to get a reaction than it is to make absolutely sure that we get a positive and pleasing reaction, or the reaction of those that are pleased by the work. Nothing is more stultifying and deadly than no reaction at all.

What do you feel are the major attributes and limitations of the musician as a communicative artist? Let me put it another way around. Instead of saying major attributes and limitations, maybe I should say major advantages and disadvantages for the musician or communicative artist. The major advantage, of course, probably lies in the fact that the musician is dealing with symbols which are ineffable, which means that they may connote certain kinds of basic meanings, but they do not denote anything specific. That gives, I believe, the musician a much greater latitude than the painter, for example, the sculptor, or the playwright, or even the opera composer, where there are some ideas that are denoted and narrative in character which may be transmitted with the music. The music itself—since it tends to be universal, as it were, and can mean so many things to so many people—gives the musician a considerable advantage and leeway in the use of his materials. The limitations, of course, are that it is very difficult for the musician to communicate a specific denotive idea—that is, to be delimiting in the definition of the symbols that he is using. For example, I would not agree with the late Richard Strauss, who claimed that by purely musical means he could convey to the audience how much water was in a tumbler full of water. He might be able to convey to the audience the idea that he had a body of water which was in turmoil or which was quite placid or which was freely flowing. But to be able to convey to the audience where that body of water was, how much water was in it, the precise size, what part of the hemisphere it was, what the color of the day was, is something that I think is beyond the normal communicative process of music, unless we insist upon reading more into music than actually exists. I make this last remark because, obviously, many of the impressionists in music believe that is possible, and we frequently (the musician and the composer frequently, and/or the music critic more likely than the other two) will borrow the vocabulary from the artists and talk about various kinds of color in music. This doesn't mean to say that by purely musical means you can paint a picture greener than another picture. I don't think this is possible. On the other hand you can give the feeling of lightness, effervescence, looking forward, striving, an ongoing feeling which one might in one way or another associate with the idea of spring, *ergo,* green. But I don't believe you can go beyond that.

As a musician, composer, conductor, or performer, what specific ends do you try to accomplish through your art? It probably would sound a little egotistical or self-centered if I would say that there are so many things in music that I enjoy, and to such a degree, that I have a kind of burning desire to share that feeling and enjoyment with other people. I suppose you might say, in the last analysis, it is a kind of missionary zeal to convert others to the point where they can get the same kind of enjoyment, although maybe in a slightly different way, but some of the same kind of enjoyment out of the same kind of music that I have been privileged to know and to understand. In connection with that, I might say here something that you know very well—that frequently the average person, in meeting a composer or artist, will say, "Well, I don't know anything about music or art, but I know what I like." I

frequently try to counter by saying, "I agree with part of your statement, but I wonder if you don't really mean that you don't know anything about music and you like what you know." I think it is characteristic of man to be a little standoffish or tend to be a little suspicious of what he does not understand. And if we are not willing to keep on with the process of learning after our high school days and to make it a lifelong experience, it is quite likely that all the most recent developments in various art forms, which take a little understanding and a little exposure to get used to, may eventually outstrip our ability to respond to them and to appreciate them. And this is why I think it is most nearly accurate to say about the person who doesn't know much about art that he has a tendency to end up liking what he knows. Anyhow, it is just for this reason that I am involved one way or another in teaching and lecturing and writing and administering: hoping I can widen the circle of appreciation for the people who come into contact with me. I suppose I am not trying necessarily to impose my taste on somebody else, but simply to say, "Look, I enjoyed this particular work and let me share that enjoyment with you; I hope you get some of the same ecstatic or uplifted feeling from it that I did." If one can accomplish this in a few cases in his life, then I think one's life in his art or whatever he is doing has been worthwhile.

THE THEATRE DIRECTOR

Interview with Richard Edelman

Richard Edelman's background in the theatre is lifelong and extremely broad. While his current concentration is exclusively in directing, he has worked as an actor since childhood, when he appeared in WPA theatre projects and radio shows in New York City. Later, in Europe he appeared on the stage and in films.

Educated at St. John's College in Annapolis, Maryland, he has pursued advanced work at Columbia University in New York and the Sorbonne in Paris. As a director he has been affiliated with New York's Neighborhood Playhouse, Living Theatre, and England's Mermaid Theatre. He also has been affiliated with many summer theatres, including the Green Mansions Camp. His directing credits, however, go far beyond legitimate English-language theatre. He has staged operas for such organizations as New York's North Shore Friends of Opera, the Mozart Opera Festival of the Brooklyn Academy, and the Buffalo Symphony, and has been involved in cross-cultural theatre, directing in French and Italian both in the United States and in Europe.

What is the relationship of the director to the playwright in the development of the theatrical artwork? Are you an artist, an interpreter, or something in between? I think no one can be just an impartial deliverer of the play as written. We fool ourselves if that is the case. In having read the play, without any attempt to add anything, we do add something, because it goes through our consciousness; it goes through our sensibilities; it goes through the specifics of our image-making process, and there is no way of avoiding that. I think that people who say that they are simply there just to do what the author wants are fooling themselves. It is impossible. The more you try to be absolutely honest and available to the author, the more likely you are to create something that is more different and unique. When I do a production, I have certain very clear ideas of what I think should happen to it. But I feel that almost every idea I have is based on what I read in the text and what I know about the particular theatre of a historical period and what the playwright's resources were. As a director, what I really want to find out is what conventions did he have in mind, what was he basing it on. Sometimes, as a director, you have to add a dimension when you enter into a collaboration, whether the writer

is there or not. If the writer is dead or not available you almost owe it to him to develop a dimension that he has not. Had you been around and worked with him as one does with a live author with whom you are collaborating, then you are making an input. There is no question about it. Somebody like Kazan made enormous inputs into the works of Tennessee Williams that did not appear in the originals of the scripts.

In this regard, how inviolable do you as a director regard the script with which you are working, especially of an author who is not available for collaboration? I tell you that this is a quirk of mine. I find it a challenge to cut as little as possible, a challenge that I want to meet. I want to find ways of making it work. I find that is the interesting challenge. I am not even sure that is an artistic challenge. Very frequently it is to my own and the play's disadvantage that I am motivated to say, "Now that line has to work some way," instead of saying, "Well, we can't handle that line; let's just cut it or let's just substitute something." Translations add another dimension, and very frequently cloud the issue. I try to find out, again, what the author really wanted. I think very frequently something like Shakespeare gets cut, because people don't take the time to find out, directors and actors, just how brilliantly constructed his plays are. Sometimes they are laid out in a triptych. You know there are three sections, even though there are five acts. He makes the statement once, then he makes it a slightly different way, then he makes it in some kind of resolution the third time. That is a structure that we do not understand in the theatre because we are much more interested in the direct narrative line. However, today I think we are a little better off; the changes of the fifties and especially of the sixties made us more open to that kind of theatrical experience. We will accept it more, but very frequently as thinkers we are not able to cut through to see what his structure is, and I think that is what a director should be about. And very frequently that doesn't happen. The director simply will cut or find a palatable coating for the pill. You put the play into antebellum Charleston because it is going to work there. Well, maybe that is sensible, or maybe it isn't. I have seen very splendid and really good productions where they have been put into other eras or where they have been modernized. More often than not, though, these are just ways of making Shakespeare palatable, meaning watering it down, meaning that they haven't really gone to the trouble to find out what the guts of that experience are.

How do you as a director view the relationships of all of the parts of a production—that is, actors, designers, and so forth? Do you see the production as a joint venture or are you like a musical conductor—that is, a dictator? I have been told that when I was young I was a dictator; I don't remember it. I have been told by actors that I have since worked with, again, that I was impossible at that point. I see myself, and I think I have always seen myself, as a collaborative director. I think it is a collaboration and I think one of the difficulties that we have is with the director who really does have very clear images of what he wants. Then he has to find people who are just going to give him what he wants, and that takes enormous organizational skills and strength, character, or extraordinarily self-centered potency. I find that I prefer to work with ideas that other people are contributing, and somehow fashion them into a joint world. The director, I think, is largely responsible for the completeness of the world that is presented on the stage at that moment. He has to find the reality of that given world— that is, the completeness of the reality, moment to moment throughout the play—the style of the piece, the form of the piece, and the life of the piece. So I see myself essentially as a collaborator. I think that happens as one gets older. I think that is a function of one's maturing and

having perhaps less energy and a little more humility concerning what one is doing—and a little more respect for the efforts of the people that one is working with. I find I modify more and more what are my original conceptions so that it is not simply a question of incorporating what somebody else has done, but incorporating what I have done into what somebody else has done. I find myself essentially a collaborative worker with the playwright if he is alive and immediately available. Or if he is dead, then I feel I have a certain commitment to find out what he had in mind.

How does the audience fit into your development of the production? Is "communication" important? The whole notion of communication is a bugaboo in the theatre, particularly for actors. Young actors, particularly, misunderstand this; they think that means that they have to show it and tell it to the audience, which is not the actors' work. The actors' work is to find the life in that particular world and if they do it fully and completely, any audience that is attentive will be able to find what has to be seen and understood. An audience sees and understands what it wants to, and not what you want it to. It is a communal experience: The audience is a community, if you like, and the actors are the other part of that community—the actors and all the support elements that go into putting the actors on the stage. It is a completed circle at that time, and I don't think a play really exists until it is in the moment of performance, and until it is experienced by the audience, which gives something back to the actors.

So are you saying, then, that when you make choices relative to what you are going to do in the production—what the set is going to look like, or the particular kind of movements that the actors are going to use—these choices are based on something other than how you want something to go across to the audience or how to get them to respond in a particular way? Or don't you care how they respond? I care how they respond, very definitely. I think the director has to be aware of a given audience. Particularly in this day and age it might be good to say there is no such thing as a vast audience. We no longer have the great popular audiences that they had in the nineteenth and early twentieth centuries. So I think you have to know which audience you are going for, and I think that in some sense that has to be considered.

You have to know which language, as it were, you are talking in when you are directing and acting and designing. Sometimes it is a little difficult. I would do a given play in different ways depending on what the audience was and what my expectations of that audience were. I don't mean I play it down to them. That is not what I am saying. I am saying that I try to find that legal binder that makes it possible for life to go on between the two—to create that union.

Pictures

Painting, Printmaking, and Photography

Pictures of family, friends, rock and sports stars, copies of artistic masterpieces, and original paintings and prints adorn our personal spaces. Dorm rooms, bedrooms, living rooms, and other places where we live seem coldly empty and depersonalized without pictures of some kind in them. Pictures have always been important to us. People who lived in caves 20,000 years ago drew pictures on their walls. In this chapter we'll learn about the many ways pictures can be made and how artists use two-dimensional qualities to speak to us.

WHAT IS IT?

Paintings, photographs, and prints are pictures, differing primarily in the technique of their execution. They are two dimensional, and their subject might be a landscape, seascape, portrait, religious picture, nonobjective (nonrepresentational) or abstract picture, still life, or something else. So, at first encounter, our response is a simple and straightforward matter of observing subject matter.

HOW IS IT PUT TOGETHER?

Medium

Our technical level of response is more complex. First of all, our response to how a work is put together is to the medium used by the artist to execute the work.

Paintings and Drawings

Paintings and drawings are executed through use of oils, watercolors, tempera, acrylics, fresco, gouache, ink, pastels, and pencils, to name just a few. An artist may combine these media and may use some others. Each medium has its own characteristics and to a great extent dictates what the artist can or cannot achieve as an end result.

Oils are perhaps the most popular of the painting media, and have been since their development near the beginning of the fifteenth century. Their popularity stems principally from the great variety of opportunity they give the painter. Oils offer a wide range of color possibilities; because they dry slowly, they can be re-worked; they present many options for textural manipulation; and they are durable. If we compare two oils, van Gogh's *The Starry Night* (Fig. 3.1) and Giovanni Vanni's *Holy Family with Saint John* (see color insert Plate 2), the medium shows its importance to the final effect of the works. Vanni creates light and shade in the baroque tradition, and his chiaroscuro (pronounced key·ahr´·uh·sku̅´·ro̅) depends on the capacity of the medium to blend smoothly among color areas. Van Gogh, in contrast, requires a medium that will stand up to form obvious brush strokes. Vanni demands the paint to be flesh and cloth. Van Gogh demands the paint to be paint and to be stars and sky, but also to call attention to itself.

Watercolor is a broad category that includes any color medium that uses water as a thinner.

However, the term has traditionally referred to a transparent paint usually applied to paper. Because watercolors are transparent, artists must be very careful to control them. If one area of color overlaps another, the overlap will show as a third area combining the previous hues. But their transparency gives watercolors a delicacy that cannot be produced in any other medium.

Tempera is an opaque watercolor medium whose use spans recorded history. It was employed by the ancient Egyptians and is still used today by such familiar painters as Andrew Wyeth. Tempera refers to ground pigments and their color binders such as gum or glue, but is best known as its egg tempera form. It is a fast-drying medium that virtually eliminates brush strokes and gives extremely sharp and precise detail. Colors in tempera paintings appear almost gemlike in their clarity and brilliance.

Figure 3.1 Vincent van Gogh, *The Starry Night* (1889). Oil on canvas, 29″ × 36¼″. Collection, The Museum of Modern Art, New York. Acquired through the Lillie P. Bliss Bequest.

Acrylics, in contrast with tempera, are modern synthetic products. Most acrylics are water soluble (that is, they dissolve in water), and the binding agent for the pigment is an acrylic polymer. Acrylics are flexible media offering artists a wide range of possibilities in both color and technique. An acrylic paint can be either opaque or transparent, depending on dilution. It is fast drying, thin, and resistant to cracking under temperature and humidity extremes. It is perhaps less permanent than some other media but adheres to a wider variety of surfaces. It will not darken or yellow with age, as will oil.

Fresco is a wall-painting *technique* in which pigments suspended in water are applied to fresh wet plaster. Michelangelo's Sistine Chapel frescoes are the best known examples of this technique. Because the end result becomes part of the plaster wall rather than being painted on it, fresco provides a long-lasting work. However, it is an extremely difficult process, and once the pigments are applied, no changes can be made without replastering the entire section of the wall.

Gouache is a watercolor medium in which gum is added to ground opaque colors mixed with water. Transparent watercolors can be made into gouache by adding Chinese white to them, a special white, opaque, water-soluble paint. The final product, in contrast to watercolor, is opaque.

Ink as a painting medium has many of the same characteristics as transparent watercolor. It is difficult to control, yet its effects are nearly impossible to achieve in any other medium. Because it must be worked quickly and freely, it has a spontaneous and appealing quality (see Fig. 3.2).

Drawing media such as ink, when applied with a pen (as opposed to a brush), pastels (crayon or chalk), and pencils all create their effect

Figure 3.2 Chu Ta (Pa-ta-shan-jen), *Lotus* (1705). Brush and ink, 61½″ × 28″. Museum of Art, The Pennsylvania State University.

through buildup of line. Each has its own characteristics, but all are relatively inflexible in their handling of color and color areas (see Fig. 3.8).

Prints

Prints fall generally into three main categories based essentially on the nature of the printing surface. First is *relief printing* such as woodcut, wood engraving, linoleum cut, and collograph. Second is *intaglio,* including etching, aquatint, drypoint, and again, collograph. Third is the *planographic process,* which includes lithography and serigraphy (silkscreen) and other forms of stenciling. In addition, other combinations and somewhat amorphous processes such as monoprinting also are used by printmakers.

To begin with, however, we need to ask, What is a print? A print is a hand-produced picture that has been transferred from a printing surface to a piece of paper. The artist personally prepares the printing surface and directs the printing process. Each step in the production of a print is accomplished by hand. In some cases a press is used, as we see later, but it is always operated by hand. The uniqueness and value of a print lie in the fact that the block or surface from which the print is made usually is destroyed after the desired number of prints has been made. In contrast, a reproduction is not an original. It is a *copy* of an original painting or other artwork, reproduced usually by a photographic process. As a copy, the reproduction does not bear the handiwork of the artist. In purchasing prints we must be sure we are buying an actual print (which has value as an artwork) and not a reproduction (which lacks such value) disguised by obscure or misleading advertising.

Note that every print has a number. On some prints the number may appear as a fraction—for example, 36/100. The denominator indicates how many prints were produced from the plate or block. This number is called the *issued number,* or *edition number.* The numerator indicates where in the series the individual print was produced. If only a single number appears, such as 500, it simply indicates the total number of prints in the series; it is also called the issue number. Printmakers are beginning to eliminate the former kind of numbering because of the misconception that the relationship of the numerator to the issue total has a bearing on a print's value. The numerator is an item of curiosity only; it has nothing to do with a print's value, monetarily or qualitatively. The issue number does have some value in comparing, for example, an issue of 25 with one of 500, and usually is reflected in the price of a print. However, the edition number is not the sole factor in determining the value of a print. The quality of the print and the reputation of the artist are more important considerations.

Relief printing. In relief printing, the image is transferred to the paper by cutting away non-image areas and inking the surface that remains. Therefore, the image protrudes, in relief, from the block or plate and produces a picture that is reversed from the image carved by the artist. This reversal is a characteristic of all printmaking media. *Woodcuts* and *wood engravings* are two popular techniques. A woodcut, one of the oldest techniques, is cut into the plank of the grain; a wood engraving is cut into the butt of the grain (Fig. 3.3). Figure 3.4 illustrates the

Figure 3.3 Wood plank and butt.

Figure 3.4 Albrecht Dürer, German (1471–1528), *Lamentation* (c. 1497–1500). Woodcut, 15½″ × 11¼″. Gift of the Friends of the Palmer Museum of Art. Palmer Museum of Art, The Pennsylvania State University.

linear essence of the woodcut and shows the precision and delicacy possible in this medium in the hands of a master. The *collograph* is a printmaking process in which assorted objects are glued to a board or plate. A collograph represents relief printing when the raised surfaces are inked and printed. When the recessed areas are inked and printed, the collograph becomes an intaglio work.

Intaglio. The intaglio process is the opposite of relief printing. The ink is transferred to the paper not from raised areas but rather from grooves cut into a metal plate. *Line engraving, etching, drypoint,* and *aquatint* are some of the methods of intaglio.

LINE ENGRAVING involves cutting grooves into the metal plate with special sharp tools. It requires great muscular control because the pressure must be continuous and constant if the grooves are to produce the desired image. The print resulting from the line-engraving process is very sharp and precise. This form of intaglio is the most difficult and demanding.

ETCHINGS are less demanding. In this process the artist removes the surface of the plate by exposing it to an acid bath. First the plate is covered with a thin waxlike substance called a *ground*. Then the artist scratches away the ground to produce the desired lines. The plate is then immersed in the acid, which burns away the exposed areas of the plate. The longer a plate is left in the acid, the deeper the resulting etches will be; the deeper the etch, the darker

the final image. So artists wishing to produce lines or areas of differing darkness must cover those lines that they do not desire to be more deeply cut before further immersions in the acid. They can accomplish this task easily. The desired number of repetitions of the process yields a plate that will produce a print with the desired differences in light and dark lines. All the details of Figure 3.5 consist of individual lines, either single or in combination. The lighter lines required less time in the acid than the darker ones. Because of the precision and clarity of the lines, it would be difficult to determine, without knowing in advance, whether this print is an etching or an engraving. Drypoint, in contrast, produces lines with less sharp edges.

Figure 3.5 Daniel Hopfer, *Ceiling Ornament.* Etching, 10″ × 8¾″. Museum of Art, The Pennsylvania State University.

DRYPOINT is a technique in which the surface of the metal plate is scratched with a needle. Unlike the line engraving, which results in a clean, sharp line, the drypoint technique leaves a ridge on either side of the groove. The resulting line is somewhat fuzzy.

Once the plate is prepared, whether by line engraving, etching, aquatint, drypoint, or a combination of methods, the artist is ready for the printing process. The plate is placed in a press and a special dampened paper is laid over it. Padding is placed on the paper and then a roller is passed over, forcing the plate and the paper together with great pressure. The ink, which has been carefully applied to the plate and left only in the grooves, is transferred as the paper is forced into the grooves by the roller of the press. Even if no ink had been applied to the plate, the paper would still receive an image. This *embossing* effect is the mark of an intaglio process; the three-dimensional *platemark* is very obvious.

AQUATINT is a difficult process to explain, and therefore to understand, without an actual print to which to refer. The intaglio methods noted thus far consist of various means of cutting lines into a metal plate. On occasion, however, an artist may wish to create large areas of subdued tonality. Such shadowlike areas cannot be produced effectively with lines. Therefore, the artist dusts the plate with a resin substance. The plate is then heated, which affixes the resin, and put into the acid bath. The result is a plate whose surface is rough in texture, like sandpaper, and a print whose tonal areas reflect that texture.

Planographic processes. In a planographic process, the artist prints from a plane surface (neither relief nor intaglio). *Lithography* (the term's literal meaning is "stone writing") is based on the principle that water and grease do not mix. To create a lithograph, artists begin with a stone, usually limestone, and grind one side until it is absolutely smooth. They then draw an image on the stone with a greasy substance. Artists can vary the darkness of the final image by the amount of grease they use: The more grease applied, the darker the image will be. After artists have drawn the image, they treat the stone with gum arabic and nitric acid and then rinse it with water. This bath fixes the greasy areas to the surface of the stone. The next step is baffling to most people. When the artist rinses the stone and fans it dry, the surface is clean! However, the water, gum, and acid have impressed the grease on the stone, and when the stone is wetted it absorbs water (limestone being porous) only in those areas that were not previously greased. Finally, a grease-based ink is applied to the stone. It, in turn, will not adhere to the water-soaked areas. As a result the stone, with ink adhering only to the areas on which the artist has drawn, can be placed in a press and the image transferred to the waiting paper. In Figures 3.6 and 3.7 we can see the characteristic most attributable to the medium of lithography—a crayon-drawing appearance. Because the lithographer usually draws with a crayonlike material on the stone, the final print has exactly that quality. Compare these prints with Figure 3.8, a pastel drawing, and the point is clear.

The *serigraphic* process (serigraphy) or silkscreening is the most common of the stenciling processes. Silkscreens are made from a wooden frame covered with a finely meshed silk fabric. The nonimage areas are blocked out with a glue mixture painted directly on the silk fabric or blocked out by a cut paper stencil. The stencil is placed in the frame and ink is applied. By means of a rubber instrument called a squeegee, the ink is forced through the openings of the stencil, through the screen, and onto the paper below. This technique allows the printmaker to achieve large, flat, uniform color areas. We can see this smooth uniformity of color areas in Figure 3.9. Here the artist, through successive applications of ink, has built up a complex composition with highly veri-similar (lifelike) detail.

Figure 3.6 Thomas Hart Benton, *Cradling Wheat* (1938). Lithograph, 9½″ × 12″. Museum of Art, The Pennsylvania State University. Gift of Carolyn Wose Hull.

Looking over Figures 3.4 through 3.9, we can see how the images of the various prints reflect recognizable differences in technique. Again, it is not always possible to discern the technique used in executing a print, and some prints reflect a combination of techniques. However, in seeking the method of execution, we add another layer of potential response to a work to those we note momentarily.

Photography

In some cases photography is not really an art at all; it is merely a matter of personal record executed with equipment of varying degrees of expense and sophistication (see Fig. 3.10). Certainly photography as a matter of pictorial record, or even as *photojournalism,* may lack the qualities we believe are requisite to art. A photograph of a baseball player sliding into second base or of Aunt Mabel cooking hamburgers at

Figure 3.7 Charles Sheeler, *Delmonico Building* (1926). Lithograph, 10″ × 7⅛″. Palmer Museum of Art, The Pennsylvania State University.

Figure 3.8 Hobson Pittman, *Violets No. 1* (1971). Pastel, 9½″ × 10¼″. Museum of Art, The Pennsylvania State University.

Figure 3.9 Nancy McIntyre (American), *Barbershop Mirror* (1976). Serigraph, 26½″ × 19″. Palmer Museum of Art, The Pennsylvania State University.

*mirror
moves up
when shutter
is released*

*pentaprism
corrects
image*

*mirror returns
instantly to
viewing
position after
exposure*

film

Figure 3.10 The single-lens reflex
(SLR) camera.

the family reunion may trigger expressive responses for us, but it is doubtful the photographers had aesthetic communication or particular design in mind when they snapped the shutter. But a carefully composed and sensitively designed and executed photograph can contain every attribute of human expression possible in any art form.

Ansel Adams saw the photographer as an interpretive artist; he likened the photographic negative to the musical score, and the print to a performance (see Fig. 3.11). In other words, despite all the choices the artist may make in committing an image to film, they are only the beginning of the artistic process. The photographer still has the choice of *size, texture,* and *value contrast,* or *tonality.* A photo of the grain of a piece of wood, for example, has an enormous range of aesthetic possibilities depending on how the artist employs and combines these three elements.

Consequently, the question "Is it art?" may have a cogent application to photography. However, the quality of our aesthetic repay-

ment from the photographic experience is higher if we view photography in the same vein as we do the other arts—as a visualization manifested through a technique and resulting in an aesthetic response or communication.

Composition

Our discussions of how any artwork is put together eventually result in a discussion of how it is composed. The elements and principles of *composition* are basic to all the arts, and we return to them time and time again as we proceed.

Elements

Line. The basic building block of a visual design is line. To most of us a line is a thin mark such as this: —————. We find that denotation in art as well. In color insert Plate 3 we find amorphous shapes. Some of these shapes are like cartoon figures; that is, they are identifiable from the background because of their *outline.* In these instances line identifies form and illustrates the first sentence of this paragraph. How-

Figure 3.11 Ansel Adams, *Moon and Half Dome, Yosemite National Park, California* (1960). © The Ansel Adams Publishing Rights Trust.

ever, the other shapes in Plate 3 also exemplify line. If we put our finger on the edge of these shapes, we have identified a second aspect of line: the boundary between areas of color and between shapes or forms. (We noted this use of line in our discussion of style in Chapter 1.) There is one further aspect of line, which is implied rather than physical. The three rectangles in Figure 3.12 create a horizontal line that extends across the design. There is no physical line between the tops of the forms, but their spatial arrangement creates one by implication. A similar use of line occurs in Figure 3.1, where we can see a definite linear movement from the upper left border through a series of swirls to the right border. That line is quite clear, although it is composed not of a form edge or outline but of a carefully developed relationship

of numerous color areas. This treatment of line is also seen in Figure 3.13, although here it is much more subtle and sophisticated. By dripping paint onto his canvas (a task not as easily executed or accidental as it might appear), the

Figure 3.12 Outline and implied line.

Figure 3.13 Jackson Pollock, *One (Number 31, 1950)* (1950). Oil and enamel on unprimed canvas, 8′ 10″ × 17′ 5⅝″. The Museum of Modern Art, New York. The Sidney and Harriet Janis Collection Fund (by exchange).

artist was able to subordinate form, in the sense of recognizable and distinct areas, and thereby *focal areas,* to a dynamic network of complex lines. The effect of this technique of execution has a very strong relationship to the actual force and speed with which the pigment was applied.

Line is used by an artist to control our vision, to create unity and emotional value, and ultimately to develop meaning. In pursuing those ends, and by employing the three aspects of line noted earlier, the artist finds that line has two characteristics: It is *curved* or it is *straight.* Whether it is expressed as an outline, as an area edge, or by implication, and whether it is simple or in combination, a line is some derivative of the characteristics of straightness or curvedness. Some people speculate whether line can also be thick or thin. Certainly that quality is helpful in describing some works of art. Those who deny that quality, however, have a point difficult to refute in asking, If line can be thick or thin, at what point does it cease to be a line and become a form?

Form. Form and line are closely related both in definition and in effect. Form is the *shape* of an object within the composition, and *shape* often is used as a synonym for form. Literally, form is that space described by line. A building is a form. So is a tree. We perceive them as buildings or trees, and we also perceive their individual details because of the line by which they are composed; form cannot be separated from line in two-dimensional design.

Color. Color characteristics differ depending on whether we are discussing color in light or color in pigment. For example, in light the primary hues (those hues that cannot be achieved by mixing other hues) are red, *green,* and blue; in pigment they are red, *yellow,* and blue. If we mix equal proportions of yellow and blue pigments we have green. Because green can be achieved by mixing, it cannot be a primary—in pigment. However, no matter how hard we try, we cannot mix any hues that will achieve green light. Inasmuch as our response to artworks most often deals with colored pigment, the discussion that follows concerns color in pigment. We do not discuss color in light.

HUE. Hue is the spectrum notation of color; a hue is a specific pure color with a measurable wavelength. The visible range of the color spectrum extends from violet on one end to red on the other. The color spectrum consists of three primary hues, blue, yellow, and red and three additional, secondary, hues that are direct derivatives of them: green, orange, and violet. These six hues are the basic hues of the spectrum, and each has a specific, measurable wavelength (Fig. 3.14). In all there are (depending on which theory one follows) from ten to twenty-four perceivably different hues, including these six. These perceptible hues are the composite hues of the color spectrum.

For the sake of clarity and illustration, let us assume twelve basic hues. Arranged in a series, they would look like Figure 3.15. However, because combinations of these hues are possible beyond the straight-line configuration of the spectrum, it is helpful to visualize color by

Figure 3.15 Color spectrum, including composite hues.

Figure 3.14 Basic color spectrum.

turning the color spectrum into a color wheel (Fig. 3.16; see also color insert Plate 4). With this visualization we now can discuss what an artist can do to and with color. First, an artist can take the primary hues of the spectrum, mix them two at a time in varying proportions, and create the other hues of the spectrum. For example, red and yellow in equal proportions make orange, a *secondary hue.* Varying the proportions—adding more red or more yellow—makes yellow-orange or red-orange, which are *tertiary hues.* Yellow and blue make green, and also blue-green and yellow-green, red and blue gives us violet, blue-violet, and red-violet. Hues directly opposite each other on the color wheel are *complementary.* When they are mixed

Figure 3.16 Color wheel. (See also color insert Plate 4.)

together in equal proportions, they produce gray (see INTENSITY).

VALUE. In discussing photography, we noted in passing the concept of value contrast—the relationship of blacks to whites and grays. The range of possibilities from black to white forms the *value scale,* which has black at one end, white at the other, and medium gray in the middle. The perceivable tones between black and white are designated light or dark (Fig. 3.17).

The application of the effects of value on color is treated in different ways by different sources. However, it appears most helpful if we approach the subject less from a theoretical point of view and more from a practical one. That is, what can painters do to color in order to create a painting that gives the effect they desire? As we indicated, they may mix primaries to create secondary and tertiary hues. Every hue has its own value; that is, in its pure state each hue falls somewhere on the value scale in Figure 3.18.

Figure 3.17 Value scale.

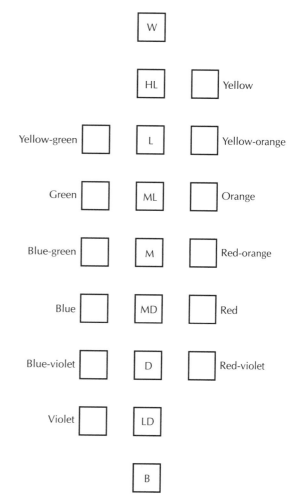

Figure 3.18 Color-value equivalents.

A broad range of color possibilities exists between high-light gray and pure white or between a pure hue and white, which does not fall on the traditional value scale. That range of possibilities is described by the term *saturation.* A saturated hue is a pure hue. An unsaturated hue is a hue to which some quantity of white alone has been added. Unsaturated hues, such as pink, are known as *tints.* What is not entirely clear is whether saturation is part of or separate from value—that is, whether the two terms should be considered as separate properties of color change or whether value includes saturation. More on this momentarily.

We can easily see that some colors are brighter than others. As we noted, the perceivable difference in brightness between primary yellow and primary blue is due to their difference in value. However, it is possible to have a *bright* yellow and a *dull* yellow. The difference in brightness between the two may be a matter of value, as we just observed—a pure yellow versus a grayed yellow. It also may be a matter of surface *brilliance,* or reflectance, a factor of considerable importance to all visual artists. A highly reflective surface creates a brighter color, and therefore a different response from the observer, than does a surface of lesser reflection, although all other color factors may be the same. This is the difference among high gloss, semigloss, and flat paints, for example. Probably surface reflectance is more a property of texture than of color. However, the term *brilliance* is often used to describe not only surface gloss but also characteristics synonymous with value. Some sources also use brilliance as a synonym for saturation; still others use saturation as a synonym for an additional color-change possibility, *intensity*.

INTENSITY. Intensity is the degree of purity of a hue. It also is sometimes called *chroma*. Returning to the color wheel (Fig. 3.16), we note that movement around the wheel creates a change in hue. Movement *across* the wheel creates a change in intensity. If we add green to red we alter its intensity. When, as in this case, hues are directly opposite each other on the color wheel such mixing has the practical effect of *graying* the original hue. Therefore, because graying a hue is a *value* change, one occasionally finds intensity and value used interchangeably. Some sources use the terms independently but state that changing a color's value *automatically* changes its intensity. Let's think about the implications of these concepts. There is a difference between graying a hue by using its complement and graying a hue by adding black (or gray derived from black and white). A gray derived from complementaries, because it *has color,* is far livelier than a gray derived from black and white, which are not colors.

The composite, or overall, use of color by the artist is termed *palette.* An artist's palette can be broad, restricted, or somewhere in between, depending on whether the artist has utilized the full range of the color spectrum and/or whether he or she explores the full range of *tonalities*—brights and dulls, lights and darks.

Mass (Space). Only three-dimensional objects have mass, that is, take up space and have den-

sity. However, two-dimensional objects give the illusion of mass, *relative* only to the other objects in the picture.

Texture. The texture of a picture is its apparent roughness or smoothness. Texture ranges from the smoothness of a glossy photo to the three-dimensionality of *impasto,* a painting technique in which pigment is applied thickly with a palette knife to raise areas from the canvas. The texture of a picture may be anywhere within these two extremes. Texture may be illusory in that the surface of a picture may be absolutely flat but the image gives the impression of three-dimensionality. So the term can be applied to the pictorial arts either literally or figuratively.

Principles

Repetition. Probably the essence of any design is repetition: how the basic elements in the picture are repeated or alternated. In discussing repetition let's consider three terms: *rhythm, harmony,* and *variation*.

RHYTHM is the ordered recurrence of elements in a composition. Recurrence may be regular or irregular. If the relationships among elements are equal, the rhythm is regular (Fig. 3.12). If not, the rhythm is irregular. However, we must examine the composition as a whole to discern if patterns of relationships exist and whether or not the *patterns* are regular, as they are in Figure 3.19.

HARMONY is the logic of the repetition. Harmonious relationships are those whose components appear to join naturally and comfortably. If the artist employs forms, colors, or other elements that appear incongruous, illogical, or out of sync with each other, then we would use a musical term and say the resulting picture is dissonant; its constituents simply do not go together in the way our cultural conditioning

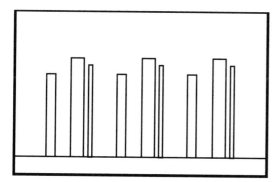

Figure 3.19 Repetition of patterns.

would describe as natural. However, we need to understand here, as we note later in music, that ideas and ideals relative to harmonious relationships in color or other elements often reflect cultural conditioning or arbitrary understandings.

VARIATION is the relationship of repeated items to each other; it is similar to theme and variation in music. How does an artist take a basic element in the composition and use it again with slight or major changes? The artist of color insert Plate 5 has taken two geometric forms, the diamond and the oval, and created a complex painting via repetition. The diamond with a circle at its center is repeated over and over to form the background. Variation occurs in the color given to these shapes. Similarly, the oval of the mirror is repeated with variations in the composition of the girl. The circular motif also is repeated throughout the painting, with variations in color and size—similar to the repetition and variation in the design of the Volkswagen noted in Figure 1.10.

Balance. The concept of balance is very important. It is not difficult to look at a composition and almost intuitively respond that it does or does not appear balanced. Most individuals have this second sense. However, *how* artists

achieve balance in their pictures is the object of our attention.

SYMMETRY. The most mechanical method of achieving balance is *symmetry,* or specifically, bilateral symmetry, the balancing of like forms, mass, and colors on opposite sides of the vertical axis of the picture. Symmetry is so precise that we can measure it. Pictures employing absolute symmetry tend to be stable, stolid, and without much sense of motion. Many works approach symmetry, but retreat from placing mirror images on opposite sides of the center-line, as do Figures 3.12, 3.20, and 3.21, all of which are symmetrical.

ASYMMETRICAL BALANCE, sometimes referred to as psychological balance, is achieved by careful placement of unlike items (Fig. 3.22). It might seem that asymmetrical balance is a matter of opinion. However, intrinsic response to what is balanced or unbalanced is relatively uniform among individuals, regardless of their aesthetic training. Every painting illustrated in this chapter is asymmetrical. Often color is used to balance line and form. Because some hues, such as yellow, have a great attraction for the eye, they can balance tremendous mass and activity on one side of a painting, by being placed on the other side.

Figure 3.20 Closed composition (composition kept within the frame).

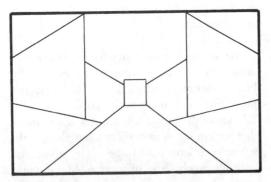

Figure 3.21 Open composition (composition allowed to escape the frame).

UNITY. With a few exceptions, we can say that artists strive for a sense of self-contained completeness in their artworks. Thus an important characteristic in a work of art is the means by which *unity* is achieved. All of the elements of composition work together to provide us with a picture that hangs together to work toward meaning. Often compositional elements are juxtaposed in unusual or uncustomary fashion to achieve a particular effect. Nonetheless, that effect usually comprises a conscious attempt at maintaining or completing a unified statement, that is, the total picture. Every element we have discussed in his section may be utilized to work with all the other elements to give us a picture that is unified. Our discussion of how an artist has employed compositional devices is not complete until we discern how the composition works as a totality.

With regard to unity, we also must consider whether or not the artist allows the composition to *escape the frame.* People occasionally speak of *closed composition,* or composition in

Figure 3.22 St. Mark and St. Luke from the Gospel Book of Godescale, 781–3. Vellum, 12¼″ × 8¼″. Bibliothèque Nationale, Paris.

Plate 1 The Church of Nikolai Khamovnik (1679–1682). Moscow, Russia.

Plate 3 Joan Miró, *Painting* (1933). Oil on canvas, 68½″ × 77¼″. The Museum of Modern Art, New York. Loula D. Lasker Bequest (by exchange).

Plate 2 Giovanni Battista Vanni, *Holy Family with St. John.* Oil on canvas, 70″ × 58″. Palmer Museum of Art, The Pennsylvania State University.

Plate 4 Color wheel.

Plate 5 Pablo Picasso, *Girl Before a Mirror* (Boisgeloup, March 1932). Oil on canvas, 64″ × 51¼″. Collection, The Museum of Modern Art, New York. Gift of Mrs. Simon Guggenheim. Photograph © 1996, The Museum of Modern Art, New York.

Plate 6 Jean-Baptiste-Camille Corot (French, 1796–1875), *A View Near Volterra* (1838). Canvas/oil on canvas, 27³⁄₈″ × 37½″. National Gallery of Art, Washington, D.C. Chester Dale Collection. Photo by Richard Carafelli.

Plate 7 Jan Vermeer (Dutch, 1632–1675), *The Girl with a Red Hat* (c. 1660). Oil on panel, unframed: 9 × 7¹⁄₁₆″; framed: 17½″ × 15½″ × 3¼″. National Gallery of Art, Washington, D.C. Andrew W. Mellon Collection. Photo by Richard Carafelli.

which use of line and form always directs the eye into the painting (Fig. 3.20), as unified, and *open composition,* in which the eye is allowed to wander off the canvas, or *escape the frame* (Fig. 3.21), as disunified. Such is not the case. Keeping the artwork within the frame is a stylistic device that has an important bearing on the artwork's meaning. For example, painting in the classical style is predominantly kept within the frame. This illustrates a concern for the self-containment of the artwork and for precise structuring. Baroque design, in contrast, tends to force the eye to escape the frame. Here the device has philosophical intent, suggesting the world or universe outside or the individual's place in an overwhelming cosmos. So unity can be achieved by keeping the composition close, but it is not necessarily lacking when the opposite state exists.

Focal area. When we look at a picture for the first time, our eye moves around it, pausing briefly at those areas that seem to be of greatest visual appeal. These are *focal areas.* A painting may have a single focal area to which our eye is drawn immediately and from which it will stray only with conscious effort. Or it may have an infinite number of focal points. We describe a picture of the latter type as "busy"; that is, the eye bounces at will from one point to another on the picture, without any attraction at all.

Focal areas are achieved in a number of ways—through confluence of line, by encirclement, (Fig. 3.23) or by color, to name just a few. To draw attention to a particular point in the picture the artist may make all lines lead to that point. He or she may place the focal object or area in the center of a ring of objects, or may give the object a color that demands our attention more than the other colors in the picture. Again, for example, bright yellows attract our eye more readily than dark blues. Artists use focal areas, of whatever number or variety, as controls over what we see and when we see it when we look at a picture.

Other Factors

Perspective

Perspective is a tool the artist uses to indicate the spatial relationships of objects in a picture. It is based on the perceptual phenomenon that causes objects farther away from us to appear smaller. If we examine a painting that has some degree of verisimilitude, we can identify, through perspective, the spatial relationship between the objects in the foreground and the objects in the background. We also can discern whether that relationship is rational—that is, whether or not the relationships of the objects appear as we see them in life. For example, paintings executed prior to the Italian Renaissance (when mechanical procedures for rendering perspective were developed) look rather strange to us because although background objects are painted smaller than foreground objects the positioning does not appear rational. So their composition strikes us as being rather primitive.

Linear perspective. Two types of perspective may be used. The first, *linear* perspective, is characterized by the phenomenon of standing on railroad tracks and watching the two rails apparently come together at the horizon. It uses *line* to achieve the sense of distance. In color insert Plate 6, the road recedes from foreground to background and becomes narrower as it does so. We perceive that recession, which denotes distance, through the artist's use of line.

Aerial perspective indicates distance through the use of light and atmosphere. For example, mountains in the background of a picture are made to appear distant by being painted in less detail; they are hazy. In the upper left of Plate 2 a castle appears at a great distance. We know it is distant because it is smaller and, more important, because it is indistinct. The same applies to the mountains in Plate 6. Another

Figure 3.23 St. Mark from the Gospel Book of St. Medard of Soissons, France (early ninth century). Paint on vellum, 14³⁄₈″ × 10¼″. Bibliothèque Nationale, Paris.

treatment of aerial perspective can be seen in the painting *Buddhist Retreat by Stream and Mountains,* attributed to the Chinese artist Juran (Fig. 3.24). This hanging scroll illustrates a device fairly common in Chinese paintings with a vertical format. The artist divides the picture into two basic units, foreground and background. The foreground of the painting consists of details reaching back toward the middle ground. At that point a division occurs, so the background and the foreground are separated by an openness in what might have been a deep middle ground. The foreground represents the nearby, and its rich detail causes us to pause and ponder on numerous elements, including the artist's use of brush stroke in creating foliage,

rocks, and water. Then there is a break, and the background appears to loom up or be suspended, almost as if it were a separate entity. Although the foreground gives us a sense of dimension—of space receding from the front plane of the painting—the background seems flat, a factor that serves to enhance further the sense of height of the mountains.

Subject Matter

We can regard treatment of subject matter as ranging from verisimilitude, or representationalism, to nonobjectivity (Fig. 3.25). We use this continuum again in later chapters, substituting the term *theatricality* for nonobjectivity. Between the two ends of this continuum are many of the

Figure 3.24 *Buddhist Retreat by Stream and Mountains.* Hanging scroll, ink on silk, height 185.4 cm. Attributed to Juran, Chinese, active c. A.D. 960–80, northern Song dynasty. The Cleveland Museum of Art. Gift of Katherine Holden Thayer.

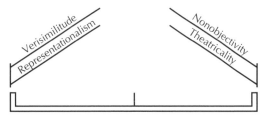

Figure 3.25 Subject-matter continuum.

isms we all are familiar with in the art world: realism, impressionism, expressionism, cubism, fauvism, and so forth. Each suggests a particular method of treatment of subject matter.

Chiaroscuro

Chiaroscuro (sometimes called *modeling*), whose meaning in Italian is "light and shade," is the device used by artists to make their forms appear *plastic,* that is, three dimensional. The problem of making two-dimensional objects appear three dimensional rests basically on the artist's ability to render highlight and shadow effectively. Without them all forms are two dimensional in appearance.

Use of chiaroscuro gives a picture much of its character. For example, the dynamic and dramatic treatment of light and shade in color insert Plate 7 gives this painting a quality quite different from what would have resulted had the artist chosen to give full, flat, front light to the face. The highlights, falling as they do, create not only a dramatic effect but also a compositional triangle extending from shoulder to cheek, down to the hand, and then across the sleeve and back to the shoulder. Consider the substantial change in character of Plate 2 had highlight and shadow been executed in a different manner. Finally, the treatment of chiaroscuro in a highly verisimilar fashion in color insert Plate 8 helps give that painting its strangely real yet dreamlike appearance.

In contrast, works that do not employ chiaroscuro have a two-dimensional quality. This can be seen to a large extent in Figure 3.1 and also in Plate 5 and Figure 3.26.

HOW DOES IT STIMULATE THE SENSES?

We do not touch pictures, and so we cannot feel their roughness or their smoothness, their coolness or their warmth. We cannot hear pictures and we cannot smell them. So, when we conclude that a picture affects our senses in a particular way, we are responding in terms of visual stimuli that are transposed into mental images of our sense of touch, taste, sound, and so forth.

Contrasts

The colors of an artist's palette are referred to as warm or cool depending on which end of the color spectrum they fall. Reds, oranges, and yellows are said to be warm colors. Those are the colors of the sun and therefore call to mind our primary source of heat. So they carry strong implications of warmth. Colors falling on the opposite end of the spectrum—blues and greens— are cool colors because they imply shade, or lack of light and warmth. As we will notice frequently, this is a stimulation that is mental but has a physical basis. Tonality and color contrast also affect our senses. The stark value contrasts of Figure 3.26 contribute significantly to the harsh

and dynamic qualities of the work. The colorlessness of this monochromatic black, white, and gray work completes its horrifying comment on the tragic bombing of the Spanish city of Guernica. In the opposite vein, the soft, yet dramatic, tonal contrasts of Plate 7 and the strong warmth and soft texture of the red hat bring us a completely different set of stimuli.

Many of the sense-affecting stimuli work in concert and cannot be separated from each other. We already have noted some of the effects of chiaroscuro, but one more will serve well. One of the most interesting effects to observe in a picture is the treatment of flesh. Some flesh is treated harshly and appears like stone. Other flesh appears soft and true to life. Our response to whatever treatment has been given is very tactile—we want to touch, or we believe we know what we would feel if we touched. Chiaroscuro is essential in an artist's achieving those effects. Harsh shadows and strong contrasts create one set of responses; diffused shadows and subdued contrasts create another. Rubens's *Assumption of the Virgin* (color insert Plate 9) presents us with softly modeled flesh whose warmth and softness come from color and chiaroscuro. Highlight and shadow func-

Figure 3.26 Pablo Picasso, *Guernica* (mural) (1937, May–early June). Oil on canvas, 11′ 6″ × 25′ 8″. Museo del Prado.

Figure 3.27 Grant Wood, American (1891–1942), *American Gothic* (1930). Oil on beaver board, 30″ × 25″. Friends of American Art Collection. Photograph © 1990. The Art Institute of Chicago. All rights reserved.

tion to create softness, and predominantly red hues warm the composition; our sensual response is heightened dramatically.

Dynamics

Although pictures are motionless, they can effectively stimulate a sense of movement and activity. They also can create a sense of stable so-lidity. The artist stimulates these sensations by using certain conventional devices. Composition that is principally vertical can express, for example, a sense of dignity and grandeur (color insert Plate 10) and Figure 3.27. A picture that is horizontal can elicit a sense of stability and placidity (Fig. 3.28). The triangle is a most interesting form in engineering because of its

Figure 3.28 Masaccio, *Tribute Money* (c. 1427). Santa Maria del Carmine, Florence. Courtesy of Heaton-Sessions, Stone Ridge, New York.

structural qualities. It is also interesting in art because of its psychological qualities. If we place a triangle so its base forms the bottom of a picture, we create a definite sense of solidarity and immovability (Fig. 3.29). If that triangle were a pyramid sitting on a level plane, a great deal of effort would be required to tip it over. If we invert the triangle so it balances on

its apex, a sensation of extreme instability results (Fig. 3.30). Although we can feel clearly the sensations stimulated by these rather simple geometric forms, we should not conclude that geometric forms used as compositional devices are either explicit or limited in communication. Nonverbal communication in the arts is not that simple. Nonetheless, the basic compo-

Figure 3.29 Upright-triangular composition.

Figure 3.30 Inverted-triangular composition.

Figure 3.31 Curved line.

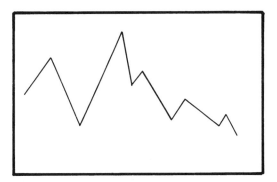

Figure 3.32 Broken line.

sitional devices do influence our response and impact on our perceptions.

The use of line also affects sense response. Figure 3.31 illustrates how this use of curved line can elicit a sense of relaxation. The broken line in Figure 3.32, in contrast, creates a more dynamic and violent sensation. We can also feel that the upright triangle in Figure 3.29, al-

though solid and stable, is more dynamic than the horizontals of Figure 3.28 because it uses stronger diagonal line, which tends to stimulate a sense of movement. Precision of linear execution also can create sharply defined forms or soft, fuzzy images. Piet Mondrian (Fig. 3.33) finds in straight lines and right angles the basic principles of life itself. Vertical

Figure 3.33 Piet Mondrian, *Composition in White, Black, and Red* (1936). Oil on canvas, 40¼" × 41". Collection, The Museum of Modern Art, New York. Gift of the Advisory Committee.

lines signify vitality and life; horizontal lines signify tranquillity and death. The intersection of vertical and horizontal line represents life's tensions.

Trompe l'oeil

Trompe l'oeil (pronounced trawmp LOY), or "trick of the eye," gives the artist a varied set of stimuli by which to affect our sensory response. Occasionally this device forms the core of a painting; at other times it is used to enhance a work's appeal. For example, all objects drawn with parallel sides recede to the same vanishing point. Some artists make subtle changes in the placement of the vanishing point, with the effect that the picture, while appearing verisimilar, gives the impression of rotating forward at the top. Its kinesthetic appeal is thereby much more dynamic.

Juxtaposition

We can also receive sense stimuli from the results of juxtaposing curved and straight lines, which results in linear dissonance or consonance. Figure 3.34 illustrates the juxtaposing of inharmonious forms, which creates instability. Careful use of this device can stimulate some very interesting and specific sense responses, as the artist has done in Plate 5.

Figure 3.34 Juxtaposition.

Objectivity

Subject matter, which involves any or all of the characteristics we have discussed, is a powerful device for effecting both sensory responses and more intense, subjective responses. The use of verisimilitude or nonobjectivity is the most noticeable stimulant of individual response. It would seem logical for individuals to respond intellectually to nonobjective pictures because the subject matter should be neutral, with no inherent expressive stimuli. However, nothing creates so extreme a *subjective* response (especially a negative one) as nonobjectivity. When asked whether they feel more comfortable with the treatment of subject matter in Plate 2 or that in Figure 3.13, most individuals choose the former, even though the latter is a product of our age, our society, our world. Does the contemporary work tell us something about ourselves we do not wish to hear?

Does an explicit appeal cause a more profound response? Or does the stimulation provided by the unfamiliar cause us to think more deeply and respond more fully because our imagination is left free to wander? The answers to these questions are worth considering as we perceive artworks, many of whose keys to response are not immediately obvious.

CHRONOLOGY OF SELECTED MAJOR PERIODS, STYLES, AND EXAMPLES FOR STUDY IN WESTERN ART

PAINTING

Prehistory–c. 4000 B.C.
   paleolithic and neolithic cave paintings

c. 4000 B.C.–c. 1000 B.C.
   Ancient Egypt
      tomb paintings

c. 3000 b.c.–c. 500 b.c.
Ancient Mesopotamia, Persia, Crete, and
Mycenae
wall and vase paintings

c. 1200 b.c.–c. 300 b.c.
Ancient Greece
vase paintings

c. 500 b.c.–c. 300 a.d.
Rome and Hellenistic Greece
vase and wall paintings

c. 300–1400
The Middle Ages
Early Christian and Byzantine Art
catacomb and wall paintings
manuscript illustration
mosaics
Romanesque Europe
manuscript illustration
Gothic
manuscript illustration
Duccio: *Majestas Altarpiece*
Martini: *Madonna in Majesty; Virgin of
Paris*
Cimabue: *Madonna Enthroned*
Giotto: *The Lamentation; Joachim and
Anna at the Beautiful Gate*
Lorenzetti: *The Birth of the Virgin*

c. 1400–c. 1500
Flanders
Martorel: *St. George and the Dragon*
Pol de Limbourg: *Les Très Riches Heures du
Duc de Berri*
Jan van Eyck: *The Arnolfini Marriage*
Roger van der Weyden: *The Descent from
the Cross*
Jerome Bosch: *Temptation of St.
Anthony*
Italy (early Renaissance)
Fra Angelico: *Annunciation*
Fra Lippo Lippi: *Adoration*

Botticelli: *Spring*
Ghirlandaio: *Old Man and Boy*
Masaccio: *Tribute Money*
Mantegna: *St. James Led to Execution*
Perugino: *Christ Delivering the Keys to St.
Peter*
The Reformation
Schongauer: *Annunciation*
Dürer: *The Four Horsemen of the
Apocalypse; The Four Apostles*
Baldung Grien: *Three Ages of Man*

c. 1480–c. 1550
High Renaissance
Leonardo da Vinci: *The Last Supper; Mona
Lisa*
Michelangelo: Sistine Chapel frescoes
Raphael: *Sistine Madonna; Madonna of the
Chair; The School of Athens*
Bellini: *Portrait of Doge Loredano*
Giorgione: *Fête Champêtre; Sleeping
Venus*
Titian: *Bacchus and Ariadne; The Young
Englishman*

c. 1510–c. 1570
Mannerism
Bronzino: *Portrait of a Young Man*
Parmigianino: *The Madonna with the Long
Neck*
Tintoretto: *The Last Supper*
Clouet: *Francis I*
Brueghel the Elder: *The Wedding Dance*

c. 1570–c. 1700
Baroque Art
Domenichino: *The Last Communion of St.
Jerome*
Caravaggio: *Bacchus: Death of the Virgin*
Velásquez: *Portrait of Philip IV; Las Meninas*
Rubens: *Assumption of the Virgin; Judgment
of Paris; The Garden of Love*
Poussin: *Orpheus and Eurydice; Funeral of
Phocian*

Lorrain: *Embarkation of the Queen of Sheba*
Hals: *Malle Babbe*
Rembrandt: *The Night Watch; Man with the Golden Helmet; Descent from the Cross*
van Ruysdael: *The Jewish Cemetery; Wheat Fields*
Vermeer: *Officer and Laughing Girl*

c. 1700–c. 1800

Rococo Art
Watteau: *Embarkation for Cythera; Giles*
Boucher: *The Toilet of Venus; Venus Consoling Love*
Chardin: *The Young Governess; Still Life Menu de Gras*
Canaletto: *Grand Canal*
Fragonard: *The Romance of Young Love; Storming the Citadel*
Social Criticism
Hogarth: *The Rake's Progress* series; *The Harlot's Progress* series
Portraiture
Gainsborough: *The Honorable Frances Duncombe*
Reynolds: *Sarah Siddons as the Tragic Muse*
Copley: *Nathaniel Hurd*
Stuart: *George Washington*
Neoclassicism
David: *The Oath of the Horatii; The Death of Socrates*

c. 1800–c. 1905

Neoclassicism
Ingres: *Odalisque*
Romanticism
Goya: *Executions of the Third of May, 1808*
Gros: *Napoleon Among the Plague-Striken at Jaffa*
Géricault: *The Raft of the "Medusa"*
Delacroix: *Massacre at Chios*

Constable: *Hampstead Heath with a Rainbow*
Turner: *The Slave Ship; Valley of Aosta*
Realism
Courbet: *The Stonebreakers; My Studio*
Manet: *Luncheon on the Grass*
Daumier: *The Third-Class Carriage*
Romantic Naturalism
Corot: *A View Near Volterra*
Impressionism
Manet: *Luncheon on the Grass*
Monet: *The River*
Renoir: *Luncheon of the Boating Party*
Degas: *Dancers Practicing at the Bar*
Postimpressionism
Seurat: *Sunday Afternoon on the Island of the Grande-Jatte*
van Gogh: *Church at Auvers; The Starry Night*
Cézanne: *Mont Sainte-Victoire Seen from Bibemus Quarry*
Gauguin: *Vision After the Sermon*

c. 1900–

Fauvism
Matisse: *The Blue Nude—Souvenir of Biskra*
Rouault: *Mr. X*
Expressionism
Beckman: *Christ and the Woman Taken in Adultery*
Kandinsky: *Improvisation; Interior*
Klee: *Actor's Mask*
Cubism
Picasso: *Les Demoiselles d'Avignon*
Braque: *Packet of Tobacco*
Léger: *Three Women*
Futurism
Severini: *Armored Train*
Suprematism
Malevich: *Suprematist Composition: White on White*
Abstract and Nonobjective Art
Mondrian: *Composition in White, Black, and Red*

Dada
  Ernst: *Woman, Old Man, and Flower*
Mechanism
  Duchamp: *The Bride*
Surrealism
  Dali: *The Persistence of Memory*
  de Chirico: *Nostalgia of the Infinite*
Precisionism
  Davis: *Lucky Strike*
Realism
  Wood: *American Gothic*
Abstract Expressionism
  De Kooning: *Excavation*
  Pollock: *Number 1*
  Rothko: *Number 10*
Pop Art
  Lichtenstein: *Whaam!*

PRINTMAKING
  Anonymous: *S. S. Christopher, Margaret and Barbara,* woodcut, c. 1420–30
  Albrecht Dürer: *St. Michael and the Dragon,* woodcut, c. 1497–98; *Adam and Eve,* copper engraving, 1504

Francisco Goya: *He Died without any Aid,* etching, aquatint, and drypoint, nineteenth century
James McNeill Whistler: *The Storm, drypoint*
Edouard Manet: *Berthe Morisot,* chalk lithograph, 1872
Georges Rouault: *Christ,* colored aquatint etching, 1935
Sam Francis: *Tokyo Mon Amour,* lithograph, 1963
Frank Kupka: *Vegetables,* silkscreen

PHOTOGRAPHY
  Matthew Brady: *Wounded Soldiers,* 1863
  Charles M. Currier: *The Bicycle Messengers, Seated,* 1900
  Lewis W. Hine: *Fresh Air for the Baby,* 1907
  Arnold Genthe: *Watching the Approach,* 1906
  Alvin L. Coburn: *The Octopus,* 1912
  Edward Weston: *Church Door, Hornitos,* 1930
  Dorothea Lange: *White Angel Breadline,* 1933
  Robert Frank: *Trolley,* 1958
  Dean Brown: *California Cows,* 1969
  Jerry Uelsmann: *Untitled,* 1972
  John Isaac: *Famine in Ethiopia,* 1984

Sculpture

Sculpture, in contrast to pictures, seems less personal and more public. In fact, we are likely to find works of sculpture mostly in public spaces. Outside city halls and in parks and corporate office buildings we find statues of local dignitaries and constructions of wood, stone, and metal that appear to represent nothing at all. We might even wonder why our tax dollars were spent to buy them. Today, as throughout history, sculpture (and other forms of art) are often the subject of public pride and controversy. Because of its permanence, sculpture often represents the only artifact of entire civilizations. In this chapter we'll not only see how sculpture is made and how it works, but our examples will reveal ideas of artists from ancient history, contemporary times, and many cultures.

WHAT IS IT?

Sculpture is a three-dimensional art. It may take the form of whatever it seeks to represent, from pure, or nonobjective form, to lifelike depiction of people or any other entity. Sometimes sculpture, because of its three-dimensionality, comes very close to reality in its depiction.

Duane Hanson and John DeAndrea, for example, use plastics to render the human form so realistically that the viewer must approach the artwork and examine it closely to determine it is not a real person.

HOW IS IT PUT TOGETHER?

Dimensionality

Sculpture may be *full round, relief,* or *linear.* Full round works are freestanding and fully three dimensional (Fig. 4.1). A work that can be viewed from only one side—that is, one that projects from a background—is said to be *in relief* (Fig. 4.2). A work utilizing narrow, elongated materials is called *linear* (Fig. 4.14). A sculptor's choice of full round, relief, or linearity as a mode of expression dictates to a large extent what he or she can and cannot do, both aesthetically and practically.

Full Round

Sculptural works that explore full three-dimensionality and are meant to be viewed from any angle are called *full round.* Some sub-

Figure 4.1 Apollo playing the lyre (Roman copy of a Greek statue), from the Temple of Apollo at Cyrene (first century A.D.). Marble, over life size. The British Museum, London.

jects and styles pose certain constraints in this regard, however. Painters, printmakers, and photographers have virtually unlimited choice of subject matter and compositional arrangements. Full round sculptures dealing with such subjects as clouds, oceans, and panoramic land-scapes are problematic for the sculptor. Because sculpture occupies real space, the use of perspective, for example, to increase spatial relationships poses obvious problems. In addition, because full round sculpture is freestanding and three dimensional, sculptors must concern themselves with the practicalities of engineering and gravity. For example, they cannot create a work with great mass at the top unless they can find a way (within the bounds of acceptable composition) to keep the statue from falling over. In numerous full round works, sculptors use small animals, branches, tree stumps, rocks, and other devices as additional support to give practical stability to a work.

Relief

Sculptors who create works in relief do not have quite so many restrictions because their work is attached to a background. Clouds, seas, and perspective landscapes are within relief sculptors' reach because their work needs only to be viewed from one side. Relief sculpture, then, is three dimensional. However, because it protrudes from a background, it maintains a two-dimensional quality, as compared to full round sculpture.

Linear

The third category of sculpture, *linear sculpture,* emphasizes construction with thin, elongated items such as wire or neon tubing. Artworks using linear materials and occupying three-dimensional space will occasionally puzzle us as we consider or try to decide whether they are really linear or full round. Here again, absolute definition is less important than the process of analysis and aesthetic experience and response.

Methods of Execution

In general, we may say that sculpture is executed using additive, subtractive, substitute, or manipulative techniques, or any combination of these. A fifth category, called *found sculpture,*

Figure 4.2 East Frieze, Halicarnassus. The British Museum, London.

may or may not be considered a method of execution, as we see later.

Subtraction

Carved works are said to be *subtractive*. That is, the sculptor begins with a large block, usually wood or stone, and cuts away (subtracts) the unwanted material. In previous eras, and to some extent today, sculptors have had to work with whatever materials were at hand. Wood carvings emanated from forested regions, soapstone carvings came from the Eskimos, and great works of marble came from the regions surrounding the quarries of the Mediterranean. Anything that can yield to the carver's tools can be formed into a work of sculpture. However, stone, with its promise of immortality, has proven to be the most popular material.

Three types of rock hold potential for the carver. *Igneous* rocks, of which granite is an example, are very hard and potentially long lasting. However, they are difficult to carve and therefore not popular. *Sedimentary* rocks such as limestone are relatively long lasting, easy to carve, and polishable. Beautifully smooth and lustrous surfaces are possible with sedimentary

rocks. *Metamorphic* rocks, including marble, seem to be the sculptor's ideal. They are long lasting, a pleasure to carve, and exist in a broad range of colors. Whatever the artist's choice, one requirement must be met: The material to be carved, whether wood, stone, or a bar of soap, must be free of flaws.

A sculptor who sets about to carve a work does not begin simply by imagining a *Samson Slaying a Philistine* (Fig. 4.3) and then attacking the stone. He or she first creates a model, usually smaller than the intended sculpture. The model is made of clay, plaster, or wax and is completed in precise detail—a miniature of the final product.

Once the likeness of the model has been enlarged and transferred, the artist begins to rough out the actual image ("knocking away the waste material," as Michelangelo put it). In this step of the sculpting process, the artist carves to within 2 or 3 inches of what is to be the finished area, using specific tools designed for the purpose. Then, using a different set of carving tools, she carefully takes the material down to the precise detail. Finishing work and polishing follow.

Figure 4.3 Giambologna, *Samson Slaying a Philistine* (c. 1562). Courtesy of The Board of Trustees of The Victoria and Albert Museum, London.

Addition

In contrast with carving from a large block of material, the sculptor using an additive process starts with raw material and *adds* element to element until the work is finished. The term *built sculpture* often is used to describe works executed in an additive technique. The materials employed in this process can be plastics, metals such as aluminum or steel, terracottas (clay), epoxy resins, or wood. Many times materials are combined (Fig. 4.4). It is not uncommon for sculptors to combine constructional methods as well. For example, built sections of metal or plastic may be combined with carved sections of stone.

Substitution

Any material that can be transformed from a plastic, molten, or fluid state into a solid state can be molded or *cast* into a work of sculpture. The creation of a piece of cast sculpture always involves the use of a mold. First, the artist creates an identically sized model of the intended sculpture. This is called a *positive*. He or she then covers the positive with a material, such as plaster of paris, that when hardened and removed will retain the surface configurations of the positive. This form is called a *negative* and becomes the mold for the actual sculpture. The molten or fluid material is poured into the negative and allowed to solidify. When the mold is removed, the work of sculpture emerges. Surface polishing, if desired, brings the work to its final form. Figures 4.5, 4.6, and color insert Plate 11 all show the degrees of complexity and variety achievable through casting.

Very often sculpture is cast so it is hollow. This method, of course, is less expensive because it requires less material. It also results in a work that is less prone to crack, since it is less susceptible to expansion and contraction resulting from changes in temperature. Finally, hollow sculpture is, naturally, lighter and thus more easily shipped and handled.

Manipulation

In this technique, materials such as clay are shaped by skilled use of the hands. A term of similar meaning is *modeling*. The difference between this technique and addition is clear when

Figure 4.4 Bakota ancestor figure from Gabon, late nineteenth century. French Congo. Ancestral figure of wood. Overlaid with copper and brass. Given by H. G. Beasley, Esq., 1924.

we watch an artist take a single lump of clay and skillfully transform it, as it turns on a potter's wheel, into a final shape.

Found

This category of sculpture is exactly what its name implies. Often natural objects, whether shaped by human hands or otherwise, are dis-

covered that for some reason have taken on characteristics which stimulate aesthetic responses. They become *objets d'art* not because an artist put them together (although an artist may combine found objects to create a work), but because an artist chose to take them from their original surroundings and hold them up to the rest of us as vehicles for aesthetic com-

Figure 4.5 Ronald J. Bennet, *Landscape #3* (1969). Cast bronze, 8″ high × 10″ wide × 7″ deep. Palmer Museum of Art, The Pennsylvania State University. Gift of the Class of 1975.

munication. In other words, an artist decided that such an object said something aesthetically and *chose* to present it in that vein.

Some may have concern about such a category, however, because it removes *techne,* or *skill,* from the artistic process. As a result, objects such as driftwood and interesting rocks can assume perhaps an unwarranted place as art products or objects. This is a touchy area. However, if a found object is altered in some way to produce an artwork, then the process would probably fall under one of our previously noted methods, and the product could be termed an artwork in the fullest sense of the word.

Ephemeral

Ephemeral art has many different expressions and includes the works of the conceptualists, who insist art is an activity of change, disorientation, and violent lack of cohesion. Designed to be transitory, ephemeral art makes its statement and then, eventually, ceases to ex-

Figure 4.6 Henry Moore, *Two Large Forms* (1969). The Serpentine, Hyde Park, London. (See also color insert Plate 11.)

ist. Undoubtedly the largest work of sculpture ever designed was based on that concept. Christo and Jeanne-Claude's *Running Fence* (Fig. 4.7) was an event and a process, as well as a sculptural work. At the end of a two-week viewing period, *Running Fence, Sonoma and Marin Counties, California (1972–76)* was removed entirely and materials were recycled.

Composition

Composition in sculpture comprises the same elements and principles as composition in the pictorial arts: mass, line, form, balance, repetition, color, proportion, and unity. Sculptors' uses of these elements are significantly different, however, because they work in three dimensions.

Elements

Mass (Space). Unlike a picture, a sculpture has literal mass. It takes up three-dimensional *space,* and its materials have *density.* Mass in pictures is

relative mass: The mass of forms in a picture has application principally in *relation to* other forms within the same picture. In sculpture, however, mass is literal and consists of actual volume and density. So the mass of a sculpture that is 20 feet high, 8 feet wide, and 6 feet deep and made of balsa wood would seem less than a sculpture 10 feet high, 4 feet wide, and 3 feet deep and made of lead. Space and density must both be considered. What if the material of a statue is disguised to look and feel like a different material? We discuss this question later in the chapter, when we look at how a sculpture affects our senses.

Line and form. As we stated in Chapter 3, line and form are highly related. We can separate them (with some difficulty) when we discuss pictures because in two dimensions an artist uses line to define form. In painting, line is a construction tool. Without using line, artists cannot reveal their forms, and when we ana-

Figure 4.7 Christo and Jeanne-Claude, *Running Fence, Sonoma and Marin Counties, California* (1972–76). Woven nylon fabric and steel cables, height 18′, length 24½ miles. © Christo, 1976. Photograph: Wolfgang Volz.

lyze a painting, line is perhaps more important to us than the actual form it reveals. However, in sculpture the case is nearly reversed. It is the form that draws our interest, and when we discuss line in sculpture, we do so in terms of how it is revealed in form.

When we view a sculpture, its elements direct our eye from one point to another, just as focal points do, via line and color, in a picture. In some works the eye is directed through the piece and then off into space. Such sculptures have an *open* form. In Figure 4.11 the eye is directed outward from the work in the same fashion as composition that escapes the frame in painting. If, however, the eye is directed continually back into the form, we say the form is *closed*. If we allow our eye to follow the linear detail of Figure 4.8, we find we are continually led back into the work. This is similar to composition kept within the frame in painting and to closed forms in music, which we discuss in Chapter 5. Often it is difficult to fit a work precisely into one or the other of these categories. For example, in Figure 4.3 there are elements of closed composition and, as indicated by the fabric flying to the left, open composition as well.

Obviously, not all sculptures are completely solid; they may have openings. We call any such holes in a sculpture *negative space,* and we can discuss this characteristic in terms of its role in the overall composition. In some works negative space is inconsequential; in others it is quite significant. It is up to us to decide which, and how it contributes to the overall piece. In figure 4.6 and Plate 11 negative space plays a significant role. In the former it might be argued that negative space is as instrumental to the overall concept of the work as is the metal form. In Figure 4.1, in contrast, negative space is clearly incidental.

Color. Perhaps color does not seem particularly important to us when we relate it to sculpture. We tend to see ancient sculpture as white and modern sculpture as natural wood or rusty iron. Color is as important to the sculptor as it is to the painter. In some cases the material itself may be chosen because of its color; in others, the sculpture may be painted. The lifelike sculptures of Duane Hanson depend on color for their effect. They are so lifelike that we easily could confuse them with real people. Finally, still other materials may be chosen or treated so that nature will provide the final color through oxidation or weathering.

Texture. Texture, the roughness or smoothness of a surface, is a tangible characteristic of sculpture. Sculpture is unique in that we can perceive its texture through our sense of touch. Even when we cannot touch a work of sculpture, we can perceive and respond to texture, which can be both physical and suggested. Sculptors go to great lengths to achieve the texture they desire for their works. In fact, much of a sculptor's technical mastery manifests itself in that final ability to impart a surface to the work. We examine texture more fully in our discussion of sense responses.

Principles

Proportion. Proportion is the relative relationship of shapes to one another. Just as we have a seemingly innate sense of balance, so we have a feeling of proportion. That feeling tells us that each form in the sculpture is in proper relationship to the others. However, as any student of art history will tell us, proportion—or the ideal of relationships—has varied from one civilization or culture to another. For example, such a seemingly obviously proportioned entity as the human body has varied greatly in its proportions as sculptors over the centuries have depicted it. Study the differences in proportion in the human body among Michelangelo's *David* (Fig. 4.8), the Chartres' *Saints* (Fig. 4.9), an ancient Greek *Kouros* figure (Fig. 4.10), and Ciacometti's *Man Pointing* (Fig. 4.11). Each depicts the human form, but with differing pro-

Figure 4.8 Michelangelo, *David* (1501–1504). Marble, 13' 5". Academy, Florence.

Figure 4.9 Jamb Statues, West Portal, Chartres Cathedral (begun 1145). Lauros-Giraudon/Art Resource.

Figure 4.10 *Kouros* figure. The Metropolitan Museum of Art, Fletcher Fund, 1932. (32.11.1)

Figure 4.11 Alberto Giacometti, *Man Pointing* (1947). Bronze, 70^1/$_2$″ × 40^3/$_4$″ × 16^3/$_8$″. Collection, The Museum of Modern Art, New York. Gift of Mrs. John D. Rockefeller 3d.

portions. This difference in proportion helps transmit the message the artist wishes to communicate about his or her subject matter.

Repetition. Rhythm, harmony, and variation constitute repetition in sculpture, as they did in the pictorial arts. However, in sculpture we must look more carefully and closely to determine how the artist has employed these elements. If we reduce a sculpture to its components of line and form, we begin to see how (as in music) rhythmic patterns—regular and irregular—occur. In Figure 4.2, for example, a regular rhythmic pattern is established in space as the eye moves from figure to figure and from leg to leg of the figures. We also can see whether the components are consonant or dissonant. For instance, in Figure 4.2 a sense of dynamics, that is, action or movement, is created by the dissonance that results from juxtaposing the strong triangles of the stances and groupings with the *biomorphic* lines of the human body. Unity of the curves in Figure 4.13, in contrast, provides us with a consonant series of relationships. Finally, we can see how line and form are used in theme and variation. We noted the repetition of triangles in Figure 4.2. In contrast, the sculptor of Figure 4.12 varies his motif, the oval, as the eye moves from the child's face to the upper arm, the hand, and finally the cat's face.

Other Factors

Articulation

Important also in viewing sculpture is noting the manner by which we move from one element to the next. That manner of movement is called *articulation,* and it applies to sculpture, painting, photography, and all the other arts. As an example, let us step outside the arts to consider human speech. Sentences, phrases, and individual words are nothing more than sound syllables (vowels) articulated (that is, joined together) by consonants. We understand what someone says to us because that individual ar-

Figure 4.12 William Zorach, *Child with Cat* (1926). Bronze, 17½″ × 10″ × 7½″. Museum of Art, The Pennsylvania State University.

ticulates as he or she speaks. Let us put the five vowel sounds side by side: Eh—EE—Ah—O—OO. As yet we do not have a sentence. Articulate those vowels with consonants, and we have meaning: "Say, she must go too." The nature of an artwork depends on how the artist has repeated, varied, harmonized, and related its parts and how he or she has articulated the movement from one part to another—that is, how the sculptor indicates where one stops and the other begins.

Focal Area (Emphasis)

Sculptors, like painters or any other visual artists, must concern themselves with drawing our eye to those areas of their work that are central to what they wish to communicate. They also must provide the means by which our eye can move around the work. However, their task is much more complicated because they deal in three dimensions and they have little control over the direction from which we will first perceive the piece; the entire 360-degree view contributes to the total message communicated by the work.

Converging lines, encirclement, and color all work for sculptors as they do for painters. The encircling line of the tree and body parts in Figure 4.13 causes us, however we proceed to scan the work, to focus ultimately on the torso of this fertility figure.

One further device is available—movement, and sculptors have the option of placing moving objects in their work. Such an object immediately becomes a focal point of the sculpture. A mobile (Fig. 4.14) presents many ephemeral patterns of focus as it turns at the whim of the breezes.

HOW DOES IT STIMULATE THE SENSES?

Touch

We can touch sculpture and feel its roughness or its smoothness, its coolness or perhaps its warmth. Even if we are prohibited by museum regulation from touching a sculpture, we can

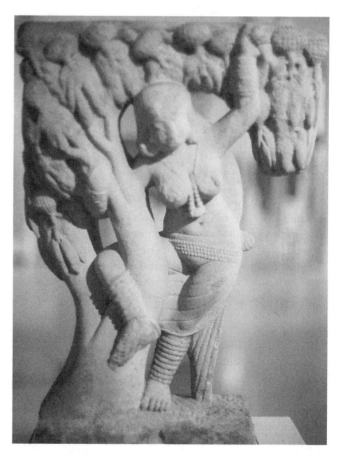

Figure 4.13 *Tree Spirit* (*Bracket Figure*), central India (first century A.D.). The British Museum, London.

Figure 4.14 Alexander Calder, *Spring Blossoms* (1965). Painted metal and heavy wire, extends 52″ × 102″. Museum of Art, The Pennsylvania State University. Gift of the Class of 1965.

see the surface texture and translate the image into an imaginary tactile sensation. Any work of sculpture cries out to be touched.

Temperature and Age

Color in sculpture stimulates our response by utilizing the same universal symbols as it does in paintings, photographs, and prints. Reds, oranges, and yellows stimulate sensations of warmth; blues and greens, sensations of coolness. In sculpture, color can result from the conscious choice of the artist, either in the selection of material or in the selection of the pigment with which the material is painted. Or, as we indicated earlier, color may result from the artist's choice to let nature color the work through wind, water, sun, and so forth.

This weathering effect, of course, creates very interesting patterns, but in addition it gives the sculpture the attribute not only of space but also of time, because the work obvi-

ously will change as nature works her wonders. A copper sculpture early in its existence will be a different work, a different set of stimuli, than it will be in five, ten, or twenty years. This is not entirely accidental; Artists choose copper, knowing what weathering will do to it. They obviously cannot predict the exact nature of the weathering or the exact hues of the sculpture at any given time in the future, but such predictability is irrelevant.

Our response to a work of art may be shaped by the effects of age on it. There is a great deal of charm and character in ancient objects. A wooden icon like Fig. 4.15 might have greater emotional impact because of the effects of age on its surfaces.

Dynamics

Line, form, and juxtaposition create dynamics in works of sculpture. The activity of a sculpture, however, tends to be heightened because

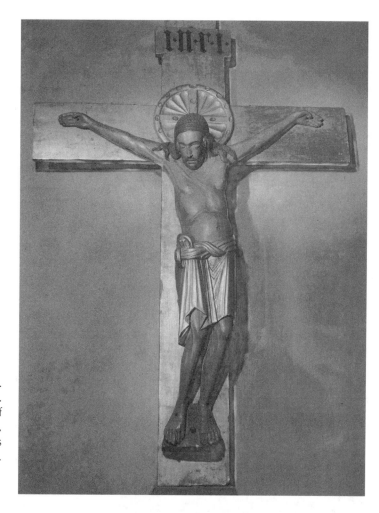

Figure 4.15 *Gero Crucifix* (c. 975–1000 A.D.). Oak, 6'2". Cologne Cathedral. Courtesy of Heaton Sessions, Stone Ridge, New York. Rheinisches Bildarchiv photo.

of its three-dimensionality. In addition, we experience a certain sense of dynamics as we walk around it. Although we are moving and not the sculpture, we perceive and respond to what seems to be movement in the work itself.

Size

Because sculpture has mass—that is, takes up space and has density—our senses respond to the weight or the size of a work. Egyptian sculpture, which is solid, stable, and oversized (see Fig. 4.16), has mass and proportion as well as line and form that make it appear heavier than a non-Egyptian work of basically the same size and material, such as in Figure 4.3. Moreover, the very same treatment of texture, verisimilitude, and subject would elicit a completely different sense response if the work were 3 feet tall than if it were 30 feet tall.

Early in the chapter we mentioned the possibility of an artist's *disguising the material* from which the work is made. Marble polished to appear like skin or wood polished to look like fabric can change the appearance of the mass of a sculpture and significantly affect our response to it.

We also must consider the purpose of disguising material. For example, does the detailing of the sculpture reflect a formal concern for design, or does it reflect a concern for greater verisimilitude? Examine the cloth represented in Figures 4.1 and 4.13. In both cases the sculptor has disguised the material by making stone appear to be cloth. In Figure 4.1 the cloth is detailed to reflect reality. It drapes as real cloth would drape, and as a result its effect in the composition depends on the subtlety of line characteristic of draped cloth. However, in Figure 4.13 the sculptor has depicted cloth in such a way that its effect in the design is not dependent on how cloth drapes, but rather on the decorative function of line as the sculptor wishes to use it. Real cloth cannot drape as the sculptor has depicted it. Nor, probably, did the sculptor care. His main concern here was for decoration, for using line (that looks like cloth) to emphasize the rhythm of the work. When sculpture de-emphasizes lifelikeness in order to draw attention to the substance from which it is made, we call it *glyptic*. Glyptic sculpture emphasizes the material from which the work is created and usually retains the fundamental geometric qualities of that material.

Lighting and Environment

One final factor that significantly influences our sense response to a sculpture, a factor we very often do not consider and is outside the control of the artist unless he or she personally supervises every exhibition in which the work is displayed, is that of *lighting and environment*. As we note in the chapter on theatre, light plays a seminal role in our perception of and thereby our response to three-dimensional objects. The direction and number of sources of light striking a three-dimensional work can change the entire composition of that work. Whether the work is displayed outdoors or indoors, the method of lighting affects the overall presentation of the work. Diffuse room lighting allows us to see all aspects of a sculpture without external influence. However, if the work is placed in a darkened room and illuminated from par-

Figure 4.16 Egyptian statuary. Sculpture made of red granite. The Metropolitan Museum of Art, New York. Gift of Edward S. Harkness, 1914 (14.7.15).

ticular directions by spotlights, it becomes much more dramatic and our response is affected accordingly.

Where and how a work is exhibited also contributes to our response. A sculpture can create a far different response if placed in a carefully designed environment that screens our vision from distracting or competing visual stimuli than if exhibited among other works amid the bustle of a public park.

CHRONOLOGY OF SELECTED MAJOR PERIODS, STYLES, AND EXAMPLES FOR STUDY IN WESTERN SCULPTURE

Prehistory–c. 4000 B.C.
paleolithic and neolithic carvings
African masks and carvings

4000 B.C.–c. 1000 B.C.
Ancient Egypt
tomb and temple sculptures

c. 3000 B.C.–c. 500 B.C.
Ancient Mesopotamia, Persia, Crete, and
Mycenae
Tell Asmar sculptures
Assyrian relief sculpture
carved figures

c. 1200 B.C.–c. 300 B.C.
Ancient Greece
The Horses of Heracles
Nike of Delos
Artemision Zeus
Polycleitus: *Lance Bearer*
Myron: *Discus Thrower*
Praxiteles: *Cnidian Aphrodite*

c. 500 B.C.–c. 300 A.D.
Rome and Hellenistic Greece
Winged Victor of Samothrace
Dying Gaul
Laocoön Group (Rhodes)

Etruscan Warrior
portrait sculpture

c. 400–c. 1400
The Middle Ages
Early Christian and Byzantine
sarcophagus sculpture
altarpiece carvings
Celtic and Germanic ornaments
Romanesque
Bronze doors of Hildesheim Cathedral
Last Judgment tympanum, Autun
Cathedral
Gothic
sculptures of Chartres Cathedral

c. 1400–c. 1500
Flanders
Claus Sluter: *The Well of Moses*
Italy (early Renaissance)
Donatello: *David; The Gattamelata*

c. 1480–c. 1550
High Renaissance
Michelangelo: *Pietà; David*

c. 1510–c. 1570
Mannerism
Giovanni da Bologna: *Mercury*
Goujon: *Fountain of the Innocents*

1570–c. 1700
Baroque Sculpture
Bernini: *Apollo and Daphne; Ecstasy of
St. Theresa*
Salvi: *Trevi Fountain,* Rome

c. 1700–c. 1800
Rococo Sculpture
Guenther: *Pietà*

c. 1800–c. 1900
Neoclassicism
Cortot: *Triumph*
Maillol: *Night*

Eclecticism
   Rodin: *Balzac*

c. 1900–c. 1960
   Zorach: *Affection*
   Epstein: *Madonna and Child*
   Lipchitz: *Seated Figure*
   Brancusi: *Bird in Space*
   Moore: *Reclining Figure*
   Calder: *7 Red, 7 Black, 1 White*
   Giacometti: *Man Pointing*
   Barlach: *Man Drawing a Sword*

c. 1960–
   Ronald Bladen: *The X*
   Claes Oldenburg: *Giant Ice Bag*
   David Smith: *Cubi Series*
   Ellsworth Kelly: *Untitled*
   Nancy Graves: *Trace*
   Duane Hanson: *Tourists*
   Judy Pfaff: *Dragons*

Music

We all have favorite forms of music. They might be tejano, reggae, rock, rhythm and blues, rap, gospel, or classical. Occasionally we are surprised to find that our favorite tune or musical form was once something else: a rock tune that first was an operatic aria, or an ethnic style that combines styles from other ethnic traditions. Whatever the case, music is music. It comprises rhythms and melodies that differ only in the ways they are put together. In this chapter we'll concentrate first on some classical forms, but after that we'll discuss qualities that apply to all music, whether classical or popular.

Music often has been described as the purest of the art forms because it is free from the physical restrictions of space that apply to the other arts. However, the freedom enjoyed by the composer becomes a constraint for us listeners because music is an art that places significant responsibility on us. That responsibility is especially critical in trying to learn and apply musical terminology, because we have only a fleeting moment to capture many of the characteristics of music. A painting or a sculpture

stands still for us; it does not change or disappear, despite the length of time it takes us to find or apply some new characteristic. Such is not the case with music.

We live in a society that is very aural in its perceptions, but these perceptions usually do not require any kind of active listening. An excellent example is the Muzak we hear in many stores, restaurants, and office buildings, which is intended solely as a soothing background designed *not* to attract attention. We hear music constantly on the radio, the television, and in the movies, but nearly always in a peripheral role. Because we are not expected to pay attention to it, we do not. Therefore, we simply do not undertake the kind of practice we need to be attentive to music and to perceive it in detail. However, like any skill, the ability to hear perceptively is enhanced through repetition and training. If we have had limited experience in responding to music, we may have some difficulty in the live concert hall hearing what there is to hear in a piece of music that passes in just a few seconds. Likewise, our ability to *remember* what we have heard is impaired if we have not practiced that skill. To deduce the structure of a musical work, we must remember at the end what we heard at the beginning. These abilities require skills that many people have not acquired.

WHAT IS IT?

Music is sound and silence. At the formal level, music may be a sonata, symphony, concerto, suite, concert overture, opera, oratorio, cantata, mass or requiem, or motet, to name only a few of the most familiar types.

Sonata

A sonata is a group of movements loosely related and played in succession. Unlike the movements of a suite, these are not all in the same key but are in related tonalities. The first movement of a sonata generally has a special form, which has taken on particular importance in musical composition—hence its name, sonata form. In discussing sonatas, we must be careful not to confuse *sonata* with *sonata form*, a particular structure we discuss later.

Symphony

The symphony is a large musical composition for orchestra that reached its full maturity in the late eighteenth century. Typically the symphony has four separate sections called *movements*. The tempos of the four movements are usually fast, slow, moderate, and fast. In addition, the first movement usually is in sonata form, sometimes with a slow introduction. The second movement generally consists of binary or sonata form; the third movement comprises a minuet and trio, in ternary form; the fourth movement explores sonata, rondo, or a combination of those forms. The symphony as a musical type has been shaped by, and to a large extent cannot be separated from, the development of the instruments for and the theories and styles of the historical periods in which it was composed. "Symphony" as a musical form may also apply to works composed for string quartet and chamber orchestra, for example. A symphony such as Beethoven's Symphony No. 9, which utilizes chorus as well as orchestra, is unique. Some symphonies have only three movements, some have more than four movements, and some do not adhere to the characteristics just noted in relation to their movements.

Concerto

The term *concerto* usually refers to a composition for solo instrument with accompaniment. It originated during the baroque era as the *concerto grosso*, which uses a solo group called the *concertino* and a full ensemble called the *ripieno*. By the end of the age the *solo concerto* emerged. The solo concerto usually has three movements, which alternate in a fast–slow–fast relationship.

Suite

If we think of the term *suite* as it is frequently used outside of music, we have an insight into its musical implications. A grouping of items of furniture in the design of a living room is called a living room *suite*. The ensemble of trousers, vest, and jacket designed in the same fabric and style and worn together is called a *suit*. The musical suite is an instrumental composition consisting of a succession of dances in the same or related keys. Suites were written primarily for keyboard instruments, specifically the harpsichord, but also for a solo instrument accompanied by harpsichord, or a group of stringed or wind instruments.

Concert Overture

An overture is customarily a single-movement introduction to, for example, an opera. However, in concert it has been popular to perform many of these introductions apart from the work they introduce. As this practice became more popular, composers began to write concert overtures—overtures with no larger work intended to follow.

Opera

Because of its special combination of music, theatre, and architecture, we discuss opera in detail later in this chapter.

Oratorio

An oratorio is a large choral work for soloists, chorus, and orchestra that was developed in the baroque period. It is usually presented in concert form—that is, there is no physical action, staging, setting, costumes, or properties. The soloists in the oratorio may take the role of characters, and the work may have a plot, although perhaps the most familiar example, Handel's *Messiah*, does neither.

Cantata

The cantata is a composition for chorus and/or solo voice(s) accompanied by an instrumental ensemble. Developed in the baroque period, it comprises several movements and uses either sacred or secular texts.

Mass

The mass as a choral type concerns itself directly with the Roman Catholic service, the mass. As such it includes six musical parts: *Kyrie, Gloria, Credo, Sanctus, Benedictus,* and *Agnus Dei.* The mass is the heart of the church rite and is based on the Last Supper of Christ. Two kinds of texts accompanied the mass, the *ordinary,* appropriate throughout the year, and the *proper,* which had texts appropriate to particular feast days. Masses may or may not be written for inclusion in the church service. The concert mass has been an important part of musical composition since the Middle Ages. Many masses have taken a special form—for example, the *requiem mass,* or mass for the dead.

Motet

A motet is a choral composition of *polyphonic* texture. Motets, like symphonies, oratorios, cantatas, masses, and so on, are associated with specific historical periods. Early motets of the thirteenth century often utilized three voices and combined sacred and secular texts. By the fifteenth and sixteenth centuries the motet was a contrapuntal work for four or five voices, usually with a sacred text. In that form it is differentiated from the *madrigal,* which utilized a secular text.

HOW IS IT PUT TOGETHER?

Understanding the vocabulary and being able to identify its application in a musical work help us comprehend the communication that uses the musical language, and thereby to understand the creative communicative intent of the composer and the musicians who bring the composition to life. The ways in which musical artists shape the characteristics that follow bring us experiences that can challenge our intellects and excite our emotions. As in all communication, meaning depends on each of the parties involved; communicators and respondents must assume responsibility for facility in the language utilized.

Music is composed through the designing of sound and silence. The latter is reasonably understandable, but what of the former? What is sound? Sound is vibration that stimulates the auditory nerves. It includes sirens, speech, crying babies, jet engines, falling trees, and so forth. We might call such sources noise. However, even noise may have a part in a musical composition. Cannons and even floor polishers have found their way into serious musical works. So we must be careful about what we include or exclude from sound in music. However, musical design does depend primarily on sound of a specific character—sound that can be controlled and shaped, sound that can be consistent in its qualities. One aspect of sound that is not limited to musical instruments but is fundamental to the designing of sound in music is tone.

Tone

Tone has four characteristics: pitch, duration, timbre, and intensity.

Pitch

Pitch is a physical phenomenon measurable in vibrations per second. So when we describe differences in pitch we are describing recognizable and measurable differences in sound waves. A pitch has a steady, constant frequency. A faster frequency produces a higher pitch; a slower frequency, a lower pitch. If a sounding body—a vibrating string, for example—is shortened, it vibrates more rapidly. Musical instruments designed to produce high pitches, such as the piccolo, therefore tend to be small. Instruments designed to produce low pitches tend to be large—for instance, bass viols and tubas.

In Chapter 3 we discussed color. Color comprises a range of light waves within a visible spectrum. Sound also comprises a spectrum, one whose audible pitches range from 16 to 38,000 vibrations per second. We can perceive 11,000 different pitches! Obviously that is more than is practical for musical composition. Therefore, *by convention* the sound spectrum is divided into roughly ninety equally spaced frequencies comprising seven and a half

octaves. The piano keyboard, consisting of eighty-eight keys (seven octaves plus two additional notes) representing the same number of equally spaced pitches, serves as an illustration (Fig. 5.1). The thirteen pitches represented by the adjacent keys of the piano from C to C constitute an octave. The distance in frequency from C to C$^\sharp$ is the same as that from C$^\sharp$ to D, and so forth. The higher C vibrates at exactly twice the frequency of the lower C. Such is the case with every note and the note one octave below it. The A one octave above the lower one shown would vibrate at twice that rate. Again by convention, each musical note is usually tuned to a specific pitch, in vibrations per second. For example, normally A is tuned to 440 vibrations per second, and its octaves to 110, 220, 880, 1,760, and so forth.

The thirteen equally spaced pitches in an octave are called a *chromatic scale.* However, the scales that sound most familiar to us are the major and minor scales, which consist of an octave of eight pitches. The distance between any two pitches is an *interval.* Intervals between two adjacent pitches are *half steps.* Intervals of two half steps are *whole steps.* The major scale—*do re mi fa sol la ti do* (recall the song, "Doe, a deer . . ." from *The Sound of Music*)—has a specific arrangement of whole and half steps (Fig. 5.2). Lowering the third and sixth notes of the

Figure 5.1 Part of the piano keyboard and its pitches.

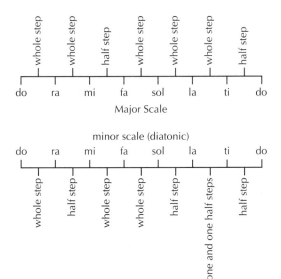

Figure 5.2 The major and minor scales.

major scale gives us the diatonic (the most common) minor scale.

To reiterate, a scale, which is an arrangement of pitches played in ascending or descending order, is a conventional organization of the frequencies of the sound spectrum. Not all music conforms to this convention. Music of Western civilization prior to approximately A.D. 1600 does not, nor does Eastern music, which makes great use of quarter tones. In addition, some contemporary Western music departs from the conventions of tonality of the major or minor scale.

Duration

A second characteristic of tone is *duration,* the length of time in which vibration is maintained without interruption. Duration in musical composition is relative and is designed within a set of conventions called musical notation (Fig. 5.3.). This system consists of a series of symbols (notes) by which the composer indicates the relative duration of each pitch. The system is progressive—that is, each note is either double or half the duration of an adjacent note. Musical notation also includes a series of symbols that denote the duration of *silences* in a composition. These symbols are called *rests,* and have the same durational values as the symbols for duration of tone.

Timbre

Timbre is the characteristic of tone that allows us to distinguish a pitch played on a violin, for example, from the same pitch played on a piano. Timbre is also referred to as *voice print* and *tone color.* In addition to identifying characteristic differences among sound-producing sources, timbre characterizes differences in quality of tones produced by the same source. Here the analogy of tone color is particularly appropriate. A tone that is produced with an excess of air—for example, by the human voice—is described as white. Figure 5.4 illustrates some of the various sources that produce musical tone and account for its variety of timbres. The following table lists some of the var-

Figure 5.3 Musical notation.

VOICE

Women's   Men's

Soprano   *Mezzo-soprano*   *Contralto*   *Tenor*   *Baritone*   *Bass*

STRINGS

Violin   *Viola*   *Cello (violoncello)*   *Bass*   *Harp*

WOODWINDS

Piccolo   *Flute*   *Oboe*   *English horn*   *Clarinet*   *Bassoon*

BRASSES

Trumpet   *Horn*   *Trombone*   *Tuba*

PERCUSSION

Bass drum   *Timpani*   *Snare drum*   *Cymbal*   *Triangle*

Figure 5.4 The key sources of musical tone in an orchestra (instruments not to scale). Calmann & King, Ltd.

ious sources that produce musical tone and account for its variety of timbres.

Voice		*Electronic*
Soprano	⎫	Synthesizer
Mezzo-sporano	⎬ Women's	
Contralto	⎭	
Tenor	⎫	
Baritone	⎬ Men's	
Bass	⎭	

Strings	*Woodwinds*	*Brasses*
Violin	Flute	Trumpet
Viola	Piccolo	Horn
Cello	Oboe	Trombone
(violoncello)		
Bass	English horn	Tuba
Harp	Clarinet	
	Bassoon	

Percussion		
Snare drum	Piano	Harpsichord
Bass drum		
Timpani		
Triangle		
Cymbal		

The piano could be considered either a stringed or a percussion instrument because it produces its sound by vibrating strings *struck* by hammers. The harpsichord's strings are set in motion by plucking.

Electronically produced music, available since the development of the RCA synthesizer at the Columbia-Princeton Electronics Music Center, has become a standard source in assisting contemporary composers (Fig. 5.5). Originally electronic music fell into two categories: (1) the electronic altering of acoustically produced sounds, which came to be labeled as *musique concrète* (see Glossary) and (2) electronically generated sounds. However, advances in technology have blurred those differences over the years.

Intensity

A final characteristic of tone is intensity. Any tone of any pitch, duration, or timbre can be loud, soft, or anywhere in between. Intensity is the *decibel* level of the tone, and depends on the physical phenomenon of *amplitude* of vibration. When greater force is employed in the

Figure 5.5 Musician at an electronic control panel. Randy Matusow/Monkmeyer Press.

production of a tone, the resulting sound waves are wider and cause greater stimulation of the auditory nerves. The *size* of the sound wave, not its number of vibrations per second, is changed.

Composers indicate intensity, or *dynamic level,* with a series of specific notations:

pp	pianissimo	very soft
p	piano	soft
mp	mezzo piano	moderately soft
mf	mezzo forte	moderately loud
f	forte	loud
ff	fortissimo	very loud

The notations of intensity that apply to an individual tone, such as *p, mp,* and *f,* also may apply to a section of music. *Dynamics* is the term used to refer to intensity levels throughout a composition. Changes in dynamics may be abrupt, gradual, wide, or small. A series of symbols also governs this aspect of music.

<	Crescendo	becoming louder
>	Decrescendo	becoming softer
> ∧ *sfz*	Sforzando	"with force"; a strong accent immediately followed by *p*

As we listen to and compare musical compositions we can consider the use and breadth of dynamics in the same sense that we consider the use and breadth of palette in painting.

Melody

Melody is a succession of sounds with rhythmic and tonal organization. We can visualize melody as linear and essentially horizontal. Thus any organization of musical tones occurring *one after another* constitutes a melody. Two

other terms, *tune* and *theme,* relate to melody as parts to a whole. For example, the *tune* in Figure 5.6 is a melody—that is, a succession of tones. However, a melody is not always a tune. For most people the term *tune* implies singability, and there are many melodies that cannot be considered singable. A *theme* is also a melody. However, in musical composition it specifically means a central musical idea, which may be restated and varied throughout a piece. Thus a melody is not necessarily a theme.

Related to theme and melody is the *motif,* or *motive,* a short melodic or rhythmic idea around which a composer may design a composition. For example, in Mozart's Symphony No. 40 the allegro movement is developed around a rhythmic motif of three notes:

In listening for how a composer develops melody, theme, and motive we can use two terms to describe what we hear: *conjunct* and *disjunct.* Conjunct melodies comprise notes close together, stepwise, on the musical scale. For example, the interval between the opening notes of the soprano line of J. S. Bach's chorale "Jesu Joy of Man's Desiring" from his Cantata 147 (Fig. 5.7) is never more than a whole step. Such melodic development is highly conjunct. Disjunct melodies contain intervals of a third or more. However, no formula determines disjunct or conjunct characteristics; there is no line at which a melody ceases to be disjunct and becomes conjunct. These are relative and comparative terms that assist us in description. For example, we would say that the opening melody of "The Star Spangled Banner" (Fig. 5.6) is more disjunct than the opening melody

Figure 5.6 "The Star Spangled Banner" (excerpt).

Figure 5.7 "Jesu Joy of Man's Desiring" (excerpt).

of "Jesu Joy of Man's Desiring"—or that the latter is more conjunct than the former.

Harmony

When two or more tones are sounded at the same time, we have harmony. Harmony is essentially a vertical arrangement, in contrast with the horizontal arrangement of melody.

However, as we shall see, harmony also has a horizontal property—movement forward in time. In listening for harmony we are interested in how simultaneous tones *sound together.*

Two tones played simultaneously are an *interval;* three or more form a *chord.* When we hear an interval or a chord our first response is to its *consonance* or *dissonance.* Consonant harmonies sound stable in their arrangement. Dissonant harmonies are tense and unstable. Consonance and dissonance, however, are not absolute properties. Essentially they are conventional and, to a large extent, cultural. What is dissonant to our ears may not be so to someone else's. What is important in musical response is determining *how* the composer utilizes these two properties. Most of our music is primarily consonant. However, dissonance can be used for contrast, to draw attention to itself, or as a normal part of *harmonic progression.*

As its name implies, harmonic progression involves the movement forward in time of harmonies. In discussing pitch we noted the convention of the major and minor scales—that is, the arrangement of the chromatic scale into a system of *tonality.* When we play or sing a major or minor scale we note a particular phenomenon: Our movement from *do* to *re* to *mi* to *fa* to *sol* to la is smooth and seems natural. But when we reach the seventh note of the scale, *ti,* something strange happens. It seems as though we must continue back to *do,* the *tonic* of the scale. Try it! Sing a major scale and stop at *ti.* You feel uncomfortable. Your mind tells you to *resolve* that discomfort by returning to *do.* That same sense of tonality—that sense of the tonic—applies to harmony. Within any scale a series of chords may be developed on the basis of the individual tones of the scale. Each of the chords has a subtle relationship to each of the other chords and to the tonic—that is, the *do* of the scale. That relationship creates a sense of progression that leads back to the chord based on the tonic.

The harmonic movement toward, and either resolving or not resolving to, the tonic is called *cadence.* Three different cadences are shown in Figure 5.8. The use of cadence is one

Figure 5.8 Full, half, and deceptive cadences.

way of articulating sections of a composition or of surprising us by upsetting our expectations. A composer using a full cadence uses a harmonic progression that resolves just as our ear tells us it should. We have a sense of ending, of completeness. However, when a half cadence or a deceptive cadence is used, the expected progression is upset and the musical development moves in an unexpected direction.

As we listen to music of various historical periods we may note that in some compositions tonal centers are blurred because composers frequently *modulate*—that is, change from one key (see Glossary) to another. In the twentieth century many composers, some of them using purely mathematical formulas to utilize equally all tones of the chromatic scale, have removed tonality as an arranging factor and have developed *atonal* music, or music without tonality. A convention of harmonic progression is disturbed when tonality is removed. However, we still have harmonic progression, and we still have harmony—dissonant or consonant.

Tonality

Utilization of pitch and tonality has taken composers in various directions over the centuries. Conventional tonality, employing the major and minor scales and keys previously mentioned, forms the basis for most pre-twentieth-century music, as well as traditionally oriented music of the twentieth century. In addition, we find *serialism* and *twelve-tone technique,* which, since World War II, have reflected a desire to exert more control and to apply a predetermined hierarchy of values to all elements of a composition. In the early twentieth century, traditional tonality was abandoned by some composers and a new *atonal* harmonic expression occurred. Exemplified in Schoenberg's "pantonality" (as he called it), atonal compositions seek the freedom to use any combination of tones without the necessity of

having to resolve chordal progressions. Schoenberg referred to this as "the emancipation of dissonance."

Texture

The aspect of musical relationships known as *texture* is treated differently by different sources. The term itself has various spatial connotations, and using a spatial term to describe a nonspatial phenomenon creates part of the divergence of treatment. Texture in painting and sculpture denotes surface quality—that is, roughness or smoothness. Texture in weaving denotes the interrelationship of the warp and the woof—that is, the horizontal and vertical threads of fibers. The organization in Figure 5.9 would be described as open or loose texture; that in Figure 5.10, closed or tight. However, there is really no single musical arrangement that corresponds to either of these spatial concepts. The characteristic called *sonority* by some comes the closest. Sonority describes the relationship of tones played at the same time. A chord with large intervals between its members would have a more open, or thinner, sonority (or texture) than a chord with small intervals between its tones; that chord would have a tight, thick, or close sonority or texture. *Sonority* is a term

Figure 5.9 Open (loose) texture.

Figure 5.10 Closed (tight) texture.

that does not have universal application; some sources do not mention it at all.

In a musical context *texture* (again, some sources do not use this term and treat the following characteristics as part of harmony) usually has two, and sometimes three, characteristics: *homophony* and *polyphony* (or *counterpoint*), and sometimes *monophony*. Monophony consists solely of one melodic line. There may be 500 voices singing a melody, but if it is the same melody it is monophonic. In homophonic music one melodic line dominates and the other voices play a subordinate or supporting role. Polyphony is the development of two or more independent melodic lines. Most music is not exclusively monophonic, homophonic, or poly-phonic. Much music alternates, especially between homophonic and polyphonic textures.

Rhythm

Rhythm comprises recurring pulses and accents that create identifiable patterns. Without rhythm we have only an aimless rising and falling of tones. Earlier we noted that each tone and silence has duration. Composing music means placing each tone into a time or rhythmical relationship with every other tone. As with the dots and dashes of the Morse code we can "play" the rhythm of a musical composition without reference to its pitches. Each symbol

(or note) of the musical notation system denotes a duration relative to every other symbol in the system.

Beat

The individual stresses we hear are called *beats.* Beats may be grouped into rhythmic patterns by placing accents every few beats. Rhythm and beat combine to form *meter.*

Meter

Normal musical practice is to group clusters of beats into units called *measures.* When these groupings are regular and reasonably equal they comprise *simple* meters. When the number of beats in a measure equals three or two it constitutes *triple* or *duple* meter. In the musical score, measures are indicated by *bar lines,* which are simple, vertical dividing lines telling the performer that a measure has just ended or begun. As listeners, we can distinguish between duple and triple meters because of their different *accent* patterns. In triple meter we hear an accent every third beat—ONE two three, ONE two three—and in duple meter the accent is every other beat—ONE two, ONE two. If there are four beats in a measure, the second accent is weaker than the first—ONE two THREE four, ONE two THREE four.

When accent occurs on normally unaccented beats, the rhythm is said to be *syncopated.*

Tempo

Tempo is the rate of speed of the composition. A composer may notate tempo in two ways. The first is by a *metronome marking,* such as ♩ = 60. This means the piece is to be played at the rate of sixty quarter notes (♩) per minute. Such notation is precise. The other method is less precise and involves more descriptive terminology in Italian.

Largo (broad)	Very slow
Grave (grave, solemn)	
Lento (slow)	Slow
Adagio (leisurely)	
Andante (at a walking pace)	
Andantino (somewhat faster than andante)	Moderate
Moderato (moderate)	
Allegretto (briskly)	
Allegro (cheerful, faster than allegretto)	Fast
Vivace (vivacious)	
Presto (very quick)	Very Fast
Prestissimo (as fast as possible)	

The tempo may be quickened or slowed, and the composer indicates this by the words *accelerando* (accelerate) and *ritardando* (retard, slow down). A performer who takes liberties with the tempo is said to use *rubato*.

Structure

Musical structure, the organization of musical elements and relationships into successive events or sections, is concerned principally with two characteristics, variety and unity. *Variety* creates interest by avoiding monotony, and composers can use variety in every musical characteristic we have discussed in order to hold our attention or pique our interest. However, because music has design, composers must also concern themselves with *coherence*. Notes and rhythms that proceed without purpose or stop arbitrarily make little sense to the listener. Therefore, just as the painter, sculptor, or any other artist must try to develop design that has focus and meaning, the musician must attempt to create a coherent composition of sounds and silences—that is, a composition that has *unity*. The principal means by which an artist creates unity is repetition. As we noted in Chapter 1, the Volkswagen (Fig. 1.10) achieved unity through strong geometric repetition that varied only in size. Music achieves unity through repetition in a similar fashion. How-

ever, because in music we are dealing with time as opposed to space, repetition in music usually involves recognizable themes.

Thus structure can be seen as organization through repetition to create unity. Structure may be divided into two categories: *closed form* and *open form*. These terms are somewhat similar to the same ones used in sculpture and to composition kept within or allowed to escape the frame in painting. Closed form directs the musical eye back into the composition by restating at the end of the thematic section that which formed the beginning of the piece. Open form allows the eye to escape the composition by utilizing repetition of thematic material only as a departure point for further development, and by ending without repetition of the opening section. A few of the more common examples of closed and open forms follow.

Closed Forms

Binary form, as the name implies, consists of two parts: the opening section of the composition and a second part that often acts as an answer to the first: AB. Each section is then repeated.

Ternary form is a three-part development in which the opening section is repeated after the development of a different second section: ABA.

Ritornello, which developed in the baroque period, and *rondo,* which developed in the classical period, employ a continuous development that returns to modified versions of the opening theme after separate treatments of additional themes. Ritornello alternates orchestral or *ripieno* passages with solo passages. Rondo alternates a main theme in the tonic key with subordinate themes in contrasting keys.

Sonata form, or *sonata-allegro form,* takes its name from the conventional treatment of the first movement of the sonata. It is also the form of development of the first movement of many symphonies. The pattern of development is ABA or AABA. The first A section is a statement of two or three main and subordinate themes, known as the *exposition.* To cement the perception of section A, the composer may repeat it: AA. The B section, the *development,* takes the original themes and develops them with several fragmentations and modulations. The movement then returns to the A section; this final section is called the *recapitulation.* Usually, the recapitulation section is not an exact repetition of the opening section; in fact, it may be difficult to hear in some pieces. In Mozart's Symphony No. 40 the opening movement (allegro) is in sonata-allegro form. However, the recapitulation section is identified only by a very brief restatement of the first theme, as it was heard in the exposition, not a repetition of the opening section. Then, after a lengthy *bridge,* the second theme from the exposition appears. Mozart closes the movement with a brief *coda,* or closing section, in the original key, based on the first phrase of the first theme.

Open Forms

The *fugue* is a polyphonic development of one, two, or sometimes three short themes. Fugal form, which takes its name from the Latin *fuga* ("flight"), has a traditional, although not a necessary, scheme of development consisting of seven elements, only some of which may be found in any given fugue. However, two characteristics are common to all fugues: (1) counterpoint and (2) a clear dominant–tonic relationship—that is, imitation of the theme at the fifth above or below the tonic. Each voice in a fugue (as many as five or more) develops the basic subject independent from the other voices, and passes through as many of the seven elements as the composer deems necessary. Unification is achieved not by return to an opening section, as in closed form, but by the varying recurrences of the subject throughout.

The *canon* is a contrapuntal form based on note-for-note imitation of one line by another. The lines are separated by a brief time interval—for example (the use of letters here does *not* indicate sectional development):

Voice 1: a b c d e f g
Voice 2:   a b c d e f g
Voice 3:   a b c d e f g

The interval of separation is not always the same among the voices. The canon is different from the *round,* an example of which is "Row, row, row your boat." A round is also an exact melodic repeat; however, the canon develops new material indefinitely; the round repeats the same phrases over and over. The interval of separation in the round stays constant—a phrase apart.

Variation form is a compositional structure in which an initial theme is modified through melodic, rhythmic, and harmonic treatments, each more elaborate than the last. Each section usually ends with a strong cadence, and the piece ends, literally, when the composer decides he or she has done enough.

HOW DOES IT STIMULATE THE SENSES?

The most obvious device for stimulating the senses is the combination of rhythm and meter. We have all at one time or another heard music that caused us involuntarily to tap our toes, drum our fingers, or bounce in our seats in a purely physical response to the strongly accented beat of the music. This involuntary motor response to a beat is perhaps the most primitive of our sensual involvements. If the rhythm is regular and the beat strong, our body may respond as a unit. However, if the rhythm is irregular or the beat divided or syncopated, we may find one part of our body doing one thing and another part doing something else. Dynamics also have much to do with our sense response to music: The way a composer manipulates volume and intensity in a piece can lull us to sleep or cause us to sit bolt upright in astonishment. A familiar example of manipulated dynamics is the second movement of

Haydn's Symphony No. 94, in which the composer relaxes his audience with very soft passages and then inserts a sudden fortissimo. The result (and the name of the symphony ever since) was *surprise!*

From time to time throughout this chapter, we have referred to certain historical conventions that permeate the world of music. Some of these have a potential effect on our sense response. Certain notational patterns, such as *appoggiaturas* (see Glossary), are a kind of musical shorthand, or perhaps mime, that conveys certain kinds of emotion to the listener. Of course, they have little meaning for us unless we take the time and effort to study music history. Some of Mozart's string quartets indulge in exactly this kind of communication. This is another illustration of how expanded knowledge can increase the depth and value of the aesthetic experience.

The timbre of a musical composition also works on our senses. A composer's use of timbre is analogous to a painter's use of palette. Only a study of an individual work will tell us how broad or narrow the composer's use of timbre is. However, the size of the musical ensemble has a nearly automatic control of our response. A large symphony orchestra can overwhelm us with diverse timbres and volumes; a string quartet cannot. Our expectations and our focus may change as we perceive the performance of one or the other. For example, because we know our perceptual experience with a string quartet will not involve the broad possibilities of an orchestra, we tune ourselves to seek the qualities that challenge the composer and performer within the particular medium. The difference between listening to an orchestra and listening to a quartet is similar to the difference between viewing a museum painting of huge dimension and viewing the exquisite technique of a miniature.

Texture, rhythm, meter, and timbre, in combination, have much to do with sensual response to a musical work. For example, the iso-lation of the woodwinds, the irregular rhythms, and the melodic development of Debussy's *Prélude à l'après-midi d'un faune* combine to ellicit images of Pan frolicking through the woodlands and cavorting with the nymphs on a sunny afternoon. Of course, much of what we see has been stimulated by the title of the composition. Our perception is heightened further if we are familiar with the poem by Mallarmé on which the symphonic poem is based. Titles and especially text in musical compositions may be the strongest devices a composer has for communicating directly with us. Images are triggered by words, and a text or title can stimulate our imaginations and senses to wander freely and fully through the musical development. Johannes Brahms called a movement in his *Ein Deutsches Requiem* "All Mortal Flesh Is as the Grass"; we certainly receive a philosophical and religious communication from that title. Moreover, when the chorus ceases to sing and the orchestra plays alone, the instrumental melodies and harmonies stimulate images of fields of grass blowing in the wind.

Harmony and tonality are both of considerable importance in stimulating our senses. Just as paintings and sculpture stimulate sensations of rest and comfort or action and discomfort, so harmonies create a feeling of repose and stability if they are consonant and a sensation of restlessness and instability if they are dissonant. Harmonic progression that leads to a full cadential resolution leaves us feeling fulfilled; unresolved cadences are puzzling and perhaps irritating. Major or minor tonalities have significantly differing effects: Major sounds positive; minor, sad or mysterious. The former seems close to home, and the latter, exotic. Atonal music sets us adrift to find the unifying thread of the composition.

Melody, rhythm, and tempo are very similar to the use of line in painting, and the term *melodic contour* could be seen as a musical analogue to this element of painting. When the tones of a melody are conjunct and undulate slowly and smoothly, they trace a pattern having the same sensual effect as their linear visual counterpart—that is, soft, comfortable, and placid.

When melodic contours are disjunct and tempos rapid, the pattern and response change:

In conclusion, it remains for us as we respond to music to analyze how each of the elements available to the composer has in fact become a part of the channel of communication, and how the composer, consciously or unconsciously, has put together a work that elicits sensory responses from us.

OPERA

Earlier, we identified opera as one of the formal divisions of music. Opera is a combination of music and drama in which music is not an equal or incidental partner but is the predominant element. The supportive elements of opera production, such as scenery, costumes, and staging, make it (although still a form of music) something apart from its musical brethren.

Traditions of opera are strong and deep. There have been attempts to make opera more like contemporary drama, with greater focus on plot, character development, and so on. Plays such as *Of Mice and Men* have been made into operas to make the form less exaggerated and implausible, a factor occasionally contributed to by singers who cannot act or who do not look the part.

Many devotees of opera regard it as the purest integration of all the arts. It contains music, drama, poetry, and in the *mise-en-scène,* visual arts. Certainly one could even include architecture, because an opera house is a particular architectural entity, with its own specific requirements for stage space and machinery, orchestra pit, and audience seating space. Because of opera's integration of art forms, much of what we respond to in opera at the formal, technical, and sensual levels is discussed in other chapters of this text. However, let us examine a few additional characteristics.

Opera is a form that also involves our sitting in the large auditorium that comprises an opera house and witnessing a musical and dramatic spectacle unfold on a stage perhaps 50 feet (15 m) wide and 70 feet (21 m) deep, filled with scenery rising 20 or 30 feet (6 or 9 m) in the air, and peopled by a chorus of perhaps 100 people, all fully costumed and singing over a full orchestra (Figs. 5.11, 5.12, and 5.13). The scope and the spectacle of such an event is *opera,* or at least comprises the circumstances of the bulk of operatic repertoire. Some operas are much more intimate. Nonetheless, listening to the music of opera on the radio or from a recording, or watching the minuscule productions brought to us through the medium of television falls short of the experience the live performance affords.

Opera can be divided more or less accurately into four varieties. *Opera* (without a qualifying adjective) is the serious or *tragic opera* that we perhaps think of immediately. This type also has been called *grand opera,* which implies to some an early operatic form consisting usually of five acts. *Opera seria* ("serious opera"), another name for tragic or grand opera, is generally highly stylized and treats heroic subjects, such as gods and heroes of ancient times.

Opéra comique, the second variety of opera, is any opera, regardless of subject matter, that has *spoken dialogue.*

The third type, *opera buffa,* is *comic* opera (do not confuse it with opéra comique), which usually does *not* have spoken dialogue. *Opera buffa* usually uses satire to treat a serious topic with humor—for example Mozart's *Marriage of Figaro.*

Figure 5.11 Giacomo Puccini, *Manon Lescaut.* Opera Company of Philadelphia. Photo by Trudy Cohen.

The fourth variety is *operetta*. Operetta also has spoken dialogue, but it has come to refer to a light style of opera characterized by popular themes, a romantic mood, and often a humorous tone. It is frequently considered more theatrical than musical, and its story line is usually frivolous and sentimental.

Opera does have some unique characteristics. The text of an opera, which is called the *libretto,* is probably the single most important

Figure 5.12 Georges Bizet, *Carmen.* Opera Company of Philadelphia. Composite photo by Trudy Cohen.

Figure 5.13 Giuseppi Galli de Bibiena (1696–1757), Scene design for an opera, 1719. Contemporary engraving. The Metropolitan Museum of Art, New York. The Elisha Whittelsey Collection, The Elisha Whittelsey Fund, 1951.

barrier to the appreciation of opera by American audiences. Because the large majority of operas in the contemporary repertoire are not of American origin, the American respondent usually has to overcome the language barrier to understand the dialogue and thereby the plot. It is not a desire for snobbery or exclusivity that causes the lack of English-translation performances; rather, opera loses much of its musical character in translation. We spoke of tone color, or timbre, earlier in this chapter. There are timbre characteristics implicit in the Russian, German, and Italian languages that are lost when they are translated into English. In addition, inasmuch as opera is in a sense the Olympic Games of the vocal music world—that is, the demands made on the human voice by the composers of opera call for the highest degree of skill and training of any vocal medium—

tone placement, and the vowels and consonants requisite to that placement, become very important to the singer. It is one thing for a tenor to sing the vowel "eh" on high B♭ in the original Italian. If the translated word to be sung on the same note employs an "oo" vowel, the technical demand is changed considerably. So the translation of opera from its original tongue into English is a far more difficult and complex problem than simply providing an accurate translation for a portion of the audience that does not know the text—as important as they may seem. Translation must concern itself with tone quality, color, and the execution of tones in the *tessitura,* or normal range of the human voice.

Experienced operagoers may study the score before attending a performance. However, every concert program contains a plot synopsis (even when the production is in English), so that even the neophyte can follow what is happening. Opera plots, unlike mysteries, have few surprise endings, and knowing the plot ahead of time does not diminish the experience of responding to the opera. To assist the audience, some opera companies have begun the practice of projecting the translated lyrics on a screen above the stage, much like subtitles in a foreign film.

The first element in opera itself is the overture. This orchestral introduction may have two characteristics. First, it may set the mood or tone of the opera. Here the composer works directly with our sense responses, putting us in the proper frame of mind for what is to follow. In his overture to *I Pagliacci*, for example, Ruggiero Leoncavallo creates a tonal story that tells us what we are about to experience. Using only the orchestra, he tells us we will see comedy, tragedy, action, and romance. If we listen to this overture, we will easily identify these elements, and in doing so understand how relatively unimportant the work's being in English is to comprehension. Add to the "musical language" the language of body and mime, and we can understand even complex ideas and character relationships—*without* words. In addition to this type of introduction, an overture may provide melodic introductions—passages introducing the arias and recitatives that will follow.

The plot is unfolded musically through *recitative*, or sung dialogue. The composer uses recitative to move the plot along from one section to another; recitative has little emotional content to speak of, and the words are more important than the music. There are two kinds of recitative. The first is *recitativo secco*, for which the singer has very little musical accompaniment, or none at all. If there is accompaniment it is usually in the form of light chording under the voice. The second type is *recitativo stromento*, in which the singer is given full musical accompaniment.

The real emotion and poetry of an opera lie in its *arias*. Musically and poetically, an aria is the reflection of high dramatic feeling. The great opera songs with which we are likely to be familiar are arias.

In every opera there are duets, trios, quartets, and other small ensemble pieces. There also are chorus sections in which everyone gets into the act. In addition, ballet or dance interludes are not uncommon. These may have nothing to do with the development of the plot, but are put in to add more life and interest to the dramatic production, and in some cases to provide a *segue* from one scene into another.

Bel canto, as its name implies, is a style of singing emphasizing the beauty of sound. Its most successful composer, Gioacchino Rossini, had a great sense of melody and sought to develop the *art song* to its highest level. In bel canto singing the melody is the focus.

Richard Wagner gave opera and theatre a prototype that continues to influence theatrical production—*organic unity*. Every element of his productions was integral and shaped to create a work of total unity. Wagner was also famous for the use of *leitmotif,* a common element in contemporary film. A leitmotif is a musical theme associated with a particular person or idea. Each time that person appears or is thought of, or each time the idea surfaces, the leitmotif is played.

Late in the nineteenth century, the *verismo* movement flourished. From the same root as the word *verisimilitude,* with which we have dealt previously, verismo opera treated themes, characters, and events from life in a down-to-earth fashion. The composer Pietro Mascagni is reported to have said, "In my operas do not look for melody or beauty . . . look only for blood!" Certainly in the works of Mascagni, Leoncavallo, and Puccini there is plenty of blood—as well as fine drama and music.

CHRONOLOGY OF SELECTED MAJOR PERIODS, STYLES, AND EXAMPLES FOR STUDY IN WESTERN MUSIC

c. 1100–c. 1400
Music of the Middle Ages
Gregorian chant
organa
minstrel songs
Machaut: *Messe de Nostre Dame*

c. 1400–c. 1600
Renaissance Music
Dufay: *Salve Regina*
Gibbons: *The Silver Swan*
Jannequin: *Chant des Oiseaux*
Josquin des Pres: *Ave Maria*
Palestrina: *Missa Salve Regina*

c. 1600–c. 1750
Baroque Music
J. S. Bach: *Brandenburg Concerto No. 2; Magnificat in D; Mass in B minor; Toccata and Fugue in D minor; Cantata No. 4.*
Corelli: *Trio Sonata in E minor, Op. 3, No. 7*
Handel: *Israel in Egypt; Concerto in B flat Major, Op. 3, No. 1; Messiah; Water Music*
Purcell: *Dido and Aeneas*
Scarlatti: *Sonata in C Major*
Schütz: *Cantiones Sacrae*
Vivaldi: *Concerto Grosso in A minor, Op. 3, No. 8; Winter Concerto Op. 8, No. 4 in F minor*

c. 1750–c. 1825
Classical Music
Haydn: *The Creation; Symphony No. 94 in G Major*
Mozart: *Cosi fan Tutte; Symphony No. 40 in G minor, K. 550; Piano Concerto in D minor, K. 466*
Transitional Music

Beethoven: *Fidelio; Missa Solemnis; Symphony No. 3; Symphony No. 5 in C Minor, Op. 67; Symphony No. 9*

c. 1825–c. 1900
Romantic Music
Berlioz: *The Damnation of Faust; Fantastic Symphony*
Brahms: *German Requiem; Symphony No. 1*
Chopin: *Étude in C minor, Op. 10, No. 12; Prelude in C minor for Piano, Op. 28*
Dvorak: *Symphony No. 9 in E minor*
Grieg: *Peer Gynt Suites*
Liszt: *Concerto No. 1 for Piano and Orchestra in E flat Major; Hungarian Rhapsodies; Les Préludes*
Mendelssohn: *Elijah; Concerto for Violin and Orchestra in E minor*
Moussorgsky: *Pictures at an Exhibition*
Schubert: *The Trout; Symphony No. 8 in B minor ("Unfinished")*
Schumann: *Symphony No. 1; Scenes of Childhood*
Smetana: *The Bartered Bride*
Tchaikovsky: *Nutcracker Suite; Symphony No. 6 ("Pathetique"); Overture 1812*
Opera
Bellini: *Sleepwalker*
Leoncavallo: *Il Pagliacci*
Rossini: *Barber of Seville*
Verdi: *Rigoletto; Aida*
Wagner: *Ring Cycle*

c. 1900–
Babbitt: *Composition for Synthesizer*
Bartók: *Concerto for Orchestra*
Berg: *Wozzeck*
Cage: *4'33"; Imaginary Landscape No. 4*
Copland: *Appalachian Spring*
Debussy: *Prélude à "L'Après-midi d'un faune"*
Gershwin: *Porgy and Bess; Rhapsody in Blue*
The Beatles: "Act Naturally," "I Want to Hold Your Hand"

Bruce Springsteen: "This Land Is Your Land"
Ives: *The Unanswered Question*
Mahler: *Symphony No. 9*
Prokofiev: *Lieutenant Kije*
Ravel: *Daphnis et Chloé*

Schoenberg: *Variations for Orchestra, Op. 31*
Sibelius: *Finlandia*
Vaughan-Williams: *English Folk Suite*
Webern: *Five Pieces for Orchestra*

6

Theatre

Of all the arts, theatre comes the closest to personalizing the love, rejection, disappointment, betrayal, joy, elation, and suffering that we experience in our daily lives. It does so because theatre uses live people acting out situations that very often look and sound like real life. Theatre once functioned in society like television and movies do today. Many of the qualities of all three forms are identical. We'll find in this chapter the ways that theatre, which frequently relies on *drama* (a written script), takes lifelike circumstances and compresses them into organized episodes. The result, although looking like reality, goes far beyond reality in order to make us find in its characters pieces of ourselves.

The word *theatre* comes from the Greek *theatron*—the area of the Greek theatre building where the audience sat. Its literal meaning is "a place for seeing." The Greeks' choice of this word suggests how they may have perceived the essence of theatre, which is to a large extent a visual experience. In addition to the words of the script, provided by the playwright, and the treatment of those words by the actors, the the-

atre artwork, the production, also involves visual messages. These include actor movement, costume, setting, lighting, and the physical relationship of the playing space to the audience.

Like the other performing arts, theatre is an interpretive discipline. Between the playwright and the audience stand the director, the designers, and the actors. Although each functions as an individual artist, each also serves to communicate the playwright's vision to the audience. Sometimes the play becomes subordinate to the expressive work of its interpreters, sometimes the concept of director as master artist places the playwright in a subordinate position. Nonetheless, a theatrical production always requires the interpretation of a concept through spectacle and sound by theatre artists.

WHAT IS IT?

Theatre represents an attempt to reveal a vision of human life through time, sound, and space. It gives us flesh-and-blood human beings involved in human action (Plate 12)—we must occasionally remind ourselves that the dramatic experience is not reality: It is an imitation of reality, acting as a symbol to communicate something about the human condition. Theatre is make-believe: Through gesture and movement, language, character, thought, and spectacle, it imitates action. However, if this were all theatre consisted of, we would not find it as captivating as we do, and as we have for more than 2,500 years.

At the formal level, theatre comprises *genre*—or type of play—from which the production evolves. *Some* of the genres of theatre are *tragedy, comedy, tragicomedy,* and *melodrama*. Some are products of specific periods of history, and illustrate trends that no longer exist; others are still developing and as yet lack definite form. Our response to genre is a bit different from our formal response or identification in music, for example, because we seldom find generic identification in the threatre program. Some plays are well-known examples of a specific genre, for example, the tragedy *Oedipus the King* by Sophocles. In these cases, as with a symphony, we can see how the production develops the conventions of genre. Other plays, however, are not well known or may be open to interpretation. As a result, we can draw our conclusions only after the performance has finished.

Tragedy

We commonly describe tragedy as a play with an unhappy ending. The playwright Arthur Miller describes tragedy as "the consequences of a man's total compulsion to evaluate himself justly, his destruction in the attempt posits a wrong or an evil in his environment." In the centuries since its inception, tragedy has undergone many variations as a means by which the playwright makes a statement about human frailty and failing.

Typically, tragic heroes make free choices that bring about suffering, defeat, and sometimes, triumph as a result of defeat. The protagonist often undergoes a struggle that ends disastrously. In Greek classical tragedy of the fifth century B.C., the hero generally was a larger-than-life figure who gained a moral victory amid physical defeat. The classical hero usually suffers from a tragic flaw—some defect that causes the hero to participate in his or her own downfall. In the typical structure of classical tragedies, the climax of the play occurs as the hero or heroine recognizes his or her role, and accepts destiny. In the years from Ancient Greece to the present, however, writers of tragedy have employed many different approaches. Playwright Arthur Miller argues the case for tragic heroes of "common stuff," suggesting tragedy is a condition of life in which human personality flowers and realizes itself.

Comedy

In many respects, comedy is much more complex than tragedy, and even harder to define. Comedy embraces a wide range of theatrical approaches, ranging from the intellectual and dialogue-centered high comedy of the seventeenth century to the slapstick, action-centered low comedy found in a variety of plays from nearly every historical period. Low comedy may include *farce,* typically a wildly active and hilarious comedy of situation, usually involving a trivial theme. We might say that the difference between comedy and farce is more than a matter of degree and includes a different point of view. Comic characters are usually sympathetic (we like them). Characters in farce are often ridiculous and, occasionally, contemptible. It is the kind of comedy we associate with actions such as pies in the face, mistaken identities, and pratfalls. Whatever happens in a farce carries little serious consequence. It perhaps provides an opportunity for the viewer to express unconscious and socially unacceptable desires without having to take responsibility for them.

Between the extremes just noted exist a variety of comic forms. One of these is the popular domestic comedy, in which family situations are the focus of attention, and in which members of a family and their neighbors find themselves in various complicated and amusing situations, for example Neil Simon's plays *Brighton Beach Memoirs* and *Broadway Bound.*

Defined in its broadest terms, comedy may not involve laughter. Many employ stinging *satire,* although we probably can say with some accuracy that humor forms the root of all comedy. In many circumstances comedy treats a serious theme, but remains basically lighthearted in spirit: Characters may be in jeopardy, but not *too* seriously so. Comedy deals with the world as we find it, focusing on everyday people through an examination of the incongruous aspects of behavior and relationships. The idea that comedy ends happily is probably due to our expectations that in happy endings everyone is left more or less to do what they please. However, happy endings often imply different sets of circumstances in different plays. Comedy appears to defy any such thumbnail definitions.

Tragicomedy

As the name suggests, tragicomedy is a mixed form of theatre, which, like the other types, has been defined in different terms in different periods. Until the nineteenth century, the ending determined the necessary criterion for this form. Traditionally, characters reflect diverse social standings—kings (like tragedy) and common folk (like comedy), and reversals went from bad to good and good to bad. It also included language appropriate to both tragedy and comedy. Tragicomedies were serious plays that ended, if not happily, then at least by avoiding catastrophe. In the last century and a half, the term has been used to describe plays in which the mood may shift from light to heavy, or plays in which endings are neither exclusively tragic or comic.

Melodrama

Melodrama is another mixed form. It takes its name from the terms *melo,* Greek for music, and "drama." Melodrama first appeared in the late eighteenth century, when dialogue took place against a musical background. In the nineteenth century, it was applied to describe serious plays without music. Melodrama uses stereotypical characters involved in serious situations in which suspense, pathos, terror, and occasionally hate are all aroused. Melodrama portrays the forces of good and evil battling in exaggerated circumstances. As a rule, the issues involved are either black or white—they are simplified and uncomplicated: Good is good and evil is evil; there are no ambiguities.

Geared largely for a popular audience, the form concerns itself primarily with situation and plot. Conventional in its morality, melodrama tends toward optimism—good always triumphs in the end. Typically, the hero or heroine is placed in life-threatening situations by the acts of an evil villain, and then rescued at the last instant. The forces against which the characters struggle are external ones—caused by an unfriendly world rather than by inner conflicts. Probably because melodrama took root in the nineteenth century, at a time when scenic spectacularism was the vogue, many melodramas depend on sensation scenes for much of their effect. This penchant can be seen in the popular nineteenth-century adaptation of Harriet Beecher Stowe's novel *Uncle Tom's Cabin,* as Eliza and the baby, Little Eva, escape from the plantation and are pursued across a raging ice-filled river. These effects taxed the technical capacities of contemporary theatres to their maximum, but gave the audience what it desired—spectacle. Not all melodramas use such extreme scenic devices, but such use was so frequent that it has become identified with the type. If we include motion pictures and television as dramatic structures, we could say that melodrama is the most popular dramatic form of the twentieth century.

HOW IS IT PUT TOGETHER?

Theatre consists of a complex combination of elements that form a single entity called a performance, or a production. Understanding the theatre production as a work of art can be enhanced if we have some tools for approaching it, which come to us from the distant past.

Writing 2,500 years ago in the *Poetics,* Aristotle argued that tragedy consisted of plot, character, diction, music, thought, and spectacle. We can use and expand on Aristotle's terminology to describe the basic parts of a production, and to use them as a set of tools for understanding theatrical productions as these six parts—and their descriptive terminology— still cover the entire theatrical product.

In the paragraphs that follow, we reshape Aristotle's terms into language that is more familiar to us, explain what the terms mean, and learn how we can use them to know how a theatrical production is put together—things to look and listen for in a production. We examine first the script, and include in that discussion Aristotle's concept of diction, or *language.* Next, we examine plot, thought—themes and ideas—character, and spectacle, which we call the visual elements. That is followed by a brief discussion of what Aristotle called music but which, to avoid confusion, we call aural elements.

The Script

A playwright creates a written document called a *script,* which contains the dialogue used by the actors. Aristotle called the words written by playwright *diction;* however, we refer to this part of a production as its *language.* The playwright's language tells us at least part of what we can expect from the play. For example, if he has used everyday speech, we generally expect the action to resemble everyday truth, or reality. In the play *Fences,* playwright August Wilson uses everyday language to bring the characters to life in the context of the period, 1957:

(*Act I, scene iii. Troy is talking to his son.*)

Like you? I go out of here every morning . . . bust my butt . . . putting up with them crackers everyday . . . cause I like you? You about the biggest fool I ever saw.

(Pause)

It's my job. It's my responsibility! You understand that? A man got to take care of his family. You live in my house . . . sleep you behind on my bedclothes . . . fill you belly up with my food . . . cause you my son.

Poetic language, in contrast, usually indicates less realism and perhaps stronger symbolism. Compare the language of *Fences* with the poetry used by Jean Racine, seventeenth-century dramatist, in *Le Cid* to create a mythical hero who is larger than life:

(*Act III, scene iv*)

Rodrigue: I'll do your bidding, yet still do I desire
To end my wretched life, at your dear hand.
But this you must not ask, that I renounce
My worthy act in cowardly repentance.
The fatal outcome of too swift an anger
Disgraced my father, covered me with shame.

In both plays, we use language and its tone to help determine the implication of the words. Language helps to reveal the overall tone and style of the play. It also can reveal character, theme, and historical context.

Plot

Plot is the structure of the play, the skeleton that gives the play shape, and on which the other elements hang. The nature of the plot determines how a play works: how it moves from one moment to another, how conflicts are structured, and how ultimately the experience comes to an end. We can examine the workings of plot by seeing the play somewhat as a timeline, beginning as the script or production begins, and ending at the final curtain, or the end of the script. In many plays plot tends to operate like a climactic pyramid (Fig. 6.1). In order to keep our attention, the dynamics of the play will rise in intensity until they reach the ultimate crisis—the *climax*—after which they will relax through a resolution called the *denouement,* to the end of the play.

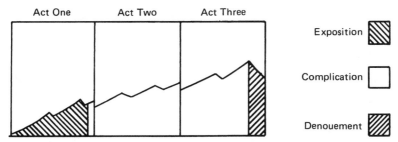

Figure 6.1 Hypothetical dynamic and structural development of a three-act play.

Depending on the playwright's purpose, plot may be shaped with or without some of the features described below. Sometimes plot may be so deemphasized that it virtually disappears. However, as we try to evaluate a play critically, the elements of plot give us things to look for—if only to note that they do not exist.

Exposition

Exposition provides necessary background information: Through it the playwright introduces the characters, their personalities, relationships, backgrounds, and their present situation. Exposition is frequently a recognizable section at the beginning of a play. It can be presented through dialogue, narration, setting, lighting, costume—or any device the playwright or director chooses. The amount of exposition in a play depends on where the playwright takes up the story, called the point of attack. A play told chronologically may need little expositional material; others require a good bit of prior summary.

Complication

Drama is about conflict. Although not every play fits that definition, in order to interest an audience, conflict of some sort is a fundamental dramatic device. At some point in the play, the normally expected course of events is usually frustrated, giving the audience a reason to be interested in what transpires. At a specific moment, an action is taken or a decision is made that upsets the current state of affairs. This is sometimes called the *inciting incident* and it opens the middle part of the plot—the complication. The complication is the meat of the play, and it comprises a series of conflicts and decisions—called *crises* (from the Greek word *krisis,* meaning "to decide")—that rise in intensity until they reach a turning point—the *climax*—that constitutes the end of the complication section.

Denouement

The denouement is the final resolution of the plot. It is the period of time during which the audience is allowed to sense that the action is ending; a period of adjustment, downward in intensity, from the climax. Ideally, the denouement brings about a clear and ordered resolution.

Exposition, complication, and denouement comprise a time frame in which the remaining parts of the play operate. The neat structural picture of plot that exposition, complication, and denouement describe will not, however, always be so neat. The fact that a play does not conform to this kind of plot structure does not make it a poorly constructed play, or one of inferior quality. Nor does it mean that these concepts cannot be used as a means for describing and analyzing how a play is put together.

Foreshadowing

Preparation for subsequent action—foreshadowing—helps to keep the audience clear about where they are at all times. Foreshadowing provides credibility for future action, keeps action logical, and avoids confusion. It builds tension and suspense: The audience is allowed to sense that something is about to happen, but because we do not know exactly what or when, anticipation builds suspense and tension. In *Jaws* a rhythmic musical theme foreshadows the presence of the shark. Just as the audience becomes comfortable with that device, the shark suddenly appears—without the music. As a result, uncertainty as to the next shark attack is heightened immensely. Foreshadowing also moves the play forward by pointing toward events that will occur later.

Discovery

Discovery is the revelation of information about characters, their personalities, relationships, and feelings. Hamlet discovers from his father's ghost that his father was murdered by Claudius, and is urged to revenge the killing, a discovery without which the play cannot proceed. The skill of the playwright in structuring the revelation of such information in large part determines the overall impact of the play on the audience.

Reversal

Reversal is any turn of fortune; for example, Oedipus falls from power and prosperity to blindness and exile; King Lear goes from ruler to disaster. In comedy, reversal often changes the roles of social classes, as peasants jump to the upper class, and vice versa.

Character

Character is the psychological motivation of the persons in the play. In most plays, the audience will focus on why individuals do what they do, how they change, and how they interact with other individuals, as the plot unfolds.

Plays reveal a wide variety of characters—both persons and motivating psychological forces. In every play we will find characters that fulfill major functions and on which the playwright wishes us to focus. We will also find minor characters—those whose actions may interact with the major characters, and whose actions constitute subordinate plot lines. Much of the interest created by the drama lies in the exploration of how persons with specific character motivations react to circumstances. For example, when Rodrigue discovers his father has been humiliated, what is it in his character that makes him decide to avenge the insult, even though it means killing the father of the woman he loves, thereby jeopardizing that love? Such responses, driven by character, are the choices that drive plays forward.

The Protagonist

Inside the structural pattern of a play some kind of action must take place. We must ask ourselves: How does this play work? How do we get from the beginning to the end? Most of the time, we take that journey via the actions and decisions of the *protagonist,* or central personage. Deciding the protagonist of a play is not always easy, even for directors. However, it is important to understand whom the play is about if we are to understand it. In Terence Rattigan's *Cause Célèbre* we could have three different responses depending on who the director decided was the protagonist. The problem is this: There are two central feminine roles. A good case could be made for either as the central personage of the play. Or they both could be equal. What we understand the play to be about depends on whom the director chooses to focus.

Thought

In order to describe the intellectual content of the play, Aristotle uses *thought,* a term we use to refer to the themes and ideas that the play communicates. In Lanford Wilson's *Burn This* (1987), for example, a young dancer, Anna, lives in a Manhattan loft with two gay roommates, Larry and Robby. As the play opens, we learn that Robby has been killed in a boating accident; Anna has just returned from the funeral and a set of bizarre encounters with Robby's family. Larry, a sardonic advertising executive, and Burton, Anna's boyfriend, maintain a constant animosity. Into the scene bursts Pale, Robby's brother and a threatening, violent figure. Anna is both afraid and irresistibly attracted to Pale; the conflict of their relationship drives the play forward to its climax.

This brief description summarizes the *plot* of a play. However, what the play is about—its thought—remains for us to discover and develop. Some might say the play is about loneliness, anger, and the way not belonging is manifested in human behavior. Others might focus on abusive relationships, and others would see a thought content dealing with hetero- and homosexual conflicts and issues. The process of coming to conclusions about meaning involves several layers of interpretation. One involves the playwright's interpretation of the ideas through the characters, language, and plot. A second layer of interpretation lies in the director's decisions about what the playwright has in mind, which will be balanced by what the director wishes to communicate, because, or in spite, of the playwright. Finally, it is important that we interpret what we actually see and hear in the production, along with what we may perceive independently from the script.

Visual Elements

The director takes the playwright's language, plot, and characters and translates them into action by using, among other things, what Aristotle called *spectacle,* or what the French call *mise-en-scène,* but which we can simply call the *visual elements.* The visual elements of a production include, first of all, the physical relationship established between actors and audience. The actor/audience relationship can take any number of shapes. For example, the audience might sit surrounding or perhaps on only one side of, the stage. The visual elements also include stage settings, lighting, costumes, and properties, as well as the actors and their movements. Whatever the audience can see contributes to this part of the theatrical production.

Part of our response to a production is shaped by the design of the space in which the play is produced. The earliest and most natural arrangement is the theatre-in-the-round, or *arena* theatre (Fig. 6.2), in which the audience surrounds the playing area on all sides. Whether the playing area is circular, square, or rectangular is irrelevant. Some argue that the closeness of the audience to the stage space in an arena theatre provides the most intimate kind of theatrical experience. A second possibility is the *thrust,* or three-quarter, theatre (Fig. 6.3), in which the audience surrounds the playing area on three sides. The most familiar illustration of this theatre is what we understand to be the theatre of the Shakespearean period. The third

Figure 6.2 Ground plan of an arena theatre.

Figure 6.3 Ground plan of a thrust theatre.

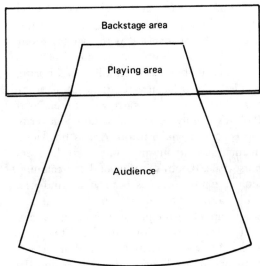

Figure 6.4 Ground plan of a proscenium theatre.

actor/audience relationship, and the one most widely used in the twentieth century, is the *proscenium* theatre, in which the audience sits on only one side and views the action through a frame (Fig. 6.4).

There are also experimental arrangements of audience and stage space. On some occasions acting areas are placed in the middle of the audience, creating little island stages. In certain circumstances, these small stages create quite an interesting set of responses and relationships between actors and audience.

Common experience indicates that the physical relationship of the acting area to the audience has a causal effect on the depth of audience involvement. Experience has also indicated that some separation is necessary for certain kinds of emotional responses. We call this mental and physical separation *aesthetic distance.* The proper aesthetic distance allows us to become involved in what we know is fictitous and even unbelievable.

The visual elements may or may not have independent communication with the audience; this is one of the options of the director

and designers. Before the nineteenth century, there was no coordination of the various elements of a theatre production. This, of course, had all kinds of curious, and in some cases catastrophic, consequences. However, for the last century, most theatre productions have adhered to what is called the *organic theory of play production:* That is, everything, visual and aural, is designed with a single purpose. Each production has a specific goal in terms of audience response, and all of the elements in the production attempt to achieve this.

Scene Design

Simply stated, the purpose of scene design in the theatre is to create an environment conducive to the production's ends. The scene designer uses the same tools of composition—line, form, mass, color, repetition, and unity—as the painter. In addition, because a stage design occupies three-dimensional space and must allow for the movement of the actors in, on, through, and around the elements of scenery, the scene designer becomes a sculptor as well. Figures 6.5, 6.6, 6.7, and 6.8 illustrate how emphasis on given elements of design highlight different characteristics in the production. C. Ricketts's design for *The Eumenides* (Fig. 6.5) stresses formality, asymmetricality, and symbolism. Charles Kean's *Richard II* (color insert Plate 13) is formal, but light and spacious. His regular rhythms and repetition of arches create a completely different feeling from the one elicited by Ricketts's design. William Telbin's *Hamlet* (color insert Plate 14), with its strong central triangle and monumental scale, creates an overwhelming weight that, while utilizing diagonal activity in the sides of the triangles, cannot match the action of Robert Burroughs's zigzagging diagonals juxtaposed among verti-

cals in his design for *Peer Gynt* (Fig. 6.6). Unlike the painter or sculptor, however, the scene designer is limited by the stage space, the concepts of the director, the amount of time and budget available for the execution of the design, and elements of practicality, for example, can the design withstand the wear and tear of the actors? A scene designer also is limited by the talent and abilities of the staff available to execute the design. A complex setting requiring sophisticated painting and delicate carpentry may be impossible to do if the only staff available are unskilled. These are the constraints, and also the challenges, of scene design.

Figure 6.5 Scene design for Aeschylus's *The Eumenides* (c. 1922). Designer: C. Ricketts. Courtesy of the Victoria and Albert Museum, London.

Figure 6.6 Scene design for Henrik Ibsen's *Peer Gynt,* the University of Arizona Theatre. Director: Peter R. Marroney. Scene designer: Robert C. Burroughs.

Lighting Design

Lighting designers are perhaps the most crucial of all the theatre artists in modern productions. Without their art nothing done by the actors, the costume designer, the property master, the director, or the scene designer would be seen by the audience. Yet lighting designers work in an ephemeral medium. They must sculpt with light and create shadows that fall where they desire them to fall; they must "paint" over the colors provided by the other designers. In doing so, they use lighting instruments with imperfect optical qualities. Lighting designers do their work in their minds, unlike scene designers, who can paint a design and then calculate it in feet and inches. Lighting designers must imagine what their light will do to an actor, to a costume, to a set. They must enhance the color of a costume, accent the physique of an actor, and reinforce the plasticity of a setting. They also try to reinforce the dramatic structure and dynamics of the play. They work within the framework of light and shade. Without shadows and highlights, the human face and body become imperceptible: A human face without shadows cannot be seen clearly more than a few feet away. In a theatre, such small movements as the raising of an eyebrow must be seen clearly as much as 100 feet away. It is the lighting designer who makes this possible.

Costume Design

One is tempted to think of the costumes of the theatre merely as clothing that has to be researched to reflect a particular historical period and constructed to fit a particular actor. But costuming goes beyond that. Costume designers work with the entire body of the actor. They design hair styles and clothing and sometimes makeup to suit a specific purpose or occasion, a character, a locale, and so forth (Figs. 6.7 and 6.8).

The function of stage costuming is threefold. First, it accents—that is, it shows the audience which personages are the most important in a scene, and it shows the relationship between personages. Second, it reflects—a particular era, time of day, climate, season, location, or occasion. The designs in Figure 6.7 reflect a historical period. We recognize different historical periods primarily through silhouette, or outline. Costume designers may merely suggest full detail or may actually provide it, as has been done in Figure 6.7. We see here the designer's concern not only for period, but also for character in her choice of details, color, texture,

Figure 6.7 Costume designs for Shakespeare's *Twelfth Night,* the Old Globe Theatre, San Diego, California. Director: Craig Noel. Costume designer: Peggy J. Kellner.

Figure 6.8 Costume designs for Shakespeare's *King Lear,* the Old Globe Theatre, San Diego, California. Director: Edward Payson Call. Costume designer: Peggy J. Kellner.

jewelry, and also hairstyle. Notice the length to which the designer goes to indicate detail, providing not only front but also back views of the costume, and also a head study showing the hair without a covering. Third, stage costuming reveals the style of the performance, the characters of the personages, and the personages' social position, profession, cleanliness, age, physique, and health. In Figure 6.8 the concern of the designer is clearly less with his-torical period than with production style and character. This costume design reveals the high emotional content of the particular scene, and we see at first glance the deteriorated health and condition of King Lear as he turns mad on the heath. The contrast provided by the king in such a state heightens the effect of the scene, and details such as the bare feet, the winter furs, and the storm-ravaged cape are precise indicators of the pathos we are expected to find and respond to. Costume designers work, as do scene and lighting designers, with the same general elements as painters and sculptors: the elements of composition. A stage costume is an actor's skin: It allows her to move as she must, and occasionally it restricts her from moving as she should not.

Properties

Properties fall into two general groups: set props and hand props. Set properties are part of the scene design: furniture, pictures, rugs, fireplace accessories, and so on. Along with the larger elements of the set, they identify the mood of the play and the character of those who inhabit the world they portray. Hand properties used by the actors in stage business also help to portray characters: cigarettes, papers, glasses, and so forth. The use of properties can be significant to our understanding of a play. For example, if at the opening curtain all properties appear to be neat and in order, but as the play develops the actors disrupt the properties, so that at the end of the play the entire scene is in disarray, that simple transition can help illustrate what may have happened in the play.

Aural Elements

What we hear also contributes to the production. Aristotle's term for the aural elements of a production is *music,* which meant something quite different from today. The aural elements, whether the actors' voices, the background music, or the clashing of swords, is an important part of the theatrical production. How a production sounds—and looks, and feels, and reads—represents a series of conscious choices on the part of all the artists involved: playwright, director, actors, and designers. Just as a composer of a musical piece creates harmonies, dynamics, rhythms, and melodies, the director, working with the actors and sound designer, makes the production develop in an aural sense so the audience is put into the proper mood,

drawn in the proper emotional direction, and captured by the proper attention points.

Dynamics

Every production has its own dynamic patterns, which we can chart (for example, as in Figure 6.1). The structural pattern of a play, about which we just spoke, is made clear to us by the dynamic patterns the director establishes. These patterns also help to hold the interest of the audience. Scientific studies indicate that attention or interest is not a constant factor; human beings are able to concentrate on specific items only for very brief periods. Therefore, to hold audience attention over the two-hour span of a production, it is essential to employ devices whereby from time to time interest or attention is allowed to peak and then relax. However, the peaks must be carefully controlled. A production should build to a high point of dramatic interest—the climax. However, each scene or act has its own peak of development—again, to maintain interest. So, the rise from the beginning of the play to the high point of dramatic interest is not a steady rise, but a series of peaks and valleys. Each successive peak is closer to the ultimate one. The director controls where and how high these peaks occur by controlling the dynamics of the actors—volume and intensity, both bodily and vocal. These are the same two qualities that make up dynamics in music.

The Actor

Although it not always easy to tell which functions in a production are the playwright's, which the director's, and which the actor's, the main channel of communication between the playwright and the audience is the actors. It is through their movements and speech that the audience perceives the play.

Our purpose is not to study acting; however, we can look for two elements in an actor's portrayal of a role that will enhance our response. The first is speech. Language is the playwright's words. Speech is the manner in which the actor delivers those words. Speech, like language, can range from high verisimilitude to high theatricality. If speech adheres to normal conversational rhythms, durations, and inflections, we respond in one way. If it utilizes extended vowel emphasis, long, sliding inflections, and dramatic pauses, we respond quite differently, even though the playwright's words are identical in both cases.

The second element of an actor's portrayal that aids our understanding is the physical reinforcement he or she gives to the character's basic motivation. Most actors try to identify a single basic motivation for their character. That motivation is called a *spine,* or *superobjective.* Everything that pertains to the decisions the person makes is kept consistent for the audience because those decisions and actions stem from this basic drive. Actors will translate that drive into something physical they can do throughout the play. For example, Blanche, in Tennessee Williams's *A Streetcar Named Desire* is driven by the desire to clean what she encounters because of the way she regards herself and the world around her. Ideally, the actress playing Blanche will discover that element of Blanche's personality as she reads the play and develops the role. To make that spine clear to us in the audience, the actress will translate it into physical action. Therefore, we will see Blanche constantly smoothing her hair, rearranging and straightening her dress, cleaning the furniture, brushing imaginary dust from others' shoulders, and so forth. Nearly every physical move she makes will relate somehow to the act of cleaning. Of course, these movements will be subtle, but if we are attentive, we can find them, thereby understanding the nature of the character we are perceiving.

Verisimilitude

In describing the relationship of the visual elements to the play, we have noted the designers' use of compositional elements. The use of these elements relative to life can be placed on a continuum, one end of which is theatricality and the other, verisimilitude. Items high in verisimilitude are those with which we deal in everyday life: language, movements, furniture, trees, rocks, and so forth. As we progress on our continuum from verisimilitude to theatricality, the elements of the production express less and less relationship to everyday life. They become distorted, exaggerated, and perhaps even nonobjective. Items far removed from verisimilitude are high in theatricality. Poetry, as we noted, is high in theatricality; everyday speech is high in verisimilitude. The position of the various elements of a production on this continuum suggests the style of the play, in the same sense that brushstroke, line, and palette indicate style in painting.

Figures 6.9 through 6.14 illustrate the range between verisimilitude and theatricality. Figure 6.9 is a proscenium setting high in verisimilitude, including a full ceiling over the setting. Figure 6.10 is an arena setting high in verisimilitude; it reflects the basically lifelike overall style of the presentation. However, the requirement of the arena configuration that there be no walls can cause problems in some productions. Note that some theatricality—specifically, the empty picture frame—is present in the decoration of this set. This is not an inconsistency because the play develops as a flashback in the mind of its main personage. In Figure 6.11 the designer has attempted to heighten the theatrical nature of the production by using set props high in verisimilitude and a setting that is representational, but pushed toward theatricality by the use of open space where one might expect solid walls in this proscenium production. The setting in Figure 6.12 moves further toward theatricality, and indicates clearly through exaggerated detail and two-dimensionality the whimsical and fun nature of the production. The designs in color insert Plate 15 and Figure 6.13 create a purely formal and theatrical environment. No locale is specifically depicted, but

Plate 8 Salvadore Dali, *The Persistence of Memory* (1931). Oil on canvas, 9½″ × 13″. The Museum of Modern Art, New York. Given anonymously.

Plate 10 Giorgio de Chirico, *Nostalgia of the Infinite* (c. 1913–14, dated on painting 1911). Oil on canvas, 53¼″ × 25½″. The Museum of Modern Art, New York. Purchase.

Plate 9 Sir Peter Paul Rubens (Flemish, 1577–1640), *The Assumption of the Virgin* (c. 1626). Oil on panel, 49³/₈″ × 37¹/₈″; framed: 62 × 49¹/₂″ × 3¹/₄″. National Gallery of Art, Washington, D.C. Samuel H. Kress Collection.

Plate 11 Henry Moore, *Two Large Forms* (1969). The Serpentine, Hyde Park, London.

Plate 12 James Earl Jones and Dianne Wiest in a 1981 production of Shakespeare's *Othello* (c. 1990 Martha Swope). Time, Inc. Photo.

Plate 13 Shakespeare's *Richard II*, Act II, scene 2: Entrance into St. Stephen's Chapel. Producer: Charles Kean, London (1857). Courtesy of The Victoria and Albert Museum, London.

Plate 14 Scene design (probably an alternate design) for Charles Fechter's revival of Shakespeare's *Hamlet*, Lyceum Theatre, London (1864). Designer: William Telbin. Courtesy of The Victoria and Albert Museum, London.

Figure 6.9 A proscenium setting for Jean Kerr's *Mary Mary,* the University of Arizona Theatre. Director: H. Wynn Pearce. Scene and lighting designer: Dennis J. Sporre.

the use of representational detail (various areas of the set served as locations and had realistic furniture) keeps the setting tied to the overall approach of the actors. Finally, in Figure 6.14, neither time nor place is indicated nor remotely suggested. Here the emphasis is on reinforcement of the high action of the production. The steep ramps throughout the set make it impossible for the actors to walk from one level to the next; the setting forces them to run.

In most arts the artist's style is unique, a recognizable mark on his or her artwork. Some artists change their style, but they do so by their own choice. Interpretive artists such as costume, scene, and lighting designers, and to a degree conductors as well, must submerge their personal style to that of the work with which they are involved. The playwright or the director sets the style, and the scene designer adapts to it and makes his or her design reflect that style.

HOW DOES IT STIMULATE THE SENSES?

In each of the elements we have just discussed, our senses are stimulated in a particular manner. We respond to the play's structure and how it works; we respond to dynamics. We are stimulated by the theatricality or verisimilitude of the language of the playwright and the movements and speech of the actors. We find our response shaped by the relationship of the stage space to the audience, and by the sets, lights, properties, and costumes. All of these elements bombard us simultaneously with complex visual and aural stimuli. How we respond, and how much we are able to respond, will determine our ultimate reaction to a production.

The theatre is unique in its ability to stimulate our senses, because only in the theatre is there a direct appeal to our emotions through the live portrayal of other individuals involved directly in the human condition. Being in the

Figure 6.10 An arena setting for Tennessee Williams's *The Glass Menagerie,* State University of New York at Plattsburgh. Director: H. Charles Kline. Scene and lighting designer: Dennis J. Sporre.

Figure 6.11 A proscenium setting for Oscar Wilde's *The Importance of Being Earnest,* the University of Arizona Theatre. Director: William Lang. Costume designer: Helen Workman Currie. Scene and lighting designer: Dennis J. Sporre.

Figure 6.12 Scene design for Jerry Devine and Bruce Montgomery's *The Amorous Flea* (musical), the University of Iowa Theatre. Director: David Knauf. Scene and lighting designer: Dennis J. Sporre.

presence of live actors gives us more of life in two hours than we could experience outside the theatre in that same time span. That phenomenon is difficult to equal. The term we use to describe our reaction to and involvement with what we experience in a theatrical production is *empathy*. Empathy causes us to cry when individuals we know are only actors become involved in tragic or emotional situations. Empathy makes us wince when an actor slaps the face of another actor or when two football players collide at full speed. Empathy is our mental and physical involvement in situations in which we are not direct participants.

Now let us examine a few of the more obvious ways a production can appeal to our senses. In plays that deal in conventions, the language may act as virtually the entire stimulant of our senses. Through the language the playwright sets the time, the place, the atmosphere, and even the small details of decoration. We become our own scene, lighting, and even costume designer, imagining what the playwright tells us ought to be there. In the opening scene of *Hamlet* we find Bernardo and Francisco, two guards. The hour is midnight; it is bitter cold; a ghost appears, in "warlike form." How do we know all of this? In a modern production we might see it all through the work of the costume and set designers. But this need not be the case, because the playwright gives us all of this information in the dialogue. Shakespeare wrote for a theatre that had no lighting save for the sun. His theatre (such as we know of it) probably used no scenery. The costumes were the street clothes of the day. The theatrical environment was the same whether the company was playing *Hamlet, Richard III,* or *The Tempest*. So what needed to be seen needed to be imagined. The language provided the stimuli for the audience.

We also respond to what we see. A sword fight performed with flashing action, swift movements, and great intensity sets us on the edge of our chair. Although we know the action is staged and the incident fictitious, we are caught in the excitement of the moment. We also can be gripped and manipulated by events

Figure 6.13 A proscenium setting for Stephen Sondheim's *Company* (musical), the University of Arizona Theatre. Director: Peter R. Marroney. Scene and lighting designer: Dennis J. Sporre.

of a quite different dynamic quality. In many plays we witness character assassination, as one life after another is laid bare before us. The intense but subtle movements of the actors—both bodily and vocal—can pull us here and push us there emotionally, and perhaps cause us to leave the theatre feeling emotionally drained. Part of our response is caused by subject matter, part by language—but much of it is the result of careful manipulation of dynamics.

Mood is an important factor in communication. Before the curtain is up, our senses are tickled by stimuli designed to put us in the mood for what follows. The houselights in the theatre may be very low, or we may see a cool or warm light on the front curtain. Music fills the theatre. We may recognize the raucous tones of a 1930s jazz piece, or a melancholy ballad. Whatever the stimuli, they are all carefully designed to cause us to begin to react the way the director wishes us to react. Once the curtain is up, the assault on our senses continues. The palette utilized by the scene, lighting, and costume designers helps communicate the mood of the play and other messages about it. The rhythm and variation in the visual elements capture our interest and reinforce the rhythmic structure of the play. In Figure 6.6, the use of line and form as well as color provides a formal and infinite atmosphere reflecting the epic grandeur of Ibsen's *Peer Gynt*.

Figure 6.14 Scene design for Euripides's *The Bacchae,* University of Illinois at Chicago. Director: William Raffeld. Scene and lighting designer: Dennis J. Sporre.

The degree of plasticity or three-dimensionality created by the lighting designer's illumination of the actors and the set causes us to respond in many ways. If the lighting designer has placed the primary lighting instruments directly in front of the stage, plasticity will be diminished and the actors will appear washed out or two-dimensional. We respond quite differently to that visual stimulant than to the maximum plasticity and shadow resulting from lighting coming nearly from the side.

We also react to the mass of a setting. Scenery that towers over the actors and appears massive in weight is different in effect from scenery that seems minuscule in comparison with the human form. The settings in Figures 6.5 and 6.11 and Plates 13 and 14 are different from one another in scale, and each places the actors in a different relationship with their surroundings. In Figure 6.11, the personages are at the center of their environment; in Plate 14 they are clearly subservient to it.

Finally, focus and line act on our senses. Careful composition can create movement, outlines and shadows that are crisp and sharp. Or it can create images that are soft, fuzzy, or blurred. Each of these devices is a stimulant; each has the potential to elicit a relatively predictable response. Perhaps in no other art are such devices so available and full of potential for the artist. We, as respondents, benefit through nearly total involvement in the life situation that comes to us over the footlights.

CHRONOLOGY OF SELECTED MAJOR PERIODS AND EXAMPLES FOR STUDY IN THEATRE

c. 500 B.C.–100 A.D..

Greek Theatre
    Aeschylus: *The Oresteia*
    Sophocles: *Oedipus the King; Antigone; Electra*
    Euripides: *Cyclops; Medea*
    Aristophanes: *The Birds; The Frogs*
Roman Theatre
    Plautus: *The Pot of Gold; Miles Gloriosus*

c. 1200–c. 1500
Medieval Theatre
mystery and miracle plays: *Everyman; Adam*
farce: *Maître Pierre Pathelin*

c. 1500–c. 1700
Italian-Renaissance Theatre
commedia dell'arte
Machiavelli: *Mandragola*
Elizabethan Theatre
Shakespeare: *Romeo and Juliet; Richard II;*
The Tempest
Beaumont and Fletcher: *The Knight of the*
Burning Pestle
Neoclassic French and Spanish Theatre
Lope de Vega: *Fuenteovejuna*
Corneille: *Le Cid*
Racine: *Phèdre*
Molière: *Tartuffe; The School for Wives*

c. 1600–c. 1800
English Restoration and Jacobean Theatre
Congreve: *The Way of the World; Love for*
Love
Cibber: *Love's Last Shift*
Sheridan: *The School for Scandal*
French Comedy
Beaumarchais: *The Marriage of Figaro*
Early American Theatre
Tyler: *The Contrast*

c. 1800–c. 1875
Alexandre Dumas *fils: La Dame aux Camélias*
Boucicault: *The Octoroon*

c. 1875–c. 1920
Ibsen: *Ghosts; Peer Gynt*
Shaw: *Pygmalion; St. Joan*
Chekhov: *The Sea Gull*
Gorki: *The Lower Depths*

c. 1920–
O'Neill: *Ah Wilderness!; Desire Under the*
Elms
Miller: *After the Fall*
Williams: *The Glass Menagerie; A Streetcar*
Named Desire
Giraudoux: *Amphitryon '38*
Brecht: *The Threepenny Opera; The Good*
Woman of Setzuan
Pinter: *The Homecoming*
Shaffer: *The Royal Hunt of the Sun*
Ionesco: *The Chairs*
Beckett: *Waiting for Godot*
Albee: *Who's Afraid of Virginia Woolf?*
Innaurato: *Gemini*
Coburn: *The Gin Game*
Pielmeier: *Agnes of God*
Simon: *Lost in Yonkers*
Albee: *Three Tall Women*
Mamet: *The Cryptogram*

*Film**

Like theatre, but without the spontaneity of "live" performers, film can confront us with life very nearly as we find it on our streets. On the other hand, through the magic of sophisticated *special effects,* film can take us to new worlds open to no other form of art.

Film is the most familiar and the most easily accessible art form; it is usually accepted almost without conscious thought, at least in terms of the story line or the star image presented or the basic entertainment value of the product. Yet all these elements are carefully crafted out of editing techniques, camera usage, juxtaposition of image, and structural rhythms, among others. It is these details of cinematic construction that can enhance our viewing of a film and can raise the film from mere entertainment into the realm of serious art. Bernard Shaw once observed that "details are important; they make comments." Our perception of the details of a film is not as easy as it might seem because at

the same time we are searching them out, the entertainment elements of the film are drawing our attention away from the search.

WHAT IS IT?

Film is aesthetic communication through the design of time and of three-dimensional space compressed into a two-dimensional image. Of all the arts discussed in this volume, film is the only one that also is an invention. Once the principles of photography had evolved and the mechanics of recording and projecting cinematic images were understood, society was ready for the production of pictures that could move, be presented in color, and eventually talk.

If we examine a strip of film, we will notice that it is only a series of pictures arranged in order of the length of the strip. Each of these pictures, or *frames,* is about four-fifths of an inch wide and three-fifths of an inch high. If we study the frames in relation to one another, we will see that even though each frame may seem to show exactly the same scene, the position of

*The text for this chapter was prepared by M. Ellis Grove. I have edited and expanded where necessary to conform to the rest of the text.

the objects in the separate frames is slightly different. When this film, which contains sixteen frames per foot of film, is run on a projecting device and passed before a light source at the rate of twenty-four frames per second (sixteen to eighteen frames per second for silent films), the frames printed on it are enlarged through the use of a magnifying lens, are projected on a screen, and appear to show movement. However, the motion picture, as film is popularly called, does not really move but only seems to. This is due to an optical phenomenon called *persistence of vision,* which according to legend was discovered by the astronomer Ptolemy sometime around the second century A.D. The theory behind persistence of vision is that the eye takes a fraction of a second to record an impression of an image and send it to the brain. Once the impression is received, the eye retains it on the retina for about one-tenth of a second after the actual image has disappeared. The film projector has built into it a device that pulls the film between the light source and a lens in a stop-and-go fashion, the film pausing long enough at each frame to let the eye take in the picture. Then a shutter on the projector closes, the retina retains the image, and the projection mechanism pulls the film ahead to the next frame. Holes, or *perforations,* along the right-hand side of the filmstrip enable the teeth on the gear of the driving mechanism to grasp the film and not only move it along frame by frame but also hold it steady in the gate or slot between the light source and the magnifying lens. It is this stop-and-go motion that gives the impression of continuous movement; if the film did not pause at each frame, the eye would receive only a blurred image.

The motion picture was originally invented as a device for recording and depicting motion. But once this goal was realized, it was quickly discovered this machine could also record and present stories—in particular, stories that made use of the unique qualities of the medium of film.

Our formal response to film recognizes three basic techniques of presentation. These are narrative film, documentary film, and absolute film.

Narrative Film

The narrative film is one that tells a story; in many ways it uses the technique of theatre. The narrative film follows the rules of literary construction in that it begins with expository material, adds levels of complications, builds to a climax, and ends with a resolution of all the plot elements. As in theatre, the personages in the story are portrayed by professional actors under the guidance of a director; the action of the plot takes place within a setting that is designed and constructed primarily for the action of the story but also allows the camera to move freely in photographing the action. Many narrative films are genre films, constructed out of familiar literary styles—the western, the detective story, and the horror story, among others. In these films the story elements are so familiar to the audience that it usually knows the outcome of the plot before it begins. The final showdown between the good guy and the bad guy, the destruction of a city by an unstoppable monster, and the identification of the murderer by the detective are all familiar plot elements that have become clichés or stereotypes within the genre; their use fulfills audience expectations. Film versions of popular novels and stories written especially for the medium of the screen are also part of the narrative-film form, but because film is a major part of the mass-entertainment industry the narrative presented is usually material that will attract a large audience and thus ensure a profit.

Documentary Film

Documentary film is an attempt to record actuality using primarily either a sociological or journalistic approach. It is normally not reenacted by professional actors and often is shot as the event is occurring, at the time and place of its occurrence. The film may use a narrative structure, and some of the events may be ordered or compressed for dramatic reasons, but its presentation gives the illusion of reality. The footage shown on the evening television news, television programming concerned with current events or problems, and full coverage either by television or film companies of a worldwide event, such as the Olympics, are all kinds of documentary film. All convey a sense of reality as well as a recording of time and place.

Absolute Film

Absolute film is simply film that exists for its own sake, for its record of movement or form. It does not tell a story, although documentary techniques can be used in some instances. Created neither in the camera nor on location, absolute film is built carefully, piece by piece, on the editing table or through special effects and multiple-printing techniques. It tells no story but exists solely as movement or form. Absolute film is rarely longer than twelve minutes (one reel) in length, and it usually is not created for commercial intent but is meant only as an artistic experience. Narrative or documentary films may contain sections that can be labeled absolute, and these sections can be studied either in or out of the context of the whole film.

HOW IS IT PUT TOGETHER?

Editing

Film is rarely recorded in the order of its final presentation; it is filmed in bits and pieces and put together, after all the photography is finished, as one puts together a jigsaw puzzle or builds a house. The force or strength of the final product depends on the editing process used, the manner in which the camera and the lighting are handled, and the movement of the actors before the camera. Naturally, the success of a film depends equally on the strength of the story presented and the ability of the writers, actors, directors, and technicians who have

worked on the film. However, this level of success is based on the personal taste of the audience and the depth of perception of the individual, and therefore does not lie within the boundaries of this discussion.

Perhaps the greatest difference between film and the other arts discussed within this volume is the use of *plasticity,* the quality of film that enables it to be cut, spliced, and ordered according to the needs of the film and the desires of the filmmaker. If twenty people were presented with all the footage shot of a presidential inauguration and asked to make a film commemorating the event, we would probably see twenty completely different films; each filmmaker would order the event according to his or her own views and artistic ideas. The filmmaker must be able to synthesize a product out of many diverse elements. This concept of plasticity is, then, one of the major advantages of the use of the machine in consort with an art form.

It is the editing process, then, that creates or builds the film, and within that process are many ways of meaningfully joining shots and scenes to make a whole. Let's examine some of these basic techniques. The *cut* is simply the joining together of shots during the editing process. A *jump cut* is a cut that breaks the continuity of time by jumping forward from one part of the action to another part that obviously is separated from the first by an interval of time, location, or camera position. It is often used for shock effect or to call attention to a detail, as in commercial advertising on television. The *form cut* cuts from an image in a shot to a different object that has a similar shape or contour; it is used primarily to make a smoother transition from one shot to another. For example, in D. W. Griffith's silent film *Intolerance,* attackers are using a battering ram to smash in the gates of Babylon. The camera shows the circular frontal area of the ram as it is advanced toward the gate. The scene cuts to a view of a circular shield, which in the framing of the shot is placed in exactly the same position as the front view of the ram.

Montage can be considered the most aesthetic use of the cut in film. It is handled in two basic ways: first, as an indication of compression or elongation of time, and, second, as a rapid succession of images to illustrate an association of ideas. A series of stills from Léger's *Ballet Mécanique* (Fig. 7.1) illustrates how images are juxtaposed to create comparisons. For example, a couple goes out to spend an evening on the town, dining and dancing. The film then presents a rapid series of cuts of the pair—in a restaurant, then dancing, then driving to another spot, then drinking, and then more dancing. In this way the audience sees the couple's activities in an abridged manner. Elongation of time can be achieved in the same way. The second use of montage allows the filmmaker to depict complex ideas or draw a metaphor visually. Sergei Eisenstein, the Russian film director, presented a shot in one of his early films of a Russian army officer walking out of the room, his back to the camera and his hands crossed behind him. Eisenstein cuts immediately to a peacock strutting away from the camera and spreading its tail. These two images are juxtaposed, and the audience is allowed to make the association that the officer is as proud as a peacock.

Camera Viewpoint

Camera position and viewpoint are as important to the structure of film as is the editing process. How the camera is placed and moved can be of great value to filmmakers as an aid in explaining and elaborating on their cinematic ideas. In the earliest days of the silent film the camera was merely set up in one basic position; the actors moved before it as if they were per-

Figure 7.1 *Ballet Mécanique* (1924). A film by Fernand Léger.

forming before an audience on a stage in a theater. However, watching an action from one position became dull, and the early filmmakers were forced to move the camera in order to add variety to the film.

The Shot

The *shot* is what is recorded by the camera over a particular period of time and is the basic unit of filmmaking. Several varieties are used. The *master shot* is a single shot of an entire piece of action, taken to facilitate the assembly of the component shots of which the scene will finally be composed. The *establishing shot* is a long shot introduced at the beginning of a scene to establish the interrelationship of details, a time, or a place, which will be elaborated on in subsequent shots. The *long shot* is a shot taken with the camera a considerable distance from the subject. The *medium shot* is taken nearer to the subject. The *close-up* is a shot taken with the camera quite near the subject. A *two-shot* is a close-up of two persons with the camera as near as possible while keeping both subjects within the frame. A *bridging shot* is a shot inserted in the editing of a scene to cover a brief break in the continuity of the scene.

Objectivity

An equally important variable of camera viewpoint is whether the scene is shot from an objective or subjective viewpoint. The *objective viewpoint* is that of an omnipotent viewer, roughly analogous to the technique of third-person narrative in literature. In this way filmmakers allow us to watch the action through the eyes of a universal spectator. However, filmmakers who wish to involve us more deeply in a scene may use the *subjective viewpoint:* The scene is presented as if we were actually participating in it, and the action is viewed from the filmmaker's perspective. This is analogous to the first-person narrative technique, and is usually found in the films of the more talented directors.

Cutting Within the Frame

Cutting within the frame is a method used to avoid the editing process. It can be created by actor movement, camera movement, or a combination of the two. It allows the scene to progress more smoothly and is used most often on television. In a scene in John Ford's *Stagecoach,* the coach and its passengers have just passed through hostile Indian territory without being attacked; the driver and his passengers all express relief. Ford cuts to a long shot of the coach moving across the desert and *pans,* or follows, it as it moves from right to left on the screen. This movement of the camera suddenly reveals in the foreground, and in close-up, the face of a hostile Indian watching the passage of the coach. In other words, the filmmaker has moved from a long shot to a close-up without the need of the editing process. He has also established a spatial relationship. The movement of the camera and the film is smooth and does not need a cut to complete the sequence. In a scene from *Jaws* (Fig. 7.2) the camera moves from the distant objects to the face in the foreground, finally including them both in the frame; the pan across the scene in so doing is accomplished without editing of the film.

Dissolves

During the printing of the film negative, transitional devices can be worked into a scene. They are usually used to indicate the end of the scene and the beginning of another. The camera can cut or jump to the next scene, but the transition can be smoother if the scene fades out into black and the next scene fades in. This is called a *dissolve.* A *lap dissolve* occurs when the fade-out and the fade-in are done simultaneously and the scene momentarily overlaps. A *wipe* is a form of optical transition in which a line moves across the screen, eliminating one shot and revealing the next, much in the way a windshield wiper moves across the windshield of a car. In silent film the transition could also

Figure 7.2 *Jaws* (1975). Universal Pictures. Director: Steven Spielberg. Copyright © by Universal Pictures, a Division of Universal City Studios, Inc. All rights reserved.

be created by closing or opening the aperture of the lens; this process is called an *iris-out* or an *iris-in*.

Movement

Camera movement also plays a part in film construction. The movement of the camera as well as its position can add variety or impact to a shot or a scene. Even the manner in which the lens is focused can add to the meaning of the scene. If the lens clearly shows both near and distant objects at the same time, the camera is using *depth of focus*. In Figure 7.2 foreground and background are equally in focus. In this way actors can move in the scene without necessitating a change of camera position. Many TV shows photographed before an audience usually use this kind of focus. If the main object of interest is photographed clearly while the remainder of the scene is blurred or out of focus, the camera is using *rack* or *differential focus*. With this technique the filmmaker can focus the audience's attention on one element within a shot.

There are many kinds of physical (as opposed to apparent) camera movement that can have a bearing on a scene. The *track* is a shot taken as the camera is moving in the same direction, at the same speed, and in the same place as the object being photographed. A *pan* is taken by rotating the camera horizontally while keeping it fixed vertically. The pan is usually used in enclosed areas, particularly TV studios. The *tilt* is a shot taken while moving the camera vertically or diagonally; it is used to add variety to a sequence. A *dolly shot* is taken by moving the camera toward or away from the subject. Modern sophisticated lenses can accomplish the same movement by changing the focal length. This negates the need for camera movement and is known as a *zoom shot*.

Of course, the camera cannot photograph a scene without light, either natural or artificial. Most television productions photographed before a live audience require a flat, general illumination pattern. For close-ups, stronger and more definitively focused lights are required to highlight the features, eliminate shadows, and add a feeling of depth to the shot. Case shadows or atmospheric lighting (in art, *chiaroscuro*) is often used to create a mood, particularly in films made without the use of color (Fig. 7.3). Lighting at a particular angle can heighten the feeling of texture, just as an extremely close

Figure 7.3 *The Birth of a Nation* (1915). Director: D. W. Griffith.

shot can. These techniques add more visual variety to a sequence.

If natural or outdoor lighting is used and the camera is hand-held, an unsteadiness in movement is found in the resulting film; this technique and effect is called *cinema veritée*. This kind of camera work, along with natural lighting, is found more often in documentary films or in sequences photographed for newsreels or television news programming. It is one of the conventions of current-events reporting and adds to the sense of reality necessary for this kind of film recording.

These techniques and many others are all used by filmmakers to ease some of the technical problems in making a film. They can be used to make the film smoother or more static, depending on the needs of the story line, or to add an element of commentary to the film. One school of cinematic thought believes that camera technique is best when it is not noticeable; another, more recent way of thinking believes the obviousness of all the technical aspects of film adds meaning to the concept of cinema. In any case, camera technique is present in every kind of film made and is used to add variety and commentary, meaning and method, to the shot, the scene, and the film.

HOW DOES IT STIMULATE THE SENSES?

The basic aim of film, as with any art, is to involve us in its product, either emotionally or intellectually. Of course, there is nothing like a good plot with well-written dialogue delivered by trained actors to create interest. But there are other ways in which filmmakers may enhance their final product, techniques that manipulate us toward a deeper involvement or a heightened intellectual response. Figure 7.4 il-

Figure 7.4 Still photo from *The Birth of a Nation* (1915). Director D. W. Griffith. The Metropolitan Museum of Art.

lustrates how angles and shadows within a frame help create a feeling of excitement and variety. An in-depth study of the films of Fellini, Hitchcock, or Bergman may indicate how directors can use some of the technical aspects of film to underline emotions or strengthen a mood or an idea in their films.

It is in the area of technical detail that perception is most important. We should begin to cultivate the habit of noticing even the tiniest details in a scene, for often these details may add a commentary that we may miss. For example, in Hitchcock's *Psycho,* when the caretaker of the motel (Tony Perkins) wishes to spy on the guests in cabin 1, he pushes aside a picture that hides a peephole. The picture is a reproduction of *The Rape of the Sabine Women.* Hitchcock's irony is obvious. Thus perception becomes the method through which viewers of film may find its deeper meanings as well as its basic styles.

Crosscutting

There are many techniques that filmmakers can use to heighten the feeling they desire for their film to convey. The most familiar and most easily identified is that of *crosscutting.* Crosscutting is an alternation between two separate actions that are related by theme, mood, or plot but are usually occurring within the same period of time. Its most common function is to create suspense. Consider this familiar cliché: Pioneers going west in a wagon train are besieged by Indians. The settlers have been able to hold them off, but ammunition is running low. The hero has been able to find a cavalry troop, and they are riding to the rescue. The film alternates between views of the pioneers fighting for their lives and shots of the soldiers galloping to the rescue. The film continues to cut back and forth, the pace of cutting increasing until the sequence builds to a climax—the cavalry arriving in time to save the wagon train. The famous chase scene in *The French Connection,* the final sequences in *Wait Until Dark,* and the sequences of the girl entering the fruit cellar in *Psycho* are built for suspense through techniques of crosscutting.

A more subtle use of crosscutting, *parallel development,* occurs in *The Godfather, Part I* (color inserts, Plates 16 and 17). At the close of that film Michael Corleone is acting as godfather for his sister's son; at the same time his men are destroying all his enemies. The film alternates between views of Michael at the religious service and sequences showing violent death. This parallel construction is used to draw an ironic comparison; actions are juxtaposed. By developing the two separate actions, the filmmaker allows us to draw our own inferences and thereby add a deeper meaning to the film.

Tension Buildup and Release

If the plot of a film is believable, the actors competent, and the director and film editor talented and knowledgeable, a feeling of tension will be built up. If this tension becomes too great, we will seek some sort of release, and an odd-sounding laugh, a sudden noise, or a loud comment from someone else may cause us to laugh, thus breaking the tension and in a sense destroying the atmosphere so carefully created. Wise filmmakers therefore build into their film a *tension release* that deliberately draws laughter from the audience, but at a place in the film where they wish them to laugh. This tension release can be a comical way of moving, a gurgle as a car sinks into a swamp, or merely a comic line. It does not have to be too obvious, but it should be present in some manner. After a suspenseful sequence the audience needs to be relaxed; once the tension release does its job, we can be drawn into another suspenseful or exciting situation.

Sometimes, to shock us or maintain our attention, a filmmaker may break a deliberately created pattern or a convention of film. In *Jaws,* for example, each time the shark is about to appear, a four-note musical *motif* is played. We thereby grow to believe we will hear this warning before each appearance, and so we relax. However, toward the end of the film the shark suddenly appears without benefit of the motif, shocking us. From that point until the end of the film we can no longer relax, and our attention is fully engaged.

Direct Address

Another method used to draw attention is that of *direct address.* It is a convention in most films that the actors rarely look at or talk directly to the audience. However, in *Tom Jones,* while Tom and his landlady are arguing over money, Tom suddenly turns directly to the audience and says, "You saw her take the money." The audience's attention is focused on the screen more strongly than ever after that. This technique has been effectively adapted by television for use in commercial messages. For example, a congenial person looks at the camera (and us) with evident interest and asks if we are feeling tired, run-down, and sluggish. He assumes we are and proceeds to suggest a remedy. In a sense, the aside of nineteenth-century melodrama and the soliloquy of Shakespeare were also ways of directly addressing an audience and drawing them into the performance.

Of course, silent films could not use this type of direct address to the audience; they had only the device of titles. However, some of the silent comedians felt they should have direct contact with their audience, and so they developed a *camera look* as a form of direct address. After an especially destructive moment in his films, Buster Keaton would look directly at the camera, his face immobile, and stare at the audience.

When Charlie Chaplin achieved an adroit escape from catastrophe he might turn toward the camera and wink. Stan Laurel would look at the camera and gesture helplessly (Fig. 7.5), as if to say, "How did all this happen?" Oliver Hardy, after falling into an open manhole, would register disgust directly to the camera and the audience. These were all ways of commenting to the audience and letting them know the comedians knew they were there. Some sound comedies adapted this technique. In the road pictures of Bob Hope and Bing Crosby, both stars, as well as camels, bears, fish, and anyone else who happened to be around, would comment on the film or the action directly to the audience. However, this style may have been equally based on the audience's familiarity with radio programs, in which the performer usually spoke directly to the home audience.

Magnitude and Convention

In considering the magnitude of a film, we must be aware of the means by which the film is to be communicated. In other words, was the film made for a television showing or for projection in a large film theatre? Due to the size of the television receiver, large panoramas or full-scale action sequences are not entirely effective on the TV—they become too condensed. TV films, to be truly effective, should be built around the close-up and around concentrated action and movement, because the TV audience is closer to the image than are the viewers in a large theater. Scenes of multiple images with complex patterns of movement or scenes of great violence will become confusing because of the intimacy of television, and will seem more explicit than they really are. On the

Figure 7.5 *Your Darn Tootin'* (1928). A Hal Roach Production for Pathe Films. Director: Edgar Kennedy.

contrary, when close shots of intimate details are enlarged through projection in a theatre they may appear ridiculous. The nuance of a slightly raised eyebrow that is so effective in the living room will appear either silly or overly dramatic when magnified on a 60-foot screen. Today's moviemakers, when creating a film, must be aware of how it will appear if translated to the home screen or enlarged in a theater; their work ought to be designed to accommodate the size of either medium.

The film, as with theatre, has certain conventions or customs that we accept without hesitation. When an exciting chase scene takes place, no one asks where the orchestra is that is playing the music which enhances the sequence; we merely accept the background music as part of the totality of the film. A film photographed in black and white is accepted as a recording of reality, even though we know the real world has color although this particular reel world does not. When a performer sings and dances in the rain in the middle of a city street, no member of the audience worries if the orchestra is getting wet or wonders if the performer will be arrested for creating a public spectacle. The conventions of the musical film are equally acceptable to an audience conditioned to accept them.

This consideration of conventions is especially important to the acceptance of the silent film as a form of art. The silent film should not be thought of as a sound film without sound but as a separate entity with its own special conventions. These conventions revolve around the methods used to indicate sound and dialogue without actually using them. The exaggerated pantomime and acting styles, the use of titles, character stereotyping, and visual metaphors are all conventions that were accepted during the silent era but appear ludicrous today because of changes in style and taste and improvements in the devices used for recording and projecting film. The action in the silent film was recorded and presented at a speed of sixteen to eighteen frames per second; when that action is presented today on a projector that operates at twenty-four frames per second, the movement becomes too fast and appears to be jerky and disconnected. However, once we learn to accept these antiquated conventions, we may find the silent film is an equally effective form of cinematic art.

Structural Rhythm

Much of the effectiveness of a film relies on its success as a form as well as a style. Filmmakers create rhythms and patterns that are based on the way they choose to tell their stories or that indicate deeper meanings and relationships. The *structural rhythm* of a film is the manner in which the various shots are joined together and juxtaposed with other cinematic images, both visual and aural.

Symbolic images in film range from the very obvious to the extremely subtle, but they are all useful to filmmakers in directing our attention to the ideas inherent in the philosophical approach underlying the film. This use of symbolic elements can be found in such clichés as the hero dressed in white and the villain dressed in black, in the more subtle use of water images in Fellini's *La Dolce Vita,* or even in the presence of an X whenever someone is about to be killed in *Scarface.*

Sometimes, symbolic references can be enhanced by form cutting—for example, cutting directly from the hero's gun to the villain's gun. Or the filmmaker may choose to repeat a familiar image in varying forms, using it as a composer would use a motif in music. Hitchcock's shower sequence in *Psycho* is built around circular images: the shower head, the circular drain in the tub, the mouth open and screaming, and the iris of the unseeing eye. In *Fort Apache* John Ford uses clouds of dust as a curtain to cover major events; the dust is also used to indicate the ultimate fate of the cavalry troop. Grass, cloud shapes, windblown trees, and patches of color have all been used symbolically and as motifs. Once they perceive such elements, serious students of film will find the deeper meanings of a film more evident and their appreciation of the film heightened.

Another part of structural rhythm is the repetition of certain visual patterns throughout a film. A circular image positioned against a rectangular one, a movement from right to left, an action repeated regularly throughout a sequence—all can become observable patterns or even thematic statements. The silent film made extreme use of thematic repetition. In *Intolerance* D. W. Griffith develops four similar stories simultaneously and continually crosscuts between them. This particular use of form enabled him to develop the idea of the similarity of intolerance throughout the ages. In their silent films Laurel and Hardy often built up a pattern of "you do this to me and I'll do that to you"; they called it "tit for tat." Their audience would be lulled into expecting this pattern, but at that point the film would present a variation on the familiar theme (a process quite similar to the use of *theme and variation* in musical composition). The unexpected breaking of the pattern would surprise the audience into laughter.

Parallel development, discussed earlier, can also be used to create form and pattern throughout a film. For example, Edwin S. Porter's *The Kleptomaniac* alternates between two stories: a wealthy woman caught shoplifting a piece of jewelry, and a poor woman who steals a loaf of bread. Each sequence alternately shows crime, arrest, and punishment; the wealthy woman's husband bribes the judge to let her off; the poor woman is sent to jail. Porter's final shot shows the statue of justice holding her scales, one weighted down with a bag of gold. Her blindfold is raised over one eye, which is looking at the money. In this case, as in others, the form is the film.

When sound films became practicable, filmmakers found many ways of using the audio track, in addition to just recording dialogue.

This track could be used as symbolism, as a motif that reinforced the emotional quality of a scene, or for stronger emphasis or structural rhythm.

Some filmmakers believe a more realistic feeling can be created if the film is cut rather than dissolved. They feel that cutting abruptly from scene to scene gives the film a staccato rhythm that in turn augments the reality they hope to achieve. A dissolve, they think, creates a slower pace and tends to make the film *legato* and thus more romantic. If the abrupt cutting style is done to the beat of the sound track, a pulsating rhythm is created for the film sequence; this in turn is communicated to us and adds a sense of urgency to the scene. In Fred Zinnemann's *High Noon* the sheriff is waiting for the noon train to arrive. The sequence is presented in *montage,* showing the townspeople, as well as the sheriff waiting. The shot is changed every eight beats of the musical track. As the time approaches noon, the shot is changed every four beats. Tension mounts. The feeling of rhythm is enhanced by shots of a clock's pendulum swinging to the beat of the sound track. Tension continues to build. The train's whistle sounds. There is a series of rapid cuts of faces turning and looking, but there is only silence on the sound track, which serves as a tension release. This last moment of the sequence is also used as transition between the music and silence. In other films the track may shift from music to natural sounds and back to the music again. Or a pattern may be created of natural sound, silence, and a musical track. All depends on the mood and attitude the filmmaker is trying to create. In Hitchcock's films music often is used as a tension release or an afterthought, as Hitchcock usually relies on the force of his visual elements to create structural rhythm.

Earlier in this chapter we mentioned the use of motif in *Jaws.* Many films make use of an audio motif to introduce visual elements or convey meaning symbolically. Walt Disney, particularly in his pre-1940 cartoons, often uses his sound track in this manner. For example, Donald Duck is trying to catch a pesky fly, but the fly always manages to elude him. In desperation Donald sprays the fly with an insecticide. The fly coughs and falls to the ground. But on the sound track we hear an airplane motor coughing and sputtering and finally diving to the ground and crashing. In juxtaposing these different visual and audio elements, Disney is using his track symbolically.

John Ford often underlines sentimental moments in his films by accompanying the dialogue of a sequence with traditional melodies; as the sequence comes to a close the music swells and then fades away to match the fading out of the scene. In *The Grapes of Wrath,* when Tom Joad says good-bye to his mother, "Red River Valley" is played on a concertina; as Tom walks over the hill the music becomes louder, and when he disappears from view it fades out. Throughout this film, this familiar folk song serves as a thematic reference to the Joad's home in Oklahoma and also boosts feelings of nostalgia for some of us. In *She Wore a Yellow Ribbon* the title of the film is underlined by the song of the same name, but through the use of different tempos and timbres the mood of the song is changed each time it is used. As the cavalry troop rides out of the fort the song is played in a strong $\frac{4}{4}$ meter with a heavy emphasis on the brass; the sequence is also cut to the beat of the track. In the graveyard sequences the same tune is played by strings and reeds in $\frac{2}{4}$ time and in a much slower tempo, which makes the song melancholy and sentimental. In the climactic fight sequence in *The Quiet Man* John Ford cuts to the beat of a sprightly Irish jig, which enriches the comic elements of the scene and plays down the violence.

Our discussion in these last few paragraphs touches only the surface of the techniques and uses of sound in film; of course, there are other ways of using sound and the other elements discussed thus far. But part of the challenge of the film as an art form is our discovery of the varying uses to which film technique can be put, and this in turn enhances further perceptions.

CHRONOLOGY AND SELECTED EXAMPLES FOR STUDY IN CINEMATOGRAPHY

1889–1914: The Growth of the Machine; Cinematic Archaeology

1895 *Baby's Lunch.* Lumierès Brothers. France.

1902 *A Trip to the Moon.* George Méliès. France.

1903 *The Great Train Robbery.* Edwin S. Porter. USA.

1905 *Rescued by Rover.* Cecil Hepworth. England.

1909 *A Corner in Wheat.* D. W. Griffith. USA.

1911 *The Lonedale Operator.* D. W. Griffith. USA

1912 *Queen Elizabeth.* Louis Mercanton. France. Starring Sarah Bernhardt.

1913 *Judith of Bethulia.* D. W. Griffith. USA.

1914 The Star System Begins

Tillie's Punctured Romance. Mack Sennett. USA. Starring Charlie Chaplin.

The Birth of a Nation. D. W. Griffith. USA.

1915–1928: The Art of the Silent Film; The Growth of the Studio System

1916 *Intolerance.* D. W. Griffith. USA.

1917 *Easy Street.* Charlie Chaplin. USA.

1919 *The Cabinet of Dr. Caligari.* Robert Weine. Germany. Expressionism.

1922 *Nanook of the North.* Robert Flaherty. USA. Documentary.

1923 *Greed.* Eric Von Stroheim. USA. Naturalism.

1924 *The Last Laugh.* F. W. Murnau. Germany. Impressionism.

1925 *Potemkin.* Sergei Eisenstein. USSR. Realism and montage.

The Gold Rush. Charlie Chaplin. USA.

1927 *Ben Hur.* Fred Nible. MGM. USA.

The Jazz Singer. Alan Crosland. Warner Brothers. USA. Starring Al Jolson.

1928 *The Lights of New York.* Bryan Foy. USA.

Steamboat Willie. Walt Disney. USA. Starring Mickey Mouse.

1929–1953: The Sound Era; Television

1929 *Un Chien Andalou.* Luis Bunuel. France. Surrealism.

1930 *Anna Christie.* Clarence Brown. MGM. USA. Starring Greta Garbo.

Little Caesar. Mervyn LeRoy. Warner Brothers. USA. Starring Edward G. Robinson.

1935 *The Thirty-Nine Steps.* Alfred Hitchcock. England.

The Informer. John Ford. RKO. USA.

1936 *Night Mail.* John Grierson. England. Documentary.

1937 *The River.* Pare Lorentz. USA. Documentary.

1939 *Gone with the Wind.* Victor Fleming. MGM-Selznick. USA.

Stagecoach. John Ford. United Artists. USA.

1941 *Citizen Kane.* Orson Welles. RKO. USA.

1945 *House on 92nd Street.* Henry Hathaway. Twentieth Century-Fox. USA. DocuDrama.

Open City. Roberto Rossellini. Italy. Neorealism.

1946 *Great Expectations.* David Lean, England.

1948 *The Bicycle Thief.* Vittorio De Sica. Italy.

1949 The Emergence of Television

1952 3-D films; Cinerama begins

1953 *The Robe.* Henry Koster. Twentieth Century-Fox. USA. CinemaScope.

The Moon is Blue. Otto Preminger. United Artists. USA. No production seal of approval.

1956–1979 Foreign Influences; Independent Studio Production

1956 *The Seventh Seal.* Ingmar Bergman. Sweden. Metaphysical allegory.

1957 *The Bridge on the River Kwai.* David Lean. Columbia. USA.

1959 *The 400 Blows.* François Truffaut. France. Auteurism.

Breathless. Jean-Luc Godard. France.

Room at the Top. Jack Clayton. England.

1960 *L'Avventura.* Michelanglo Antonioni. Italy. Subjective realism.

Psycho. Alfred Hitchcock. Paramount. USA.

1963 *8 .* Federico Felini. Italy. Abstraction.

Tom Jones. Tony Richardson. England.

1967 *Bonnie and Clyde.* Arthur Penn. Warner Brothers-Seven Arts. USA.

1968 *2001.* Stanley Kubrick. MGM. USA.

1969 *M.A.S.H.* Robert Altman. Twentieth Century-Fox. USA.

1972 *The Godfather, Part I.* Francis Ford Coppola. Paramount. USA.

1975 *Jaws.* Steven Spielberg. Universal. USA.

1978 *Superman.* Richard Donner. Warner Brothers. USA. The force of special effects.

1979 *All That Jazz.* Bob Fosse. Twentieth Century-Fox-Columbia. USA. Biographical surrealism.

Manhattan. Woody Allen. United Artists. USA. The film is the man.

1980: The Box Office and Mass Audiences

1980 *Elephant Man.* Paramount. USA.

The Empire Strikes Back. Twentieth Century-Fox.

Ordinary People. Paramount. USA.

The Shining Mirror. Warner Brothers. USA.

1981 *Four Seasons.* Universal. USA.

The French Lieutenant's Woman. United Artists. USA.

On Golden Pond. Universal. USA.

Ragtime. Paramount. USA.

Chariots of Fire. Warner Brothers. USA.

Raiders of the Lost Ark. Paramount. USA.

1982 *E. T.* Universal. USA.

Gandhi. Columbia. USA.

Sophie's Choice. Universal. USA.

Tootsie. Columbia. USA.

1983 *The Dresser.* Columbia. USA.

Fanny and Alexander. Embassy Pictures. USA.

Terms of Endearment. Paramount. USA.

Silkwood. Twentieth Century-Fox. USA.

1984 *Indiana Jones and the Temple of Doom.* Paramount. USA.

The Bounty. Dino De Laurentiis. USA.

The Natural. Tri-Star. USA.

Never Cry Wolf. Buena Vista. USA.

1990: A Worldwide Cinema

Age of Innocence. Martin Scorsese. Columbia. USA.

Bad Behavior. Les Blair, Parallax. UK.

Naked. Mike Leigh. Thin Man Films. USA.

The Piano. Jane Campion. Jan Chapman Productions. UK.

The Stolen Children. Gianni Amelio. Erre Produzioni. Italy.

The Story of Qiu Ju. Zang Yimou. Sil-Metropole. People's Republic of China.

Un Coeur en Hiver. Claude Saute. Film par Film. France.

8

Dance

Every December, Tchaikovsky's "Nutcracker Ballet" rivals Handel's *Messiah* and television reruns of the Jimmy Stewart movie, *It's a Wonderful Life,* as a holiday tradition. Nevertheless, ballet and dance in general seem remote from most people. Ballet, in particular, evokes strong personal opinions of like or dislike. Why this is so and what those opinions are create spirited classroom discussion.

Dance is one of the most natural and universal of human activities. In virtually every culture, regardless of location or level of development, we find some form of dance. Dance appears to have sprung from human religious needs. For example, scholars are relatively sure the theatre of ancient Greece developed out of that society's religious, tribal dance rituals. There can be no doubt that dance is part of human communication at its most fundamental level. We can see this expression even in little children, who, before they begin to paint, sing, or imitate, begin to dance.

WHAT IS IT?

Dance focuses on the human form in time and space. In general it follows one of three traditions: ballet, modern dance, and folk dance. Other forms or traditions of dance exist including jazz dance, tap, and musical comedy. Their properties or qualities as concert dance are often debated. We note jazz dance in passing later in the chapter and focus our brief discussion on ballet, modern dance, and folk dance.

Ballet

Ballet comprises what can be called classical, or formal dance; it is rich in tradition and rests heavily on a set of prescribed movements and actions, as we shall see. In general, ballet is a highly theatrical dance presentation consisting of solo dancers, duets, and choruses, or *corps de ballets.* According to Anatole Chujoy in the *Dance Encyclopedia,* the basic principle in ballet is "the reduction of human gesture to bare essentials, heightened and developed into meaningful patterns." George Balanchine saw the single steps of a ballet as analogous to a single frame in a motion picture. Ballet, then, became a fluid succession of images, all existing within specialized codes of movement. As with all dance and all the arts, ballet expresses basic human experiences and desires.

Modern Dance

Modern dance is a label given to a broad variety of highly individualized dance works limited to the twentieth century, essentially American in derivation, and antiballetic in philosophy. It began as a revolt against the stylized and tradition-bound elements of the ballet. The basic principle of modern dance probably could be stated as an emphasis on natural and spontaneous or uninhibited movement, in strong contrast with the conventionalized and specified movement of the ballet. The earliest modern dancers found stylized ballet movement incompatible with their need to communicate in twentieth-century terms. As Martha Graham characterized it, "There are no general rules. Each work of art creates its own code." Nonetheless, in its attempt to be nonballetic, certain conventions and characteristics have accrued to modern dance. Although narrative elements do exist in many modern dances, there may be less emphasis on them than in traditional ballet. There also are differences in the use of the body, the use of the dance floor, and the interaction with the mise-en-scène.

Folk Dance

Folk dance, somewhat like folk music, is a body of group dances performed to traditional music. It is similar to folk music in that we do not know the artist who developed it; there is no choreographer of record for folk dances. The dances began as a necessary or informative part of certain cultures, and their characteristics are stylistically identifiable with a given culture. They developed over a period of years, without benefit of authorship, passing from one generation to another. They have their prescribed movements, rhythms, and music and costume. At one time or another they may have become formalized—that is, committed to some form of record. But they are part of a heritage, and usually not the creative result of an artist or a group of interpretative artists, as is the case with the other forms of dance. Likewise, they exist more to involve participants than to entertain an audience.

Folk dancing establishes an individual sense of participation in society, the tribe, or a mass movement. "The group becomes one in conscious strength and purpose, and each individual experiences a heightened power as part of it . . . [a] feeling of oneness with one's fellows which is established by collective dancing."*

HOW IS IT PUT TOGETHER?

Dance is an art of time and space that utilizes many of the elements of the other arts. In the mise-en-scène and in the line and form of the human body it involves many of the compositional elements of pictures, sculpture, and theatre. Dance also relies heavily on the elements of music—whether or not music accompanies the dance presentation. However, the essential ingredient of dance is the human body and its varieties of expression.

Formalized Movement

The most obvious repository of formalized movement in dance is ballet. All movement in ballet is based on five basic leg, foot, and arm positions. In the *first position* (Fig. 8.1) the dancer stands with weight equally distributed

*John Martin, *The Dance* (New York: Tudor, 1946), p. 26.

Figure 8.1 First position. Linda Rich photo.

Figure 8.2 Second position. Linda Rich photo.

between the feet, heels together, and toes open and out to the side. In ballet all movements evolve from this basic *open* position; the feet are never parallel to each other and both point straight forward. The *second position* (Fig. 8.2) is achieved by opening the first position the length of one's foot, again with the weight placed evenly on both feet. In the *third position* (Fig. 8.3) the heel of the front foot touches the instep of the back foot; the legs and feet must be well turned out. In the *fourth position* (Fig. 8.4) the heel of the front foot is opposite the toe of the back foot. The feet are parallel and separated by the length of the dancer's foot; again, the weight is placed evenly on both feet. The *fifth position* (Fig. 8.5) is the most frequently used of the basic ballet positions. The feet are close together with the front heel touching the toe of the back foot. The legs and

the feet must be well turned out to achieve this position correctly, and the weight is placed evenly on both feet. As we can see in Figures 8.1 through 8.5, each position changes the attitude of the arms as well as that of the legs and feet. From these five basic positions a series of fundamental movements and poses is developed; these are the core of every movement of the human body in formal ballet.

Some of the fundamental ballet poses and movements can be recognized throughout a dance work, including modern dance; a few lend themselves to photographic illustration. Figure 8.6 shows a *demi-plié* in first position. This half-bend of the knees can be executed in any position. The *grand plié* shown in Figure 8.7, also in first position, carries the bend to its maximum degree. The *arabesque* is a pose executed on one foot with arms and foot extended. It can appear in a variety of positions; it is shown in Figure 8.8 in the *penché,* or leaning position. The *port de bras* (Fig. 8.9) is simply the technique of moving the arms correctly. As we might imagine, many variations can be made on the five basic positions. For example, the *grande seconde* (Fig. 8.10) is a variation on second position in which the leg is elevated to full height. The leg also is elevated in the *demi-hauteur,* or "half height" (Fig. 8.11). Full height requires extension of the leg at a 90-degree angle to the ground; half height requires a 45-degree extension. Movements carry the same potential for variety. For example, in the *ronds de jambe à terre* (Fig. 8.12) the leg from the knee to and including the foot is rotated in a semicircle. Other basic movements (defined in the Glossary) include the *assemblé, changement de*

pied, jeté, pirouette, and *relevé.* As we develop expertise in perceiving dance it will become obvious to us in watching formal ballet (and to a lesser degree, modern dance) that we see a limited number of movements and poses, turns and leaps, done over and over again. In this sense these bodily compositions form a kind of theme and variation, and they are interesting in that right alone.

In addition, it is possible for us to find a great deal of excitement in the bodily movements of formal ballet if for no other reason than the physical skills required for their execution. The standards of quality applied to a ballet dancer are based on the ability of the dancer to execute these movements properly. Just as in gymnastics or figure skating, the strength and grace of the individual in large part determines his or her qualitative achievement. It goes without

Figure 8.3 Third position. Linda Rich photo.

Figure 8.4 Fourth position. Linda Rich photo.

Figure 8.5 Fifth position. Linda Rich photo.

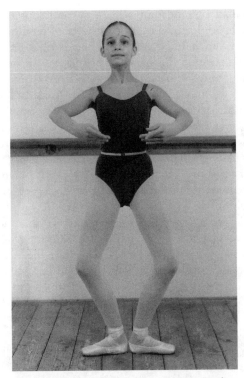

Figure 8.6 *Demi-plié* in first position. Linda Rich photo.

saying, however, that ballet is far more than just a series of gymnastic exercises.

Perhaps the most familiar element of ballet is the female dancer's toe work or dancing *on point* (Fig. 8.13). A special kind of shoe is required for toe work (Fig. 8.14). Dancing on point is a fundamental part of the female dancer's development. It usually takes a minimum of two years of thorough training and development before a dancer can begin to do toe work. Certain kinds of turns are not possible without toe shoes and the technique for using them—for example, spinning on point or being spun by a partner.

We have focused on ballet in this discussion of formalized movement because it is the most familiar of the traditional, formalized dance forms. Ballet, however, is not alone in adhering to formalized patterns of movement. It is,

in part, formalized movement that allows us to distinguish among folk and other dances, such as the *pavane,* the *galliard,* the *waltz,* and the *mambo.* All have formal or conventional patterns of movement. Perhaps only modern dance resists formal movement, and even then not completely.

Line, Form, and Repetition

The compositional elements of the line, form, and repetition apply to the use of the human body in exactly the same sense that they apply to those elements in painting and sculpture—the latter especially. The body of the dancer can be analyzed as sculptural, three-dimensional form that reflects the use of line, even though the dancer is continually in motion. The body as a sculptural form moves from one pose to another, and if we were to take a stop-action movie of a dance, we could analyze, frame by frame or second by second, the compositional qualities of the human body. The human form in every illustration in this chapter, including those that show groupings of dancers, can be analyzed as a composition of line and shape. Dance, therefore, can be seen at two levels: first, as a type of pictorial communication employing symbols that occur only for a moment, and, second, as the design of transition with movement between these movements.

Because the dancer moves through time, the concept of repetition becomes an important consideration in analyzing how a dance work is put together. The relationship of the movements to each other as the dance progresses from beginning to end shows us a repetitional pattern that is very similar to theme and variation in music. So, *choreographers* concern themselves with the use of the individual dancer's body as well as combinations of dancers' bodies in duets, trios, or the entire corps de ballet (Figs. 8.15 and 8.16 and color insert, Plate 18).

Rhythm

As we watch a dance we can see the steps are related and coherent. Dance phrases are held together in their rhythm, in the same sense as occurs in musical rhythm. Sequences of long and short motions occur that are highlighted by accents. In a visual sense dance rhythms occur in spatial arrangements, up and down, back and forth, curved and linear, large and small. We also can perceive rhythmic relationships in the

Figure 8.7 *Grand plié* in first position. Linda Rich photo.

Figure 8.8 *Arabesque (penché)*. Linda Rich photo.

Figure 8.9 *Port de bras.* Linda Rich photo.

Figure 8.10 *Grande seconde.*
Linda Rich photo.

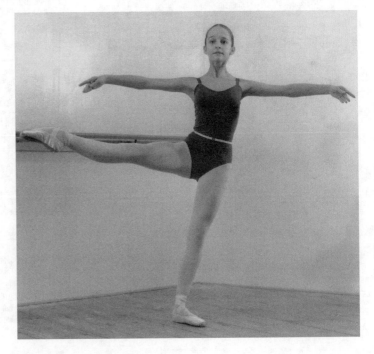

ebb and flow of dancers' energy levels. Energy, of course, calls to mind dynamics in the same sense that we discussed the term in music and theatre.

Mime and Pantomime

Within any dance form, modern dance included, there may be elements of bodily movement we call *mime* and *pantomime*. Bodily movement is *mimetic* whenever it suggests the kinds of movements we associate with people or animals. It is also mimetic if it employs any of the forms of conventional sign language, such as the Delsarte system. Of course, if there are narrative elements in the dance and the dancer actually portrays a character in the theatrical sense, there also may be pantomimetic action. Pantomime is the acting out of dramatic action without words. In the Romantic style of ballet from the nineteenth century, for example, pantomime helps to carry forward the story line. We sense the emotions, the feelings, and the character relationships in the dancers' steps, gestures, movements, and facial expres-

Figure 8.11 *Demi-hauteur.* Linda Rich photo.

Figure 8.12 *Ronds de jambe à terre.* Linda Rich photo.

sions. Only when the movement of the dance is purely an emotional expression of the dancer can we say it is free of mime.

Idea Content

Our consideration of the presence or absence of mime leads us to a consideration of how dance communicates its idea content. There are three general possibilities. First, the dance may contain *narrative* elements; that is, it may tell a story. Second, the dance may communicate through *abstract* ideas. There is a specific theme to be communicated in this case, but no story line. The ideas are abstract and general and relate to some aspect of human emotion or the human condition. Modern dance, especially, tends to deal with human psychology and behavior. Social themes occur frequently, as do impressions or expressions from plays, poems, and novels. Religious themes as well as folk

themes can be found in the wide treatments and explorations of subject ideas in modern dance. The third possibility is the absence of narrative or abstract communication. The work may be a *divertissement,* or diversion. Romantic ballet usually has strong narrative elements. However, some ballets are divertissements. Modern ballet (that is, twentieth-century ballet) has dealt increasingly with abstract ideas. Modern dance often concerns itself with abstract ideas; it may have narrative elements as well.

A final variable of idea content in dance is the presence or absence of *ethnic influence.* It is interesting to note how elements of dance reflect sociocultural background. Jazz dance, for example, may stimulate us to consider the African heritage in America. Jazz dance has emerged strongly in the twentieth century, and many would include it as a form equal to ballet, modern, and folk. Jazz dance has its own history, which is linked closely with the African experience in America, show business, and jazz as a musical idiom.

Music

We associate music with dance as a matter of course. Most of the time music serves as a basis for the bodily movement of the work we are perceiving, although it is not necessary for dance to be accompanied by music. However, it is impossible to have dance without one element of music—rhythm, as we noted previously. Every action of the dancer's body has some relationship in time to every other movement, and those relationships establish rhythmic patterns that are musical regardless of the presence or absence of auditory stimuli.

When we hear music accompanying a dance we can respond to the relationship of the dance to the musical score. The most obvious relationship we will see and hear is the one between the gestures and footfalls of the dancer and the beat of the music. In some cases the two are in strict accord; the *beat-for-beat* relationship is one to one. In other cases there may be virtually no perceivable beat-for-beat relationship between the dancer's movements and the accent or rhythmic patterns of the musical score.

Another relationship is that of the *dynamics* of the dance to those of the music. Of prime importance in this relationship is the intensity, or *force,* of the dance movement. Moments of great intensity in a dance can manifest themselves in rapid movement and forceful leaps. Or they may be reflected in other qualities. We must discern how the actual performance employs dynamics.

We can use the same kind of analysis in dance as we did in theatre in plotting dynamic levels and overall structure. For maximum in-

Figure 8.13 On point. Linda Rich photo.

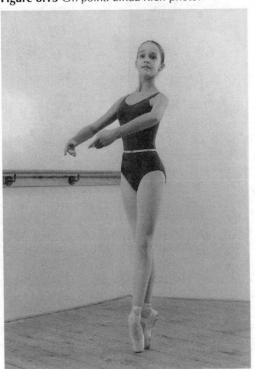

Figure 8.14 Toe shoes. Linda Rich photo.

Figure 8.15 *Nameless Hour,* Jazz Dance Theatre at Penn State, Pennsylvania State University. Choreographer: Jean Sabatine. Photo by Roger Greenawalt.

terest there must be variety of intensity. So if we chart the relationship of the peaks and valleys of dynamic levels, we are likely to conclude that the dynamic structure of a dance is quite similar to the dynamic structure of a play in that it tends to be pyramidal: It builds to a high point and then relaxes to a conclusion. This kind of analysis applies whether or not narrative elements are present.

Mise-en-Scène

Because dance is essentially a visual and theatrical experience, part of our response must be to those theatrical elements of dance that are manifested in the environment of the presentation. In other words, we can respond to the *mise-en-scène* of the dance (Figs. 8.16 and Plate 18). We can note the elements of verisimilitude in the mise-en-scène and how those elements reflect or otherwise relate to the aural and visual elements of the dance. A principal consideration here is the interrelationship of the dance with properties, settings, and the floor of the theatrical environment. The dance may use *properties* in significant or insignificant ways. As for *settings,* some dances employ massive stage designs. Others have no setting at all; they are performed in a neutral environment. Again,

Figure 8.16 *A Family Tree,* Jazz Dance Theatre at Penn State, The Pennsylvania State University. Choreographer: Jean Sabatine. Photo by Roger Greenawalt.

part of our response is to the relationship of the elements of the setting to the rest of the dance.

A principal difference between formal ballet and modern dance lies in the use of the *dance floor.* In formal ballet the floor acts principally as an agent from which the dancer springs and to which the dancer returns. But in modern dance the floor assumes an integral role in the dance, and we are likely to see the dancers sitting on the floor, rolling on it—in short, *interacting with* the floor. So, consideration of the use of the floor in dance concerns not only whether or not it is employed as an integral part of a dance, but also how the use of the floor relates to the idea content of the dance.

In discussing the relationship of *costume* to dance, we would do well to return to the section on costume design in Chapter 6 to note the purposes of costume, because those purposes apply to the dance in the same manner that they apply to a theatre production. In some dances costume will be traditional, conventional, and neutral. There would be little representation of story line or character in the tights and *tutu* of the female dancer shown in Figure 8.17. However, in many dances we are likely to see costumes high in verisimilitude. Costumes may help portray character, locality, and other aspects of the dance (Figs. 8.15 and 8.16).

In addition, it is especially important that the costume allow the dancer to do whatever it is that the choreographer expects him or her to do. In fact, costume may become an integral

Figure 8.17 Traditional tights and tutu. Linda Rich photo.

part of the dance itself. An extreme example of this is Martha Graham's *Lamentation,* in which a single dancer is costumed in what could be best described as a tube of fabric—no arms, no legs, just a large envelope of cloth. Every movement of the dancer stretches that cloth so the line and form of the dancer is not the line and form of a human body but rather the line and form of a human body enveloped in a moving fabric.

The final element of the dance costume to be considered, and one of great significance, is footgear. Dancers' footgear ranges from the simple, soft, and supple ballet slipper to the very specialized toe shoe of formal ballet, with street shoes, character oxfords, and a variety of representational or symbolic footwear in between. In addition, modern dance often is done in bare feet. Of course, the fundamental require-

ments of footgear are comfort and enough flexibility to allow the dancer to do whatever he or she must do. Footgear, whether it be toe shoe, ballet slipper, character oxford, or bare feet, must be appropriate to the surface of the stage floor. Great care must be taken to ensure the dance floor is not too hard, too soft, too rough, too slippery, or too sticky. The floor is so important that many touring companies take their own floor with them to ensure they will be able to execute their movements properly. There have been cases in which professional dance companies refused to perform in local auditoriums because the floor was dangerous for the dancers.

Lighting

Inasmuch as the entire perception of a dance relies on perception of the human body as a three-dimensional form, the work of the lighting designer is of critical importance in the art of dance. How we perceive the human form in space depends on how that body is lit. Certainly our emotional and sense response is highly shaped by the nature of the lighting that plays on the dancer and the dance floor.

HOW DOES IT STIMULATE THE SENSES?

The complex properties of the dance make possible perhaps the most diverse and intense communicative stimuli of any of the arts. We noted earlier that opera is a synthesis of all of the arts. The dance, as well, integrates elements of all of the arts, and it does so in such a way as to communicate in a highly effective symbolic and nonverbal manner.

We noted previously that it is possible to respond at different levels to an artwork. To some extent we can respond even at a level of total ignorance. In many ways artworks are like onions. If they lack quality we can call them rotten. But more important, and more seriously, an artwork, like an onion, has a series of layers. As we peel away one that is obvious to us, we reveal another and another and another, until we have gotten to the core. There will be levels of understanding, levels of meaning, levels of potential response for the uninitiated as well as the thoroughly sophisticated viewer. The more sophisticated a *balletomane* one becomes, the fuller one's understanding and response.

Moving Forms

Like every other artwork that exists in space, the dance appeals to our senses through the compositional qualities of line and form. These qualities exist not only in the human body but in the visual elements of the mise-en-scène. Essentially, horizontal line stimulates a sense of calm and repose. Vertical lines suggest grandeur and elegance. Diagonal lines stimulate a feeling of action and movement (Fig. 8.16), and curved lines, grace. As we respond to a dance work we respond to how the human body expresses line and form, not only when it is standing still but also when it moves through space. If we are alert and perceptive we will recognize not only how lines and forms are created, but also how they are repeated from dancer to dancer and from dancer to mise-en-scène.

Often, the kind of line created by the body or body characteristics of the dancer is a key to understanding the work of the choreographer. George Balanchine, for example, insisted that his dancers be almost skin and bone; you would not see a corpulent or overly developed physique in his company. So, bodies themselves appeal to our senses, and choreographers capitalize on that appeal in their dance conceptions.

Force

We noted in Chapter 5 that the beat of music is a fundamental appeal to our senses. Beat is the aspect of music that sets our toes tapping and our fingers drumming. Probably our basic response to a dance is to the dynamics expressed by the dancers and in the music. A dancer's use of vigorous and forceful action,

high leaps, graceful turns, or extended pirouettes appeals directly to us, as does the tempo of the dance. Variety in dynamics—the louds and softs and the highs and lows of bodily intensity as well as musical sound—is the dancer's and choreographer's means of providing interest, just as it is the actor's, the director's, and the painter's.

Sign Language

The dancer, like the actor, can stimulate us directly because he or she is another human being and can employ many symbols of communication (Fig. 8.15). Most human communication requires us to learn a set of symbols, and therefore, we can respond to the dance at this level only when we have mastered this language. There are systems of sign language, such as the Delsarte, in which the positions of the arms, the hands, and the head have meanings. Likewise, in our response to the hula dance, experts tell us, we ought not concentrate on the vigorous hip movements of the dancer but rather on the hand movements, each of which communicates an idea. But until we learn what each of these movements means, we cannot respond in any significant way. However, there is a set of universal body symbols to which all of us respond (so psychologists tell us), regardless of our level of familiarity or understanding. For example, the gesture of acceptance in which the arms are held outward with the palms up has the same universal meaning. The universal symbol of rejection is the hands held in front of the body with the palms out as if to push away. When dancers employ universal symbols we respond to their appeal to our senses just as we would to the nonverbals or body language in everyday conversation.

Color

Although the dancer uses facial and bodily expressions to communicate some aspect of the human condition, we do not receive as direct a message from them as we do from the words of the actor. So, to enhance the dancer's communication the costume, lighting, and set designers must strongly reinforce the mood of the dance through the mise-en-scène they create. The principle means of expression of mood is color. In dance, lighting designers are free to work in much more obvious ways with color because they do not have to create patterns of light and shadow as high in verisimilitude as those of their counterparts in the theatre. As a result, they do not have to worry if the face of a dancer is red or blue or green, an attribute that would be disastrous in a play. Thus we are apt to see much stronger, colorful, and more suggestive lighting in the dance than in theatre. Colors will be more saturated, intensity will be much higher, and the qualities of the human body, as form, will be explored much more strongly by light from various directions. The same is true of costumes and settings. Because dancers obviously do not portray a role in a highly verisimilar way, their costume can be very communicative in an abstract way. On the other hand, scene designers must be careful to utilize color in such a way that the dancer receives the focus in the stage environment. In any but the smallest of stage spaces it is very easy for the human body to be overpowered by the elements of the mise-en-scène because it occupies much more space. So, scene designers, in contrast with lighting designers, must be careful to provide a background against which the dancer will stand out in contrast unless a synthesis of the dancer with the environment is

intended, as in the case, for example, of some works by choreographer Merce Cunningham. Nevertheless, scene designers use color as forcefully as they can to help reinforce the overall mood of the dance.

The examples of how dance affects our senses that we have just noted are rudimentary ones. Perhaps more than any other art, dance causes us to ascend beyond our three cognitive questions—What is it? How is it put together? How does it affect the senses?—and dwell in that fourth level of meaningful response: What does it mean?

SELECTED EXAMPLES FOR STUDY IN DANCE

Dance Music
    Stravinsky: *The Firebird; The Rite of Spring*
    Copland: *Appalachian Spring*
Films
    Ballet with Edward Villella (LCOA). Contains
        excerpts—*Pas de Deux, Giselle, Apollo,* and
        Rubies—choreographed by George
        Balanchine.
Dance: *Anna Sokolow's "Rooms"* (IU).
Dance: *Echoes of Jazz* (IU).
Dance: *Four Pioneers* (IU).
Dance: *New York City Ballet* (IU).
Dance: *Robert Joffrey Ballet* (IU).
Seraphic Dialogue (Martha Graham) (IU).
Martha Graham Dance Company (Parts 1, 2, and
    3) (IU).

9

Landscape
Architecture*

With the exception of architecture, we come into contact with landscape architecture more than any other art form. Arguably, perhaps, landscape architecture makes a minimal conscious impact on us while it makes a maximum contribution to our well-being. Cities without parks seem unlivable, and every drab apartment building cries out for a bed of flowers.

WHAT IS IT?

Landscape architecture as an art and science is the design of three-dimensional outdoor space. Its purposes are to accommodate people's functions, improve their relationship with their artificial and natural environments, and enhance their pursuit of their activities. Typical landscape designs include streetscapes, malls, urban plazas, shopping centers, parks and playscapes, and residential, commercial, and industrial areas. The discipline, then, includes large and small spaces, rural, suburban, and urban spaces,

*The text for this chapter was prepared by Donald Girouard. I have edited and arranged it to conform to the rest of the book.

and public as well as private areas. As a science and an art the design and planning process that takes place in landscape architecture manifests reasoned judgments as well as intuitive and creative interpretation.

The purpose and design structure of contemporary landscape design trace their roots to early history. The concept of private gardens arranged in formal geometric patterns appeared in early Egyptian times and found its way into classical Greek and Roman civilization. Eventually the Moorish influences in Spain resulted in a transition from rigid, confined spaces to designs that included views beyond the garden walls (Fig. 9.1). The Renaissance gardens of France and Italy continued the formal geometric and symmetrical arrangements. We find the same concept of formality in Middleton Place, Charleston, South Carolina, America's oldest landscaped gardens. The gardens, laid out in 1741 by Henry Middleton, president of the First Continental Congress, are part of the restored plantation (color insert, Plate 19).

The antithesis of formal landscape design can be traced to the early Chinese and Japa-

Figure 9.1 Moorish influence in Spain.

nese gardens. The veneration of nature in these two cultures promoted the development of a very informal, natural landscape with emphasis on the use of the natural elements of ground form, stone, sand, plants, and water. The influence of this informal, natural setting was evident in a style of landscape design that evolved in England during the eighteenth century (Fig. 9.2). The style was one that exemplified asymmetrical arrangements and informality. The English parks designed in this style formed the basis for the concept of Central Park in New York City, designed in the 1850s by the father of landscape architecture in America, Frederick Law Olmsted, and his partner, Calvert Vaux.

The twentieth century revolted against the *eclecticism* of preconceived symmetrical forms and patterns of design. The concept of functionalism—signified by the maxim "form follows function"—left its mark on present-day landscape design. In fact, contemporary landscape architecture reflects to some degree all of these influences.

What has evolved from this history is an art form that embraces the organization and arrangement of land and the spaces above it, including the natural and artificial physical elements that give form and character to the spaces on the land. The result is a three-dimensional pattern of elements and spaces that have functional and visual *harmony* and create meaningful experiences for the people using them.

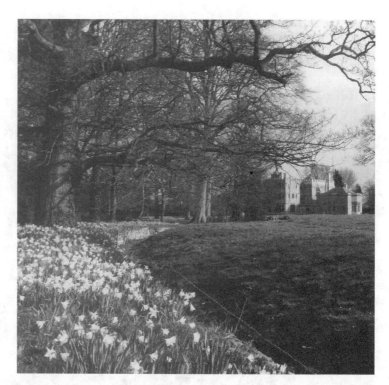

Figure 9.2 Informal design in eighteenth-century England.

HOW IS IT PUT TOGETHER?

Several factors link the landscape architecture of the past and present. These include *the function of the design, the people for whom the spaces are created,* and *the influences of the particular site and its surroundings.* In addition, the compositional elements of unity, scale, time, space and mass, light and shade, and texture and color persist in landscape architecture.

Space

The landscape designer assumes an intermediary role between the client and the eventual users of the space or spaces he or she creates. *Space,* then, is a basic medium of landscape design. It can take its form from the arrangement of living walls of plants, from concave or convex land forms, from structural walls of brick or concrete, or from buildings. The floor of the space and the overhead plane of sky or tree canopy form the other units of spatial definition.

Intent

An important aspect of space is its character, or quality. *Character* refers to the *intent* of the designer to create a landscape whose elements are harmonious and unified and support intended functions and experiences. For example, the spatial character of an area designed to support quiet park activities might use natural colors and textures, flowing landforms, indigenous plants, curving forms, lines and spaces, and soothing sounds. In addition, the *scale,* or size, of the elements and spaces, if appropriate to humans, may create a feeling of intimacy rather than of grandeur or monumentality.

Sequence

Another basic consideration in landscape design is *time and space,* or *sequence.* Sequence involves movement through space and movement from space to space. Designers can control a desired response by the way they organize this movement. Spaces can be connected in sequential movement up or down, from narrow to wide, from closed to open, from large to small, or in controlled random movement, depending on the function and experiences desired.

Within a given space, landscape designers can create light or dark spaces depending on the *density,* mass, texture, and color of the enclosing elements. In addition, they can induce sequential movement through space by contrasting dark with light, shade with sun, and so forth, in their design of spaces.

The Floor

In most landscape design the *floor* of the space becomes a basic organizational element. The floor contains the walks or roads that define movement, and the linear qualities of these arteries—free flowing or rigid and straight—form the backbone of spatial function and our experience of the designed spaces.

The Design Process

The Client

The process of designing outdoor spaces can be thought of as including three phases. Phase one is the analysis of the client's program of functions to determine their interrelatedness and how they should be organized in a logical sequence. The design of a shopping area, for example, would consider the main entry drive leading to the parking area near the stores, an area close to the stores for pickup of passengers, a walk from the parking area to the stores, and so forth. The designer must consider the logic of the sequence as well as ensuring that the change from driver to pedestrian is a safe yet pleasant experience.

The Site

Second, the site and its surroundings must be analyzed. This entails looking at the natural or deliberately constructed landscape and its existing character to determine whether it is strong enough to manifest itself in the design character to be established. In the case of a rugged, mountainous area with craggy, steep slopes, angular forms, and heavy natural forests, the designer can complement these qualities with the form, materials, textures, and colors he or she uses in the design. Or the designer can use delicate curving forms, smooth textures, and vivid colors as a contrast with the natural backdrop, creating a foil that enhances both what exists and what is designed (Fig. 9.3). Other aspects of the site that the landscape designer must consider include views into and from the site; the climatic influences of sun and wind exposure to determine orientation; and the topographic limitations or potentials of the site.

Synthesis

Having analyzed these factors, the landscape architect *synthesizes* the functions with the site and produces the final three-dimensional form.

HOW DOES IT STIMULATE THE SENSES?

The analysis of how a landscape design is synthesized does not consist merely of an explanation of the factors we have mentioned. Landscape architecture is a space-time experience that includes people as participants. Therefore, readers must project themselves into space and time and become a participant in the spaces. The effects of landscape design on the senses can then become more meaningful and understandable.

Formality

Villa Lante, created in 1564 for a wealthy cardinal, is an excellent example of formal symmetrical design (Figs. 9.4–9.8). Set outside Rome, the villa served as a summering place where one could escape the heat of the city. It was sited on a hillside so it could capture welcome breezes.

Figure 9.3 Frank Lloyd Wright, Kaufmann House, "Falling Water," Bear Run, Pennsylvania, 1936–37.

Figure 9.4 Formal symmetry in landscape design. Villa Lante, Rome. First level.

Figure 9.5 Villa Lante.

Figure 9.6 Villa Lante. Second level.

Figure 9.7 Villa Lante. Third level.

The designer's inheritance of the time was *formal composition,* an arrangement that tends to express and emphasize human will by announcing clear order and the relationship of parts in achieving unity and balance. The relationship of the design to the hillside is crisply delineated vertically and horizontally by dividing the hillside into four specific levels that are separated twice by vertical walls and twice by clearly defined geometric shapes.

A single, dominant centerline forms the spine of the design, but almost without exception one cannot walk along it. Consequently, one views the central focal points on a diagonal, which yields far less awareness of the overall symmetry. In most cases the strongest organizational factor of landscape design is the path or road system that guides people through space.

The first level of the villa (Fig. 9.4), near a village, is monumental in scale and is well juxtaposed with the adjoining buildings in the composition. The gate and broad expanse of the floor of the space are conventions used to create the relationship of *scale* between humans and the space. The gate also creates a transition

Figure 9.8 Villa Lante.

from the village to the villa. The pool and fountain begin to set the theme of a summering
place and to complement the red and green
colors of the garden beds. The chromatic effects
are subdued. The water becomes a definite link
between the various levels of the design, and
this repetition of an element also helps to create unity.

Looking in the other direction up the hill
(Fig. 9.5), we find two twin structures tucked
into the base of the slope. This architectural
treatment creates a strong definition between
the hillside and the level plane. In addition, it
narrows the space to form an entry, which emphasizes movement up the hill. Sloping planes
of lawn lead to the second level.

The second level (Fig. 9.6) has a fountain as
a *focal point* along the centerline axis and introduces sound as a part of the experience. In addition, the design incorporates an overhead
canopy of trees to create a more intimate scale
and to introduce a change from the light, open
space below. Moving into and through the
space, one becomes more aware of and comes
into closer contact with the textural qualities of
the materials of the design.

The third level (Fig. 9.7) is reached by a set
of stairways, and again the convention of a focal area in the center of the space is used. The
long basin gives added depth to the illusion of
perspective. Space encloses more, water continues, space modulates in size and feeling be-

tween levels, and our attention is drawn upward.

Above this level is a sloping cascade of water that directs our attention to yet another focal point, which in turn leads to a backdrop in the wooded hillside (Fig. 9.8). This progression of space also must be viewed and experienced as one moves in the opposite direction, down to the open terrace below. The water, which begins in a natural grotto, eventually finds itself in the quiet basin below. The downward progression allows for looking down and across the town, and the spaces continually open up to reveal the countryside. This movement from beginning to end in landscape design is planned as such; it does not just happen.

Informality

Let's look now at a pleasure garden designed in the 1960s in Montreal, Canada (Figs. 9.9–9.12). The finished design was to be primarily a sensory experience. The design expresses *informality*. Focal points are introduced on an informal axis, a walkway, but not on any centerline of vision. They are casually dispersed, but controlled. Water, plants, and natural elements dominate the design. The scale is decidedly intimate: The designer puts us in close contact with the textures, sounds, and colors of nature.

The view in the illustration (Fig. 9.9) is not seen as one enters the space of the design, but attention is drawn to this part of the garden by

Figure 9.9 Informality in landscape design. Garden, Place Bonaventure, Montreal, Canada. Architects: Sasaki, Dawson, DeMay Associates. Quebec Government House.

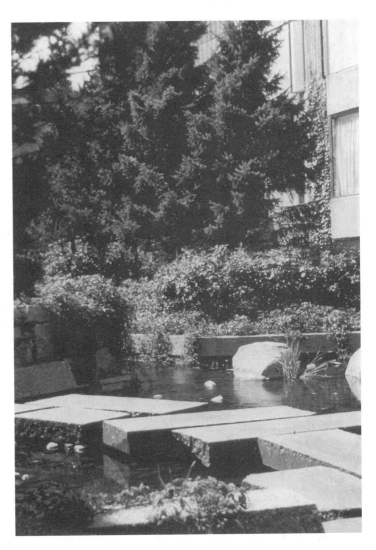

Figure 9.10 Garden, Place Bonaventure.

its sounds. The experience of this part of the garden sets the theme for what is to occur as one moves through the sequence. The plants introduce a play of shade and shadow, darks and lights, and all elements seem in harmony with one another.

Movement through the space changes gradually, and at times the walls seem alive (Fig. 9.10). The axis of the design is informal and moves us at a casual pace. The walkway through the garden is designed at points to reinforce the slow pace and informality so as to encourage close union with the elements. Plants are used as accents and masses throughout the composition. Openings focus attention or allow the eye to explore the effects that have been created (Fig. 9.11). Very little use of color is made; earth tones, grays, and greens dominate and

Figure 9.11 Garden, Place Bonaventure. Quebec Government House.

unify the composition and our experience of it. The spatial qualities and the character of the design are easily perceived in its theme, and the cadence of movement supports the sensory experience.

The final point of focus is contained in a larger space with a major backdrop of greenery and architecture (Fig. 9.12). One could easily compare this part of the garden to a painted landscape with foreground, middle ground, and background. Turning back in the sequence, one would find it hard to imagine this rooftop garden surrounded by hotel rooms and lobbies.

Composition

In both Villa Lante and the garden in Place Bonaventure, *focal points* are distributed along a sequence. Moreover, *spatial size* is varied in

both designs, and there are similarities in the use of *materials.* The opening and closing of space, the use of overhead planes, shade and shadows, and darks and lights, and emphasis on contact with sound and texture are realized in each design. However, the garden exhibits no obvious order or pattern and is continuously intimate in scale, whereas the villa contrasts monumentality with intimacy, for emphasis.

Function

The sculpture in Figure 9.13 identifies a playground space designed in Washington, D.C., in the 1960s (Figs. 9.14–9.17). The client was a government body. The site was near an urban school. The goal was to provide for recreational needs of various age groups in a densely populated area where daily access to large attractive state parks miles away is impossible. A play-

Figure 9.12 Garden, Place Bonaventure.

ground at this site would provide facilities where they were needed and be accessible on a daily basis. The potential users of the space spent most of their recreational energy on sidewalks, in streets, and on vacant lots. Fulfilling a social function, therefore, was the major consideration in this design.

The urban setting, with its familiar rectangular forms and concrete, brick, wood, and steel materials, represented an existing environmental character that would give substance and form to the final design (Fig. 9.14). To meet the requirements of providing activities for various age groups on a small site, different levels were provided for different spaces; walks and steps serve as transitions between spaces (Fig. 9.15). The steps also function as places

from which to observe the various activities. The older group can enjoy basketball, the younger group the play-apparatus area, and families or other groups picnics or seating under the shade of the roof. These uses are compatible with one another. Moreover, the spaces are close to one another so a variety of experiences can be enjoyed and are sequenced for easy movement from one to the next. The organization is decidedly informal: It reflects free movement and choice, in direct contrast with the walks and streets that govern most experiences in the city.

The use of *scale* in the design—that is, the use of spaces and objects appropriate to the size and age of the persons using them—creates *harmony* between the playground and its users (Fig.

Figure 9.13 Sculpture at site of playground illustrated in Figures 9.14–9.17.

9.16). Children can easily orient themselves to the space and objects. They are not awed by their size, but rather are invited to carry on their activities because the designer's use of scale adds to the experience of the space and enhances relationships among user, objects, and spaces.

We might characterize the design quality of the space in this playground as one of dynamic action (Fig. 9.17). The solid materials of stone, concrete, wood, and steel, the forms of varying height, the texture and colors, the play of horizontal, vertical, and angled lines and forms, the variety of enclosed and open space, the play of shade and shadows and of dark and light areas—all embody the designer's expression and composition, support human usage, and provide sensual pleasure.

SUMMARY

A landscape design comes from the analysis of the client's expressed needs, the users, the site, and its environment. Reason and intuition combine to create functional spaces and at the same time exhibit an artist's appreciation for the use of artistic elements to create not only unity and harmony among geometric forms but also functional and visual variety and interest. The result is a stimulation of a *predetermined response from the user.*

All the factors, then—space and time, people, functions and experiences, site and surroundings, plus the designer's sensitivity to creating appropriate design qualities—are interrelated. Landscape design is unique in that it can stimulate the senses only by the full participation of the "audience" in the use of its spaces. A person's reaction to the various stimuli in the landscape can encourage active or passive participation. The medium of space—the elements constituting its boundaries or existing within it—create the atmosphere for reaction. Large open spaces can produce fright unless a scale suitable to humans is used. Dark, poorly lit, narrow spaces can cause one to hurry ahead to the relief of an area open to the sky. Active forms and bright colors can stimulate playful participation. Horizontal forms and planes, curving lines and spaces, the dappled shade of a tree, the warmth of the sun, and quiet natural colors can combine to create a feeling of relaxation. Dynamic forms, bold colors, elements in motion, looping paths, the sounds of voices, music, and water, intersecting planes, and large and small spaces, apparently unorganized—all can stimulate the senses and create the setting for yet another type of experience.

Figure 9.14 Function in landscape design. Playground, Washington, D.C. Designer: M. Paul Friedberg.

Figure 9.15 Playground, Washington, D.C.

Figure 9.16 Playground, Washington, D.C.

Figure 9.17 Playground, Washington, D.C.

Landscape designers usually try to stimulate a predetermined response by their organizational pattern, definition of form and spaces, use of lines, textures, and scale, and choice of natural or synthetic materials. They are responsible for functional as well as sensual qualities. However, the true test of landscape design rests with the people who use and experience the space.

SELECTED EXAMPLES FOR STUDY IN LANDSCAPE ARCHITECTURE

1000–1600

Alhambra and Generalife, Granada. c. 1240.
Villa Medici, Rome. c. 1540.
Villa D'Este, Tivoli. c. 1549.

1600–1800

Vaux-le-Vicomte, Melun, France. Le Nôtre. 1656.

Versailles, France. Le Nôtre. c. 1661–1662.
Hampton Court, London. Christopher Wren. 1699.
Mount Vernon, Potomac River. 1743.
Villa Balbianello, Lake Como. c. 1785.

1800–1900

Birkenhead Park, near London. John Paxton. 1843
Central Park, New York City. Frederick Law Olmsted and Calvert Vaux. 1868.

1900–

Mellon Square, Pittsburgh, Simonds and Simonds.
Constitution Plaza, Hartford. Sasaki, Dawson, DeMay Associates. 1960s.
Copley Square, Boston, Sasaki, Dawson, DeMay Associates. 1960s.
Ghirardelli Square, San Francisco. Lawrence Halprin and Associates. 1960s.

10

Architecture

Every street in our towns represents a museum of ideas and engineering. The houses, churches, and commercial buildings we pass every day reflect appearances and techniques that may be as old as the human race itself. We go in and out of these buildings, often without notice, and yet they engage us and frequently dictate actions we can or cannot take.

In approaching architecture as an art, it is virtually impossible for us to separate aesthetic properties from practical or functional properties. In other words, architects first have a practical function to achieve in their buildings, which is their principal concern. The aesthetics of the building are important, but they must be tailored to overall practical considerations. For example, when architects set about to design a 110-story skyscraper, they are locked into an aesthetic form that will be vertical rather than horizontal in emphasis. They may attempt to counter verticality with strong horizontal elements, but the physical fact that the building will be taller than it is wide is the basis from which the architects must work. Their structural design must take into account all the

practical needs implicit in the building's use. Nonetheless, considerable room for aesthetics remains. Treatment of space, texture, line, and proportion can give us buildings of unique style and character or buildings of unimaginative sameness.

Architecture often is described as the art of sheltering. To consider it as such we must use the term *sheltering* very broadly. Obviously there are types of architecture within which people do not dwell and under which they cannot escape the rain. Architecture encompasses more than buildings. So, we can consider architecture as the art of sheltering people both physically and spiritually from the raw elements of the unaltered world.

WHAT IS IT?

As we noted, architecture can be considered the art of sheltering. In another large sense, it is the design of three-dimensional space to create practical enclosure. Its basic forms are residences, churches, and commercial buildings. Each of these forms can take innumerable shapes, from single-family residences to the ornate palaces of kings to high-rise condominiums and apartments. We also could expand our categorization of architectural forms to include bridges, walls, monuments, and so forth.

HOW IS IT PUT TOGETHER?

In examining how a work of architecture is put together we limit ourselves to ten fundamental elements: structure, materials, line, repetition, balance, scale, proportion, context, space, and climate.

Structure

There are many systems of construction or systems of structural support. We deal with only a few of the more prominent. *Post-and-lintel, arch,* and *cantilever* systems can be viewed, essentially, as historical systems. Contemporary architecture, however, can better be described by two additional terms, which to some extent overlap the others. These contemporary systems are *bearing-wall* and *skeleton frame.*

Post-and-Lintel

Post-and-lintel structure (Figs. 10.1–10.4) consists of horizontal beams (lintels) laid across the open spaces between vertical supports (posts). In this architectural system the traditional material is stone. Post-and-lintel structure is similar to *post-and-beam* structure, in which series of vertical posts are joined by horizontal members, traditionally of wood. The wooden members of post-and-beam

Figure 10.1 Stonehenge, Salisbury Plain, England (c. 1800–1400 B.C.). British Information Services photo.

Figure 10.2 The Parthenon, Acropolis, Athens (448–432 B.C.). AC&R photo.

Figure 10.3 The Nereid Monument, c. 400 B.C. The British Museum, London.

structure are held together by nails, pegs, or lap joints.

Because of the lack of tensile strength in its fundamental material, stone, post-and-lintel structure is limited in its ability to define space. *Tensile strength* is the ability of a material to withstand bending. If we lay a slab of stone across an open space and support it only at each end, we can span only a narrow space before it cracks in the middle and falls to the ground. However, stone has great *compressive strength*— the ability to withstand compression or crushing.

A primitive example of post-and-lintel structure is Stonehenge, that ancient and mysterious religious configuration of giant stones in Great Britain (Fig. 10.1). The ancient Greeks refined this system to high elegance; the most familiar of their post-and-lintel creations it the Parthenon (Fig. 10.2). A more detailed view of this style and structure can be seen in Figures 10.3 and 10.4.

The Greek refinement of post-and-lintel structure is a *prototype* for buildings throughout the world and across the centuries. So it makes sense to pause to examine the Greek style in more detail. One of the more interesting aspects of the style is its treatment of columns and *capitals*. Figure 10.5 shows the three basic Greek orders: Ionic, Doric, and Corinthian. These, of course, are not the only styles of post-and-lintel structure. Column capitals can be as varied as the imagination of the architect who designed them. Their primary purpose is to act as a transition for the eye as it moves from post to lintel. Columns also may express a variety of detail—for example, Figures 10.6 and 10.7. A final element, present in some columns, is *flut-*

Figure 10.4 The Nereid Monument, c. 400 B.C. (roof detail). The British Museum, London.

A	Entablature	D	Frieze	G	Shaft	1	Guttae	4	Abacus	7	Fluting
B	Column	E	Architrave	H	Base	2	Metope	5	Echinus	8	Dentils
C	Cornice	F	Capital	I	Plinth	3	Triglyph	6	Volute	9	Fascia

Figure 10.5 Greek columns and capitals: (left) Doric, (center) Ionic, (right) Corinthian. Calmann & King, Ltd.

Figure 10.6 Column capital, Central portal, Westminster Cathedral, London.

Figure 10.7 Column capital, Egypt (eighth century A.D.). The British Museum, London.

ing—vertical ridges cut into the column (Fig. 10.4).

Arch

A second type of architectural structure is the arch. As we indicated earlier, post-and-lintel structure is limited in the amount of un-encumbered space it can achieve. The arch, in contrast, can define large spaces because its

stresses are transferred outward from its center (the *keystone*) to its legs. So it does not depend on the tensile strength of its material.

There are many different styles of arches, some of which are illustrated in Figure 10.8. The characteristics of different arches may have structural as well as decorative functions.

The transfer of stress from the center of an arch outward to its legs dictates the need for a strong support to keep the legs from caving outward. Such a reinforcement is called a *buttress* (Fig. 10.9). The designers of Gothic cathedrals sought to achieve a sense of lightness. Because stone was their basic building material, they recognized some system had to be developed that would overcome the bulk of a stone buttress. Therefore, they developed a system of buttresses that accomplished structural ends but were light in appearance. These structures are called *flying buttresses* (Fig. 10.10).

Arches placed back to back to enclose space form a *tunnel vault* (Fig. 10.12). Several arches placed side by side form an *arcade* (Fig. 10.11). When two tunnel vaults intercept at right angles,

Figure 10.8 The Arch. *A*. Round (Roman) arch. *B*. Horseshoe (Moorish) arch. *C*. Lancet (pointed, Gothic) arch. *D*. Ogee arch. *E*. Trefoil arch. *F*. Tudor arch.

Figure 10.9 Buttress.

Figure 10.10 Flying buttresses.

as they do in the floor plan of the traditional Christian cathedral, they form a *groin vault* (Fig. 10.13). The protruding masonry indicating diagonal juncture of arches in a tunnel vault or the juncture of a groin vault is *rib vaulting* (Fig. 10.14).

When arches are jointed at the top with their legs forming a circle, the result is a *dome*

(Fig. 10.15). The dome, through its intersecting arches, allows for more expansive, freer space within the structure. However, if the structures supporting the dome form a circle, the result is a circular building such as the Pantheon (color insert, Plate 20). To permit squared space beneath a dome, the architect can

Figure 10.11 Arcade.

Figure 10.12 Tunnel vault.

Figure 10.14 Ribbed vault.

transfer weight and stress through the use of *pendentives* (Fig. 10.16).

Cantilever

A *cantilever* is an overhanging beam or floor supported only at one end (Fig. 10.17). Although not a twentieth-century innovation—many nineteenth-century barns in the central and eastern parts of the United States employed it—the most dramatic uses of cantilever have emerged with the introduction of modern materials such as steel beams and prestressed concrete (Fig. 10.18).

Bearing Wall

In the bearing-wall system, the wall supports itself, the floors, and the roof. Log cabins are examples of bearing-wall construction; so

are solid masonry buildings, in which the walls are the structure. In variations of bearing-wall construction, such as Fig. 10.30, the wall material is continuous, that is, not jointed or pieced together. This variation is called *monolithic* construction.

Skeleton Frame

When a skeleton frame is used, a framework supports the building; the walls are attached to the frame, thus forming an exterior skin. When skeleton framing utilizes wood, as in house

Figure 10.15 Dome, St. Paul's Cathedral, London (1675–1710). British Tourist Authority.

Figure 10.13 Groin vault.

Figure 10.16 Dome with pendentives (P).

construction, the technique is called *balloon construction*. When metal forms the frame, as in skyscrapers, the technique is known as *steel cage construction*.

Building Materials

Historic and contemporary architectural practices and traditions often center on specific materials, and to understand architecture further, we need to note a few.

Stone

The use of stone as a material turns us back to post-and-lintel systems and Figures 10.1 through 10.4. When stone is used together with mortar, for example, in arch construction, that combination is called *masonry* construction. The most obvious example of masonry, however, is the brick wall, and masonry construction is based on that principle. Stones, bricks, or blocks are joined together with mortar, one on top of the other, to provide basic, structural, weight-bearing walls of a building, a bridge, and so forth (Fig. 10.19). There is a limit to what can be accomplished with masonry because of the pressures that play on the joints between blocks and mortar and the foundation on which they rest. However, when one considers that office buildings such as Chicago's Monadnock Building (Fig. 10.20) are skyscrapers and their walls are completely masonry (that is, there are no hidden steel reinforcements in the walls), it becomes obvious that much is possible with this elemental combination of stone and mortar.

Concrete

The use of concrete is central to much contemporary architectural practice, but it was also significant as far back in the past as ancient Rome. The Pantheon (Plate 20) comprises a masterful structure of concrete with a massive

Figure 10.17 Cantilever.

Figure 10.18 Grandstand, Zarzuela Race Track, Madrid (1935). Architect: Eduardo Torroja.

concrete dome, 142 feet in diameter, resting on concrete walls 20 feet thick. In contemporary architecture, we find *precast* concrete, which is concrete cast in place using wooden forms around a steel framework. We also find *ferro-concrete* or *reinforced concrete,* which utilizes metal reinforcing embedded in the concrete. Such a technique combines the tensile strength of the metal with the compressive strength of the concrete. *Prestressed* and *post-tensioned* concrete use metal rods and wires under stress or tension to cause structural forces to flow in predetermined directions. Both comprise extremely versatile building materials.

Wood

Whether in balloon framing for houses or in laminated beaming for modern churches, wood has played a pivotal role, especially in the United States. As new technologies emerge in making engineered beams from what once was scrap wood, wood's continuation as a viable building product will probably remain—with less negative impact on the environment.

Steel

The use of steel comprises nearly endless variation and almost limitless possibilities for construction. Its introduction into the nineteenth-century industrial age forever changed

Figure 10.19 Masonry wall.

Figure 10.20 Monadnock Building, Chicago, Illinois (1891). Architects: Burnam and Root.

style and scale in architecture. *Steel cage* construction and cantilever construction were noted earlier. *Suspension* construction in bridges, superdomes, aerial walkways, and so on, has carried architects to the safe limits of space spansion and, sometimes, beyond those limits. The *geodesic dome* (Fig. 10.21) is a unique use of materials invented by an American architect, R. Buckminster Fuller. Consisting of a network of metal rods and hexagonal plates, the domes is a light, inexpensive, yet strong and easily assembled building. Although it has no apparent size limit (Fuller claims he could roof New York City, given the funds), its potential for variation and aesthetic expressiveness seems somewhat limited.

Line, Repetition, and Balance

Line and repetition perform the same compositional functions in architecture as in painting and sculpture. In his Marin County Courthouse (Fig. 10.22), Frank Lloyd Wright takes a single motif, the arc, varies only its size, and repeats it almost endlessly. The result, rather than being monotonous, is dynamic and fascinating.

Let's look at three other buildings. The main gate of Hampton Court Palace (Fig. 10.23), built in the English Tudor style around 1515 by Thomas Wolsey, at first appears haphazard to us because we seem to see virtually no repetition. Actually, this section of the palace is quite symmetrical, working its way left and right of the central gatehouse in mirror images. However, the myriad of chimneys, the imposition of the main palace, which is not centered on the main gate, and our own vantage point cause an apparent clutter of line and form that prompts our initial reaction. Line and its resultant form give Hampton Court Palace the appearance of a substantial castle.

Although it seems impossible, Figure 10.24 is the same Hampton Court Palace. Figure 10.24 reflects the style and taste of England during the reign of Henry VIII (who appropriated the palace from its original owner, Cardinal Wolsey). Later monarchs found the cumbersome and primitive appearance unsuited to their tastes, and Christopher Wren was commissioned to plan a new palace. So, in 1689, in the reign of William and Mary, renovation of the palace proper began. The result was a new and classically oriented facade in the style of the English baroque.

As we can see in Figure 10.24, Wren has designed a sophisticated and overlapping system of repetition and balance. Note first that the facade is symmetrical. The outward wing at the far left of the photograph is duplicated at the right (but not shown in the photo). In the center of the building are four attached columns surrounding three windows. The middle win-

Figure 10.21 Geodesic dome. Climatron, St. Louis, Missouri (1959). Architect: R. Buckminster Fuller. Wayne Andrews/Esto Photographics.

dow forms the exact center of the design, with mirror-image repetition on each side. Now note that above the main windows is a series of relief sculptures, pediments (triangular casings), and circular windows. Now return to the main row of windows at the left border of the photo and count toward the center. The outer wing contains three windows; then seven windows; then the central three; then seven; and finally the three of the unseen outer wing. Patterns of threes and sevens are very popular in architecture and carry religious and mythological sym-

Figure 10.22 Marin County Courthouse, California (1957–1963). Architect: Frank Lloyd Wright. Ezra Stoller/Esto Photographics.

Figure 10.23 Hampton Court Palace, England. Tudor entry (c. 1515).

bolism. Wren has established a pattern of three in the outer wing, repeated it at the center, and then repeated it within each of the seven-window groups to create yet three additional patterns of three! How is it possible to create three patterns of three with only seven windows? First, locate the center window of the seven. It has a pediment and a relief sculpture above it. On each side of this window are three windows (a total of six) without pediments. So, we have *two* groupings of three windows each. Above each of the outside four windows is a circular window. The window on each side of the center window does not have a circular window above it. Rather, it has a relief sculpture, the presence of which joins these two windows with the center window to give us our third grouping of three. Line, repetition, and balance in this facade form a marvelous perceptual exercise and experience.

Buckingham Palace (Fig. 10.25 and the Palace of Versailles (Fig. 10.26) illustrate different treatments of line and repetition. Buckingham Palace uses straight line exclusively, with repetition of rectilinear and triangular form. Like Hampton Court Palace, it exhibits *fenestration* groupings of threes and sevens, and the building itself is symmetrically balanced and divided by three pedimented, porticolike protrusions. Notice how the predominantly horizontal line of the building is broken by the three major pediments and given interest and contrast across its full length by the window pediments and the verticality of the attached columns.

Contrast Buckingham Palace with the Palace of Versailles, in which repetition occurs in groupings of threes and fives. Contrast is provided by juxtaposition and repetition of curvilinear line in the arched windows and baroque statuary. Notice how the horizontal line of the building, despite three porticoes, remains vir-

Plate 15 A thrust setting for Shakespeare's *King John,* University of Illinois at Chicago. Director: H. Don Dickenson. Scene and lighting designer: Dennis J. Sporre.

Plate 16 and Plate 17 In films the cross-cutting technique enables viewers to experience very dramatic contrasts, as in these scenes from *The Godfather, Part I.* (Courtesy of Paramount Pictures. *The Godfather* copyright © 1972 by Paramount Pictures. All rights reserved.)

Plate 18 Dancers of the Joffrey Ballet rehearse with choreographer Gerald Arpino to achieve desired line and form. (© Migdoll).

Plate 19 Formal gardens of Middleton Place, Charleston, South Carolina, a restored plantation of the Old South. They were laid out in 1741 by Henry Middleton, president of the first Continental Congress, and are the oldest landscaped gardens in the United States. (Courtesy Middleton Place, S.C.)

Plate 20 Giovanni Paolo Panini (Roman, 1691–1765), *Interior of the Pantheon, Rome* (c. A.D. 1734). Oil on canvas, 50½″ × 39″; framed: 56¾″ × 45″. 1995 Board of Trustees, National Gallery of Art, Washington, D.C. Samuel H. Kress Collection. Photo by Richard Carafelli.

Plate 21 Renzo Piano and Richard Rogers, Pompidou Center, Paris, 1971–78. Spectators in plaza near Pompidou Center can view unique architectural feature of engineering support appearing on exterior of structure. (Charles Kennard/Stock Boston)

Plate 22 Renzo Piano and Richard Rogers, Pompidou Center, Paris, 1971–78. Escalator bearing passengers skyward in Pompidou Center. (David Simpson/Stock Boston)

Plate 23 Charles Moore, Piazza d'Italia, New Orleans, 1978–79. (R. Pasley/Stock Boston)

Figure 10.24 Hampton Court Palace, England. Wren facade (1689).

Figure 10.25 Buckingham Palace, London. British Tourist Authority.

Figure 10.26 Palace of Versailles, France (1669–1685). Architects: Louis LeVau and Jules Hardouin-Mansart. Pan American World Airways photo.

tually undisturbed, in contrast with Buckingham Palace.

Scale and Proportion

The mass, or *scale,* and proportion of a building and its component elements are very important compositional qualities. Scale refers to the building's size and the relationship of the building and its decorative elements to the human form.

Proportion, or the relationship of individual elements in a composition to each other, also plays a role in the overall analysis and appearance of a design. Let's step outside architecture for a familiar example. The Concorde supersonic airliner appears to be a rather large plane when we view it on the movie screen or on television. Yet if we were to see the plane in actuality, we would be surprised to find that it is not particularly large—in comparison with a

DC–10, a Boeing 747, or even a Boeing 707. The proportion of the Concorde's window area to its overall size is misleading when we see the plane out of context with the human body. The Concorde's windows are very small, much smaller than in other airliners. So when we see the Concorde in a newsreel we immediately equate the window size with which we are familiar with the windows in the Concorde. We assume the relationship or *proportion* of window size to overall fuselage is conventional, and that assumption gives us a larger–than–actual image of the size of the plane. In terms of architecture, proportion and scale are tools by which the architect can create relationships that may be straightforward or deceptive. We must decide how these elements are used and to what effect. In addition, proportion in many buildings is mathematical: The relationships of one part to another often are based on ratios of three to two, one to two, one to three, and so on, as were the parts of the chest of drawers discussed in Chapter 1. Discovering such relationships in the buildings we see is one of the fascinating ways in which we can respond to architecture.

Context

An architectural design must take into account its context, or environment. In many cases context is essential to the statement made by the design. For example, Chartres Cathedral (Fig. 10.27) sits at the center of and on the highest point in the village of Chartres. Its placement at that particular location had a purpose for the medieval artisans and clerics responsible for its design. The centrality of the cathedral to the community was an essential

Figure 10.27 Exterior, Chartres Cathedral, France (1145–1220). Photo: Giraudon/Art Resource, N.Y.

statement of the centrality of the church to the life of the medieval community. Context also has a psychological bearing on scale. A skyscraper in the midst of skyscrapers has great mass but does not appear as massive in scale when overshadowed by another, taller skyscraper. A cathedral, when compared with a skyscraper, is relatively small in scale. However, when standing at the center of a community of small houses, it appears quite the opposite.

Two additional aspects of context concern the design of line, form, and texture relative to the physical environment of the building. On one hand, the environment can be shaped according to the compositional qualities of the building. Perhaps the best illustration of that principle is Louis XIV's palace at Versailles, whose formal symmetry is reflected in the design of thousands of acres around it. On a more modest scale, the formal gardens of Hampton Court (Fig. 10.28) reflect the line and form of the palace.

In contrast, a building may be designed to reflect the natural characteristics of its environment. Frank Lloyd Wright's *Falling Water* (Fig. 9.3) illustrates this principle. Such an idea has been advanced by many architects and can be seen especially in residences in which large expanses of glass allow us to feel a part of the outside while we are inside. The interior decoration of such houses often takes as its theme the colors, textures, lines, and forms of the environment surrounding the home. Natural fibers, earth tones, delicate wooden furniture, pictures that reflect the surroundings, large open spaces—together they form the core of the design, selection, and placement of nearly every item in the home, from walls to furniture to silverware. Sometimes a building seems at odds with its context. Situated in the middle of historic Paris near the old marketplace, Les Halles, the Pompidou Centre (color inserts, Plates 21 and 22), an art museum whose brightly painted infrastructure appears on the outside of the

Figure 10.28 Three views of formal landscaping. Hampton Court Palace, England.

building, seems out of place beside its more ancient neighbors.

Space

It seems almost absurdly logical to state that architecture must concern space—for what else, by definition, is architecture? However, the world is overwhelmed with examples of architectural design that have not met that need. Design of space essentially means the design and flow of contiguous *spaces* relative to function. Take, for example, a sports arena. Of primary concern is the space necessary for the sports intended to occupy the building. Will it play host to basketball, hockey, track, football, or baseball? Each of these sports places a design restriction on the architect, and there may be curious results when functions not intended by the design are forced into its parameters. When the Brooklyn Dodgers moved to Los Angeles, they played for a time in the Los Angeles Coliseum, a facility designed for the Olympic games and track and field and reasonably suited for the addition of football. However, the imposition of baseball created ridiculous effects; the left-field fence was only slightly over 200 feet from home plate!

In addition to the requirements of the game, a sports arena must also accommodate the requirements of the spectators. Pillars that obstruct the spectator's view do not create goodwill and the purchase of tickets. Likewise, attempting to put more seats in a confined space than ought to be there can create great discomfort. Determining where to draw the line between more seats and fan comfort is not easy. The Montreal Forum, in which anyone over the height of 5 feet 2 inches is forced to sit with the knees under the chin, has not proven to be deleterious to ticket sales for the Montreal Canadiens hockey team. However, such a design of space might be disastrous for a franchise in a less hockey-oriented city.

Finally, the design of space must concern the relationship of various needs peripheral to the primary functions of the building. Again, in a sports arena the sport and its access to the spectator are primary. However, the relationship of access to spaces such as rest rooms and concession stands must also be considered. I once had season basketball tickets in an arena seating 14,000 people in which access to the *two* concession stands required standing in a line that, because of spatial design, intersected the line to the rest rooms! If the effect was not chaotic, it certainly was confusing, especially at half time of an exciting game.

Climate

Climate always has been a factor in architectural design in zones of severe temperature, either hot or cold. As the world's energy supplies diminish, this factor will grow in importance. In the temperate climate of much of the United States, solar systems and designs that make use of the moderating influence of the earth are common. These are passive systems—that is, their design accommodates natural phenomena rather than adding technological devices such as solar collectors. For example, in the colder sections of the United States a building can be made energy efficient by being designed with no glass, or minimal glass, on its north-facing side. Windows facing south can be covered or uncovered to catch existing sunlight, which even in midwinter provides considerable warmth. Also, because temperatures at the shallow depth of 3 feet below the earth's surface rarely exceed or go below 50 degrees regardless of season, the earth presents a gold mine of potential for design. Houses built into the sides of hills or recessed below the earth's surface require much less heating or cooling than those standing fully exposed—regardless of climate extremes. Even in zones of uniform and moderate temperature, climate is a design factor. The "California lifestyle," as it often is known, is responsible for design that accommodates easy access to the out-of-doors, and large, open spaces with free-flowing traffic patterns.

HOW DOES IT STIMULATE THE SENSES?

As should be clear at this point, our sensual response to a form of aesthetic design is a composite experience. To be sure, the individual characteristics we have discussed previously are the stimuli for our response. Lately, color has become an important tool to the postmodern architect in stimulating our sense responses. The effects of color in the Plaza d'Italia (color insert, Plate 23) turn architecture into an exotic sensual experience.

Controlled Vision and Symbolism

The Gothic cathedral has been described as the perfect synthesis of intellect, spirituality, and engineering. The upward, striving line of the Gothic arch makes a simple yet powerful statement of medieval people's striving to understand their earthly relation to the spiritual unknown. Even today the simplicity and grace of that design have an effect on most who view a Gothic cathedral. Chartres Cathedral (Figs. 10.27 and 10.29), unlike the symmetry of other gothic churches, has an asymmetrical design, arising from the replacement of one of its steeples because of fire. The new steeple reflects a later and more complex Gothic style, and as a result impedes the eye as it progresses upward. Only after some pause does the eye reach the tip of the spire, the point of which symbolizes the individual's escape from the earthly known to the unknown.

Included in this grandeur of simple vertical line is an ethereal lightness that defies the material from which the cathedral is constructed. The medieval architect has created in stone not the heavy yet elegant composition of the early Greeks, which focused on treatment of stone, but rather a treatment of stone that focuses on space—the ultimate mystery. Inside the cathedral the design of stained glass kept high above the worshipers' heads so controls the light entering the cathedral that the overwhelming ef-

Figure 10.29 Interior, Chartres Cathedral, France.

fect is, again, one of mystery. Line, form, scale, color, structure, balance, proportion, context, and space all combine to form a unified composition that has stood for seven hundred years as a prototype and symbol of the Christian experience.

Style

The Christian experience is also the denominator of the design of the Holy Family Church (Fig. 10.30). However, despite the clarity of line and the upward striving power of its composition, this church suggests modern sophistication through its style, perhaps speaking more of our own conception of space, which to us is less unknowable and more conquerable, than seemed to our medieval predecessors. The juxtaposing of rectilinear and

Figure 10.30 The Church of the Holy Family, Parma, Ohio (1965). Architects: Conrad and Fleishman.

curvilinear line creates an active and dynamic response, one that prompts in us abruptness rather than mystery. The composition is cool, and its material calls attention to itself—to its starkness and to its lack of decoration.

Each part of the church is distinct and is not quite subordinate to the totality of the design. This building perhaps represents a philosophy intermediate between the philosophy underlying the Chartres Cathedral, whose entire design can be reduced to a single motif—the Gothic arch—and the philosophy such as the baroque style, as seen in the Hall of Mirrors of the Palace of Versailles (Fig. 10.31). No single part of the design of this hall epitomizes the whole, yet each part is subordinate to the whole. Our response to the hall is shaped by its ornate complexity, which calls for detachment and investigation and intends to overwhelm us with its opulence. Here, as in most art, the

expression and the stimuli reflect the patron. Chartres Cathedral reflects the medieval church, the Church of the Holy Family, the contemporary church, and Versailles, King Louis XIV. Versailles is complex, highly active, and yet warm. The richness of its textures, the warmth of its colors, and its curvilinear softness create a certain kind of comfort despite its scale and formality.

In the U.S. Capitol, a neoclassic house of government (Fig. 10.32), formality creates a foursquare, solid response. The symmetry of its design, the weight of its material, and its coldness give us a sense of impersonal power, which is heightened by the crushing weight of the dome. Rather than the upward-striving spiritual release of the Gothic arch, or even the powerful elegance of the Greek post-and-lintel, the Capitol building, based on a Roman prototype, elicits a sense of struggle. This

Figure 10.31 Hall of Mirrors, Palace of Versailles, France (1680). Architects: Jules Hardouin-Mansart and Charles LeBrun. French Government Tourist Office.

Figure 10.32 United States Capitol Building (1792–1856). Washington Area Convention and Visitors Association Photo.

is achieved through upward columnar thrust (heightened by the context provided by Capitol Hill) and downward thrust (of the dome) focused toward the interior of the building.

Apparent Function

The architect Louis Sullivan, of whom Frank Lloyd Wright was a pupil, is credited with the concept that form follows function. To a degree we have seen that concept in the previous examples, even though, with the exception of the Church of the Holy Family, they all precede Sullivan in time. A worthy question concerning the Guggenheim Museum (Fig. 10.33) might be how well Wright followed his teacher's philosophy. There is a story that Wright hated New York City because of unpleasant experiences he had had with the city fathers during previous projects. As a result, the Guggenheim, done late in his life, became his final gesture of derision to the city. This center of contemporary culture and art, with its single, circular ramp from street level to roof, was built (so the story goes) from the plans for a parking garage! Be that as it may, the line and form of this building create a simple, smoothly flowing, leisurely, upward movement juxtaposed against a stark and dynamic rectilinear form. The building's line and color and the feeling they produce are contemporary statements appropriate to the contemporary art the museum houses. The modern design of the Guggenheim is quite in contrast with the classical proportions of the Metropolitan Museum of Art, just down the street, which houses great works of ancient and modern art. The interior design is outwardly expressed in the ramp, and one can speculate that the slowly curving, unbroken line of the ramp is highly appropriate to the leisurely pace that one should follow when going through a museum.

Dynamics

Leisurely progress through the Guggenheim is diametrically opposite the sensation stimulated by the cantilevered roof of the grandstand at Zarzuela Race Track in Spain (Fig. 10.18). Speed, power, and flight are its preeminent concerns. The sense of dynamic instability inherent in the structural form—that is, cantilever, and this particular application of that form—mirror the dynamic instability and forward power of the race horse at full speed. However, despite the form and the strong diagonals of this design, it is not out of control; the architect has unified the design through repetition of the track-level arcade in the arched line of the cantilevered roof. The design

Figure 10.33 Guggenheim Museum, New York City (1942–1959). Architect: Frank Lloyd Wright. David Heald/The Solomon R. Guggenheim Museum Photo.

is dynamic and yet humanized in the softness of its curves and the control of its scale.

Scale

Nothing suggests the technological achievement of modern humans more than the overwhelming scale of the skyscraper. Also, nothing symbolizes the subordination of humans to their technology more than the scale of this, the world's tallest building (Fig. 10.34). Designed of rectangular components placed side by side, the Sears Tower is a glass and steel monolith overwhelming in its scale and proportion and cold in its materials. As a point of departure, its appeal to our senses raises the question of what comes next, the conquest of space or a return to respect for its natural mysteries?

Figure 10.34 Sears Tower, Chicago, Illinois (1971). Architects: Skidmore, Owings, and Merrill. Sears Roebuck & Co. Photo.

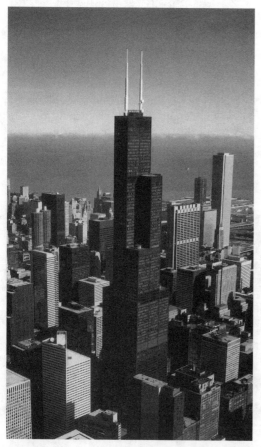

CHRONOLOGY OF SELECTED MAJOR PERIODS AND EXAMPLES FOR STUDY IN ARCHITECTURE

c. 4000 B.C.–c. 1000 B.C.
Ancient Egypt
  pyramids
  tombs

c. 1200 B.C.–c. 300 B.C.
Ancient Greece
  Parthenon
  Temple of Athena
  Theater of Dionysus

c. 500 B.C.–c. 300 A.D.
Roman Architecture
  Colosseum
  Pantheon
  Baths of Diocletian
  aqueduct, Segovia, Spain

c. 300 A.D.–c. 1500
Early Christian and Byzantine Architecture
  Old St. Peter's Basilica, Rome
  Hagia Sophia, Constantinople

c. 900–c. 1200
Romanesque Europe
  St. Trophime, Arles
  St. Sernin, Toulouse
  St. Pierre, Angoulême
  Leaning Tower, Pisa
  Cathedral of Worms

c. 1200–c. 1400
Gothic Architecture
  Chartres Cathedral
  Cathedral of Notre Dame de Paris

Amiens Cathedral
Exeter Cathedral

c. 1400–c. 1500
Italy (early Renaissance)
Cathedral of Florence
Brunelleschi: Pazzi Chapel
Michelozzo: Medici-Riccardi Palace

c. 1480–c. 1550
High Renaissance
Bramante: Tempietto, Rome
Michelangelo: apse, St. Peter's, Rome

c. 1510–c. 1570
Mannerism
Château of Chambord
Lescot: Lescot Wing of the Louvre

c. 1570–c. 1700
Baroque Architecture
Ribera: Hospicio de San Fernando, Madrid
Perrault: East Facade of the Louvre
Le Vau, Hardouin-Mansart: Palace of
Versailles

c. 1700–1800
Neoclassical Architecture
Jefferson: Rotunda, University of Virginia
Gabriel: Petit Trianon, Versailles
Soufflot: Pantheon, Paris
Rococo Architecture
Pöppelmann: Zwinger Palace, Dresden
Zimmermann: Church at Die Weis, Bavaria

c. 1800–
Neoclassical Revival (Romantic Classicism)
La Madeleine, Paris
Arc de Triomphe de l'étoile, Paris
Capitol Building, Washington, D.C.
Romanticism
Berry: Houses of Parliament, London
Gilbert: Woolworth Building, New York City
Nash: Royal Pavilion, Brighton, England
Art Nouveau
Horta: Tassel House, Brussels
Jourdain: Samartine Department Store, Paris
"Modern"
Behrens: Turbin Factory, Berlin
Gropius: Bauhaus, Dessau, Germany
Le Corbusier: Savoye House, Poissy-sur-
Seine, France
Skidmore, Owings, and Merrill: Lever
House, New York City
Sullivan: Prudential Building, Buffalo, New
York
Wright: Robie House, Chicago; Falling
Water, Bear Run, Pennsylvania
Postmodern
Bofill: The Palace of Abraxis, Marne-la-
Vallée, near Paris.
Graves: Portland Public Office Building,
Portland, Oregon.
Piano and Rogers: Pompidou Center, Paris.
Moore: Piazza d'Italia, New Orleans.

Literature

Read any good books lately? Ever tried to write poetry? From the earliest of times, cultures have been defined by their literature. Even before the invention of writing, myths and legends in prose and poetry told people who they were and where they came from. Today, before there can be a movie or a soap opera, there must be a story and, usually, a script. Such things comprise literature, our last subject for discussion.

WHAT IS IT?

In the same sense that all artworks communicate through a particular medium someone's perception of reality or truth, so literature communicates using the forms we examine momentarily. There is a difference between literature that some call utilitarian and literature that may be called creative. Creative literature has a different approach than utilitarian literature. The approach determines the category in the same sense that a picture composed of line, form, and color is termed art, whereas another picture, composed of those same characteristics but whose purpose is merely to provide a visual copy, is termed "illustration."

The formal divisions of literature are fiction, poetry, biography, essay, and drama.

Fiction

Fiction is a work created from the author's imagination rather than from fact. Normally it takes one of two approaches to its subject matter: *realistic,* that is, the appearance of observable, true-to-life details; or *nonrealistic,* that is, fantasy. Other literary forms such as narrative poetry and drama can also be fiction, and fictional elements can be introduced into forms such as biography and epic poetry. Fiction traditionally is divided into novels and short stories.

Novels

The *novel* is a prose narrative of considerable length which has a plot that unfolds from the actions, speech, and thoughts of the characters. Normally the novel treats events within the range of ordinary experience and draws on original subject matter rather than traditional or mythic subjects. Novels typically have numerous characters and employ normal, daily speech. The subject matter of novels can be divided into two general categories, *sociological-panoramic,* covering a wide-ranging story of many years and various settings, and *dramatic-intimate,* which is restricted in time and setting.

Often, novels are formally classified by their subject matter. A few of these categories are as follows:

picaresque: the adventures of a rogue
manners: problems of personal relations
sentimental: the development of emotionality, especially a sentimental appreciation of simplicity
gothic: the trials of a pure, sensitive, and noble heroine who undergoes terrifying experiences, emerging undamaged. Usually this type of novel is stilted, melodramatic, and exploitive of the darker side of emotional psychology
historical: intertwines historical events and fictional characters
realistic: focuses on familiar situations and ordinary people
lyrical: a short work with a metaphoric structure and a limited number of characters

Short Stories

As the name implies, short stories are short prose fictional works focusing on unity of characterization, theme, and effect.

Poetry

Poetry is a type of work designed to convey a vivid and imaginative sense of experience. Poetry uses condensed language selected for its sound, suggestive power, and meaning, and employs specific technical devices such as meter, rhyme, and metaphor. Poetry can be divided into three major types: narrative, dramatic, and lyric.

Narrative

Narrative poetry tells a story. *Epic* poetry is narrative poetry of substantial length and elevated style. It uses strong symbolism and has a central figure of heroic proportions. A *ballad* is a sung or recited narrative. A *metrical romance* is a long narrative, romantic tale in verse.

Dramatic

Dramatic poetry utilizes dramatic form or dramatic technique. Its major form is the dramatic monologue.

Lyric

Lyric poetry was originally intended to be sung and accompanied by a lyre. It is a brief, subjective work employing strong imagination, melody, and feeling to create a single, unified, and intense impression of the personal emotion of the poet.

Biography

Over the centuries, biography has taken many forms and witnessed many techniques and intentions, including literary narratives, catalogues of achievement, and psychological portraits. Biography is a written account of a person's life. Accounts of the lives of the saints and other religious figures are called *hagiographies.*

Essays

The essay traditionally is a short literary composition on a single subject, usually presenting the personal views of the author. The word comes from the French, meaning "to try" and the vulgar Latin, meaning "to weigh." Essays include many subforms and a variety of styles, but they uniformly present a personal point of view with a conscious attempt to achieve grace of expression. Essays characteristically are marked by clarity, grace, good humor, wit, urbanity, and tolerance.

An essay is a work of nonfiction reflecting the author's attitudes toward a specific subject. In so doing, it may reveal the author's personality or speculations. For the most part, essays are brief, but occasionally much longer works such as John Locke's treatise *Essay Concerning*

Human Understanding (1690) have appeared. Traditionally, essays fall into two categories: formal or informal.

Informal

Informal essays tend to be brief and very personal. They are conversational in tone and loose in structure. This type of essay can be further divided into categories called *familiar* or *personal* and *character.* The personal essay presents an aspect of the author's personality as he or she reacts to an event. Character essays describe persons, isolating their dominant traits, for example.

Formal

Formal essays are longer and more tightly structured than informal essays. Formal essays tend to focus on impersonal subjects and place less emphasis on the personality of the author.

Drama

Drama is the written script, or play, on which a theatre performance may be based. We examined this genre in Chapter 6.

HOW IS IT PUT TOGETHER?

Fiction

Point of View

Fiction is a story told by someone at a particular time and place to a particular audience. So it has a definite perspective, and, therefore, certain limitations of objectivity. It raises questions about the right way of seeing things. For the story to achieve credibility as fiction, the author must appear to distance himself or herself from the representative truth of the story and the reader. The "point of view" is a device to objectify the circumstances. Four types of narrative point of view are (1) *first person;* (2) *epistolary,* that is, told through the use of letter written by the characters; (3) *omniscient narration* or "third person"; and (4) *stream of consciousness* or "interior monologue," wherein a flow of thoughts, feelings, and memories come from a specific character's psyche. These arbitrary definitions regarding point of view may vary or be combined by authors to suit their own purposes. Point of view, as we have discussed it here, means merely that one of the means by which fiction is put together is usable by an author in several ways, at several levels, to communicate meaning.

Appearance and Reality

Fiction claims to be true to actuality, but it is built on invented sequences of events. It refers back on itself, layering the fictional and the factual.

Tone

Tone may also be called the atmosphere of the story. In essence, it is the author's attitude toward the story's literal facts. Reading is much like listening to conversation. That is, the words carry meaning, but the way in which they are said—their tone—shapes meaning much more effectively. In addition, the atmosphere of the story sometimes includes the setting or the physical environment. In many stories, atmosphere is psychological as well as physical, and when all of these characteristics of tone are taken together, they provide subtle and powerful suggestions leading to our fuller understanding of the work.

Character

What gives literature its appeal is people, but not just people alone. Our interest is drawn because we see a human character involved in some kind of conflict—that is, a struggle with some important human problem. Authors write to that potential interest and usually strive to focus our attention, and to achieve unity, by drawing a central character with whose actions, decisions, growth, and development we can identify, and in whom we can find an indication of some broader aspect of the human condition. As we noted in the chapter on theatre, the term *character* goes beyond the mere identification of a "person." Character means the psychological spine of the individual, the driving force which makes that individual respond the way he or she does when faced with a given set of circumstances. Character is what we are interested in: Given a set of troubling or challenging circumstances, what does the character of the individual lead him or her to do?

In developing character, an author has numerous choices, depending, again, on his or her purposes. Character may be fully three-dimensional and highly individualistic—that is, as complex as the restrictions of the medium allow. Novels, because of their length and the fact that the reader can go back to double-check a fact or description, allow much more complex character development or individuality than do plays, whose important points must be found by the audience the moment they are presented. However, the author's purpose may be served by presenting character, not as a fully developed individual, but as a type. Whatever the author's choice, the nature of character development tells us much about the meaning we are to find in the work.

Plot

Plot is the structure of the work. It is more than the story line or the facts of the piece. In literature, as in the theatre, we find our interest depends on action. We are here to witness character in action. Plot is the structure of that action. It creates unity in the work and thereby helps us find meaning. Plot is the skeleton that determines the ultimate shape of the piece, once the elements of flesh have been added to it. The action of a literary work is designed to dramatize a fully realized theme, situation, or character.

Plot may be the major or subordinate focus in a work, and it can be open or closed. Closed plots rely on the Aristotelian model of pyramidal action with exposition, complication, and resolution or denouement. An open plot has little or no resolution. We merely leave the characters at a convenient point and imagine them continuing on as their characters will dictate.

Theme

Most good stories have an overriding idea or theme by which the other elements are shaped. Quality in works of art may rest on the artist's ability to utilize the tools of his or her medium and on whether the artist has something worthwhile to say. Some critics argue that the quality of a theme is less important than what the author does with it. Yet the conclusion is inescapable: The best artworks are those in which the author has taken a meaningful theme and developed it exceptionally. So the theme or idea of a work is what the author has to say. The other devices of the piece will help us understand the ultimate idea. Theme may mean a definite intellectual concept, or it may indicate a highly complex situation. Clues to understanding the idea can come as early as our exposure to the title. Beyond that, the theme is usually revealed in small pieces as we move from beginning to conclusion.

Symbolism

Every work of literature is symbolic to one degree or another. It stands for something greater than its literal reality. Words are symbols, as is language. So any story is symbolic inasmuch as it reveals human experience. Often the symbols that occur in a story are cultural in derivation. That is why we often have difficulty understanding the levels of meaning in works from other cultures. We also find it difficult to grasp the symbols in works from our own tradition. The more we know about our culture and its various points of view through history, the more we are able to grasp the symbolism, and thereby the meaning, of the great thinkers, writers, and artists whose insights into the human condition can help us cope with the significant questions of our time and our personal condition.

Sometimes symbols are treated as if they are private or esoteric. In other words, sometimes writers will purposely try to hide some levels of meaning from all but the thoroughly initiated or truly sophisticated. Sometimes authors will try to create new symbol systems. Whatever the case, symbolism gives the story its richness and much of its appeal. When we realize a character, for example, is a symbol, regardless of how much of an individual he or she may be, the story takes on new meaning for us. We often discover that every character in the story symbolizes us—that is, some aspect of *our* complex and often contradictory characters. Symbols can be hidden, profound, or simple. When we discover them and unlock their revelations, we have made a significant stride toward understanding meaning.

Poetry

Language

Rhythm in poetry consists of the flow of sound through accents and syllables. For example, in Robert Frost's *Stopping by Woods on a Snowy Evening* (see the end of the chapter) each line contains eight syllables with an accent on every other syllable. Rhythms, like Frost's, that depend on a fixed number of syllables in each line, are called *accentual-syllabic.* Contrast that with the freely flowing rhythm of Shakespeare's "The Seven Ages of Man" in which rhythmic flow uses naturally occurring stresses in the words. This use of stress to create rhythm is called *accentual.*

Imagery comprises a verbal representation of a sensory experience. It can be literal or figurative. In the former, there is no change or extension in meaning; for example, "green eyes" are simply eyes that are a green color. In the latter, there is a change in literal meaning; for example, green eyes might become "green orbs."

Figures, like images, take words beyond their literal meaning. Much of poetic meaning comes in comparing objects in ways that go beyond the literal. For example, in Robert Frost's "Stopping by Woods on a Snowy Evening," snowflakes are described as *downy,* which endows them with the figurative quality of soft, fluffy feathers on a young bird. In the same sense, Frost uses "sweep" and "easy" to describe the wind.

Metaphors are figures of speech by which new implications are given to words. For example, the expression "the twilight of life" takes the word *twilight* and applies it to the concept of life to create an entirely new image and meaning.

Symbols also are often associated with figures of speech, but not all figures are symbols, and not all symbols are figures. Symbolism is critical to poetry, which uses compressed language to express, and carry us into, its meanings. In poetry "the whole poem helps to determine the meaning of its parts, and in turn, each part helps to determine the meaning of the whole poem" (K. L. Knickerbocker and W. Willard Reninger, *Interpreting Literature,* p. 218).

Structure

Form or structure in poetry derives from fitting together lines of similar structure and length tied to other lines by end rhyme. For example, the sonnet has fourteen lines of iambic pentameter rhymed 1–3, 2–4, 5–7, 6–8, 9–11, 10–12, 13–14.

Stanzas, which are any recurring groupings of two or more lines in terms of length, meter, and rhyme, are part of structure. A stanza usually presents a unit of poetic experience, and if the poem has more than one stanza, the pattern is usually repeated.

Sound Structures

Rhyme is the most common sound structure. Rhyme is, of course, the coupling of words that sound alike. Its function in poetry is to tie the sense together with the sound. Rhyme can be masculine, feminine, or triple. Masculine rhyme is based on single-syllable vowels such as "hate" and "mate." Feminine rhyme is based on sounds between accented and unaccented syllables, for example, "hating" and "mating." Triple rhyme comprises a correspondence among three syllables such as "despondent" and "respondent."

Alliteration is a second type of sound structure in which an initial sound is repeated for effect—for example, *fancy free*.

Assonance is a similarity among vowels but not consonants.

Meter

Meter comprises the type and number of rhythmic units in a line. Rhythmic units are called *feet*. Four common kinds of feet are *iambic, trochaic, anapestic,* and *dactyllic.* Iambic meter alternates one unstressed and one stressed syllable; trochaic meter alternates one stressed and one unstressed syllable; anapestic alternates two unstressed and one stressed syllables; and dactyllic meter alternates one stressed and two unstressed syllables.

Line, also called verse, determines the basic rhythmic pattern of the poem. Lines are named by the number of feet they contain. One foot is monometer; two, dimeter; three, trimeter; four, tetrameter; five, pentameter; six, hexameter; seven, heptameter; and eight, octameter.

Biography

Facts

Facts are the verifiable details around which a biography is shaped. However, facts, other than matters such as birth, death, marriage, and other date-related occurrences, often have a way of becoming elusive. "Facts" often turn out to be observations filtered through the personality of the observer. Incontrovertible facts may comprise a chronological or skeletal framework for a biography, but often they do not create much interest. Often they do not provide much of a skeleton either. Many individuals about whose lives we would like to learn more have few facts recorded about them. In contrast, the lives of other important individuals have been chronicled in such great detail that too many facts exist. Artistry entails selection and composition, and in the latter case, interest may require leaving many facts out of the narrative. Of course, another issue related to facts and biography is the question of what the author should do with the facts. If the facts are injurious, should they be used? In what context should they be used? Whatever the situation, facts alone do not comprise a sufficient quality for an artistic or interesting biography.

Anecdotes

Anecdotes are stories or observations about moments in a biography. Anecdotes take the basic facts and expand them for illustrative purposes, thereby creating interest. Anecdotes may be true or untrue. Their purpose, often, is to create a memorable generalization. They may also generate debate or controversy.

Quotations form part of anecdotal experience. Their purpose is to create interest by changing the presentational format to that of dialogue. In one sense, dialogue brings us closer to subjects of the biography by helping to create the impression that we are part of the scene, as opposed to being third parties listening to someone else describe a situation.

HOW DOES IT APPEAL TO THE SENSES?

The following selections serve as illustrations of literature. Literature appeals to our senses by the way in which the writer uses the tools of the medium. We have applied the formal and technical elements of the arts enough times now that to do so again would be to restate the obvious. Read the following examples and de-cide for yourself how your response is manip-ulated by the author's use of the devices we have discussed. Discuss each example with a friend to see if your reactions were similar or different. Where differences arise, try to deter-mine why.

FICTION

THE SOFT-HEARTED SIOUX

Zitkala-Sa [Gertrude Bonnin]

I

Beside the open fire I sat within our tepee. With my red blanket wrapped tightly about my crossed legs, I was thinking of the coming sea-son, my sixteenth winter. On either side of the wigwam were my parents. My father was whistling a tune between his teeth while pol-ishing with his bare hand a red stone pipe he had recently carved. Almost in front of me, be-yond the centre fire, my old grandmother sat near the entranceway.

She turned her face toward her right and ad-dressed most of her words to my mother. Now and then she spoke to me, but never did she al-low her eyes to rest upon her daughter's hus-band, my father. It was only upon rare occa-sions that my grandmother said anything to him. Thus his ears were open and ready to catch the smallest wish she might express. Sometimes when my grandmother had been saying things which pleased him, my father used to comment upon them. At other times, when he could not approve of what was spoken, he used to work or smoke silently.

On this night my old grandmother began

Source: Zitkala-sa (Gertrude Bonnin), "The Soft-Hearted Sioux." Reprinted from *The Singing Spirit*, edited by Bernd C. Peyer. Copyright 1989 The Arizona Board of Regents.

her talk about me. Filling the bowl of her red stone pipe with dry willow bark, she looked across at me.

"My grandchild, you are tall and are no longer a little boy." Narrowing her old eyes, she asked, "My grandchild, when are you going to bring here a handsome young woman?" I stared into the fire rather than meet her gaze. Waiting for my answer, she stooped forward and through the long stem drew a flame into the red stone pipe.

I smiled while my eyes were still fixed upon the bright fire, but I said nothing in reply. Turn-ing to my mother, she offered her the pipe. I glanced at my grandmother. The loose buck-skin sleeve fell off at her elbow and showed a wrist covered with silver bracelets. Holding up the fingers of her left hand, she named off the desirable young women of our village.

"Which one, my grandchild, which one?" she questioned.

"Hoh!" I said, pulling at my blanket in con-fusion. "Not yet!" Here my mother passed the pipe over the fire to my father. Then she too began speaking of what I should do.

"My son, be always active. Do not dislike a long hunt. Learn to provide much buffalo meat and many buckskins before you bring home a wife." Presently my father gave the pipe to my grandmother, and he took his turn in the ex-hortations.

"Ho, my son, I have been counting in my heart the bravest warriors of our people. There is not one of them who won his title in his six-teenth winter. My son, it is a great thing for some brave of sixteen winters to do."

Not a word had I to give in answer. I knew well the fame of my warrior father. He had earned the right of speaking such words, though even he himself was a brave only at my age. Refusing to smoke my grandmother's pipe because my heart was too much stirred by their words, and sorely troubled with a fear lest I should disappoint them, I arose to go. Drawing my blanket over my shoulders, I said, as I stepped toward the entranceway: "I go to hobble my pony. It is now late in the night."

II

Nine winters' snows had buried deep that night when my old grandmother, together with my father and mother, designed my future with the glow of a camp fire upon it.

Yet I did not grow up the warrior, huntsman, and husband I was to have been. At the mission school I learned it was wrong to kill. Nine winters I hunted for the soft heart of Christ, and prayed for the huntsmen who chased the buffalo on the plains.

In the autumn of the tenth year I was sent back to my tribe to preach Christianity to them. With the white man's Bible in my hand, and the white man's tender heart in my breast, I returned to my own people.

Wearing a foreigner's dress, I walked, a stranger, into my father's village.

Asking my way, for I had not forgotten my native tongue, an old man led me toward the tepee where my father lay. From my old companion I learned that my father had been sick many moons. As we drew near the tepee, I heard the chanting of a medicine-man within it. At once I wished to enter in and drive from my home the sorcerer of the plains, but the old warrior checked me. "Ho, wait outside until the medicine-man leaves your father," he said. While talking he scanned me from head to feet. Then he retraced his steps toward the heart of the camping-ground.

My father's dwelling was on the outer limits of the round-faced village. With every heart-throb I grew more impatient to enter the wigwam.

While I turned the leaves of my Bible with nervous fingers, the medicine-man came forth from the dwelling and walked hurriedly away. He head and face were closely covered with the loose robe which draped his entire figure.

He was tall and large. His long strides I have never forgot. They seemed to me then as the uncanny gait of eternal death. Quickly pocketing my Bible, I went into the tepee.

Upon a mat lay my father, with furrowed face and gray hair. His eyes and cheeks were sunken far into his head. His sallow skin lay thin upon his pinched nose and high cheek-bones. Stooping over him, I took his fevered hand. "How, Ate?" I greeted him. A light flashed from his listless eyes and his dried lips parted. "My son!" he murmured, in a feeble voice. Then again the wave of joy and recognition receded. He closed his eyes, and his hand dropped from my open palm to the ground.

Looking about, I saw an old woman sitting with bowed head. Shaking hands with her, I recognized my mother. I sat down between my father and mother as I used to do, but I did not feel at home. The place where my old grandmother used to sit was now unoccupied. With my mother I bowed my head. Alike our throats were choked and tears were streaming from our eyes; but far apart in spirit our ideas and faiths separated us. My grief was for the soul unsaved; and I thought my mother wept to see a brave man's body broken by sickness.

Useless was my attempt to change the faith in the medicine-man to that abstract power named God. Then one day I became righteously mad with anger that the medicine-man should thus ensnare my father's soul. And when he came to chant his sacred songs I pointed toward the door and bade him go! The man's eyes glared upon me for an instant. Slowly gathering his robe about him, he turned his back upon the sick man and stepped out of our wigwam. "Hā, hā, hā! my son, I cannot live without the medicine-man!" I heard my father cry when the sacred man was gone.

III

On a bright day, when the winged seeds of the prairie-grass were flying hither and thither, I walked solemnly toward the centre of the camping-ground. My heart beat hard and ir-regularly at my side. Tighter I grasped the sa-cred book I carried under my arm. Now was the beginning of life's work.

Though I knew it would be hard, I did not once feel that failure was to be my reward. As I stepped unevenly on the rolling ground, I thought of the warriors soon to wash off their war-paints and follow me.

At length I reached the place where the peo-ple had assembled to hear me preach. In a large circle men and women sat upon the dry red grass. Within the ring I stood, with the white man's Bible in my hand. I tried to tell them of the soft heart of Christ.

In silence the vast circle of bareheaded war-riors sat under an afternoon sun. At last, wip-ing the wet from my brow, I took my place in the ring. The hush of the assembly filled me with great hope.

I was turning my thoughts upward to the sky in gratitude, when a stir called me to earth again.

A tall, strong man arose. His loose robe hung in folds over his right shoulder. A pair of snap-ping black eyes fastened themselves like the poisonous fangs of a serpent upon me. He was the medicine-man. A tremor played about my heart and a chill cooled the fire in my veins.

Scornfully he pointed a long forefinger in my direction and asked,

"What loyal son is he who, returning to his father's people, wears a foreigner's dress?" He paused a moment, and then continued: "The dress of that foreigner of whom a story says he bound a native of our land, and heaping dry sticks around him, kindled a fire at his feet!" Waving his hand toward me, he exclaimed, "Here is the traitor to his people!"

I was helpless. Before the eyes of the crowd the cunning magician turned my honest heart into a vile nest of treachery. Alas! the people frowned as they looked upon me.

"Listen!" he went on. "Which one of you who have eyed the young man can see through

his bosom and warn the people of the nest of young snakes hatching there? Whose ear was so acute that he caught the hissing of snakes whenever the young man opened his mouth? This one has not only proven false to you, but even to the Great Spirit who made him. He is a fool! Why do you sit here giving ear to a fool-ish man who could not defend his people be-cause he fears to kill, who could not bring venison to renew the life of his sick father? With his prayers, let him drive away the enemy! With his soft heart, let him keep off starvation! We shall go elsewhere to dwell upon an un-tainted ground."

With this he disbanded the people. When the sun lowered in the west and the winds were quiet, the village of cone-shaped tepees was gone. The medicine-man had won the hearts of the people.

Only my father's dwelling was left to mark the fighting-ground.

IV

From a long night at my father's bedside I came out to look upon the morning. The yellow sun hung equally between the snow-covered land the cloudless blue sky. The light of the new day was cold. The strong breath of winter crusted the snow and fitted crystal shells over the rivers and lakes. As I stood in front of the tepee, thinking of the vast prairies which separated us from our tribe, and wondering if the high sky likewise separated the soft-hearted Son of God from us, the icy blast from the north blew through my hair and skull. My neglected hair had grown long and fell upon my neck.

My father had not risen from his bed since the day the medicine-man led the people away. Though I read from the Bible and prayed be-side him upon my knees, my father would not listen. Yet I believed my prayers were not un-heeded in heaven.

"Hā, hā, hā! my son," my father groaned upon the first snowfall. "My son, our food is gone. There is no one to bring me meat! My son, your soft heart has unfitted you for everything!" Then covering his face with the buffalo-robe, he said no more. Now while I stood out in that cold winter morning, I was starving. For two days I had not seen any food. But my own cold and hunger did not harass my soul as did the whining cry of the sick old man.

Stepping again into the tepee, I untied my snow-shoes, which were fastened to the tent-poles.

My poor mother, watching by the sick one, and faithfully heaping wood upon the centre fire, spoke to me:

"My son, do not fail again to bring your father meat, or he will starve to death."

"How, Ina," I answered, sorrowfully. From the tepee I started forth again to hunt food for my aged parents. All day I tracked the white level lands in vain. Nowhere, nowhere were there any other footprints but my own! In the evening of this third fast-day I came back without meat. Only a bundle of sticks for the fire I brought on my back. Dropping the wood outside, I lifted the door-flap and set one foot within the tepee.

There I grew dizzy and numb. My eyes swam in tears. Before me lay my old gray-haired father sobbing like a child. In his horny hands he clutched the buffalo-robe, and with his teeth he was gnawing off the edges. Chewing the dry stiff hair and buffalo-skin, my father's eyes sought my hands. Upon seeing them empty, he cried out:

"My son, your soft heart will let me starve before you bring me meat! Two hills eastward stand a herd of cattle. Yet you will see me die before you bring me food!"

Leaving my mother lying with covered head upon her mat, I rushed out into the night.

With a strange warmth in my heart and swiftness in my feet, I climbed over the first hill, and soon the second one. The moonlight upon the white country showed me a clear path to the white man's cattle. With my hand upon the knife in my belt, I leaned heavily against the fence while counting the herd.

Twenty in all I numbered. From among them I chose the best-fattened creature. Leaping over the fence, I plunged my knife intoit.

My long knife was sharp, and my hands, no more fearful and slow, slashed off choice chunks of warm flesh. Bending under the meat I had taken for my starving father, I hurried across the prairie.

Toward home I fairly ran with the life-giving food I carried upon my back. Hardly had I climbed the second hill when I heard sounds coming after me. Faster and faster I ran with my load for my father, but the sounds were gaining upon me. I heard the clicking of snow-shoes and the squeaking of the leather straps at my heels; yet I did not turn to see what pursued me, for I was intent upon reaching my father. Suddenly like thunder an angry voice shouted curses and threats into my ear! A rough hand wrenched my shoulder and took the meat from me! I stopped struggling to run. A deafening whir filled my head. The moon and stars began to move. Now the white prairie was sky, and the stars lay under my feet. Now again they were turning. At last the starry blue rose up into place. The noise in my ears was still. A great quiet filled the air. In my hand I found my long knife dripping with blood. At my feet a man's figure lay prone in blood-red snow. The horrible scene about me seemed a trick of my senses, for I could not understand it was real. Looking long upon the blood-stained snow, the load of meat for my starving father reached my recognition at last. Quickly I tossed it over my shoulder and started again homeward.

Tired and haunted I reached the door of the wigwam. Carrying the food before me, I entered with it into the tepee.

"Father, here is food!" I cried, as I dropped the meat near my mother. No answer came. Turning about, I beheld my gray-haired father dead! I saw by the unsteady firelight an old gray-haired skeleton lying rigid and stiff.

Out into the open I started, but the snow at my feet became bloody.

V

One the day after my father's death, having led my mother to the camp of the medicine-man, I gave myself up to those who were searching for the murderer of the paleface.

They bound me hand and foot. Here in this cell I was placed four days ago.

The shrieking winter winds have followed me hither. Rattling the bars, they howl unceasingly: "Your soft heart! your soft heart will see me die before you bring me food!" Hark! something is clanking the chain on the door. It is being opened. From the dark night without a black figure crosses the threshold. . . . It is the guard. He comes to warn me of my fate. He tells me that tomorrow I must die. In his stern face I laugh aloud. I do not fear death.

Yet I wonder who shall come to welcome me in the realm of strange sight. Will the loving Jesus grant me pardon and give my soul a soothing sleep? or will my warrior father greet me and receive me as his son? Will my spirit fly upward to a happy heaven? or shall I sink into the bottomless pit, an outcast from a God of infinite love?

Soon, soon I shall know, for now I see the east is growing red. My heart is strong. My face is calm. My eyes are dry and eager for new scenes. My hands hang quietly at my side. Serene and brave, my soul awaits the men to perch me on the gallows for another flight. I go.

They have their exits and their entrances,
And one man in his time plays many parts,
His acts being seven ages. At first the infant,   5
Mewling[1] and puking in the nurse's arms.
Then the whining schoolboy, with his satchel
And shining morning face, creeping like snail
Unwillingly to school. And then the lover,
Sighing like furnace, with a woeful ballad[2]   10
Made to his mistress' eyebrow. Then a soldier,
Full of strange oaths and bearded like the pard,[3]
Jealous in honor,[4] sudden and quick in quarrel,
Seeking the bubble reputation[5]
Even in the cannon's mouth. And then the justice,   15
In fair round belly with good capon lined,[6]
With eyes severe and beard of formal cut,
Full of wise saws[7] and modern instances;[8]
And so he plays his part. The sixth age shifts
Into the lean and slippered Pantaloon,[9]   20
With spectacles on hose and pouch on side;
His youthful hose, well saved, a world too wide
For his shrunk shank, and his big manly voice,
Turning again toward childish treble, pipe
And whistles in his sound. Last scene of all,   25
That ends this strange eventful history,
Is second childishness and mere oblivion,
Sans[10] teeth, sans eyes, sans taste, sans everything.
                    —*As You Like It,* II. vii. 139–166

POETRY

THE SEVEN AGES OF MAN

William Shakespeare
1564–1616

All the world's a stage,
And all the men and women merely players.

[1]Whimpering. [2]Poem. [3]Leopard. [4]Sensitive about honor. [5]As quickly burst as a bubble. [6]Magistrate bribed with a chicken. [7]Sayings. [8]Commonplace illustrations. [9]The foolish old man of Italian comedy. [10]Without.

STOPPING BY WOODS ON A SNOWY EVENING

Robert Frost
1874–1963

Whose woods these are I think I know.
His house is in the village though;
He will not see me stopping here
To watch his woods fill up with snow.

My little horse must think it queer   5
To stop without a farmhouse near
Between the woods and frozen lake
The darkest evening of the year.

He gives his harness bells a shake
To ask if there is some mistake.   10
The only other sound's the sweep
Of easy wind and downy flake.

The woods are lovely, dark and deep.
But I have promises to keep,
And miles to go before I sleep,   15
And miles to go before I sleep.

Source: Robert Frost, "Stopping by Woods on a Snowy Evening" from *The Poetry of Robert Frost,* edited by Edward Connery Lathem. Copyright 1923 © 1969 by Henry Holt and Co., Inc. Reprinted by permission of Henry Holt and Co., Inc.

THEME FOR ENGLISH B

Langston Hughes
1902–67

The instructor said,
    Go home and write
    a page tonight.
    And let that page come out of you—
    Then it will be true.
I wonder if it's that simple?

I am twenty-two, colored, born in Winston-Salem.

I went to school there, then Durham, then here
to this college on the hill above Harlem.
I am the only colored student in my class.
The steps from the hill lead down into Harlem
through a park, then I cross St. Nicholas.
Eighth Avenue. Seventh, and I come to the Y,
the Harlem Branch Y, where I take the elevator
up to my room, sit down, and write this page:
It's not easy to know what is true for you or me
at twenty-two, my age. But I guess I'm what
I feel and see and hear, Harlem, I hear you:
hear you, here me—we two—you, me, talk on
    this page.
(I hear New York, too) Me—who?

Well, I like to eat, sleep, drink, and be in love.
I like to work, read, learn, and understand life.
I like a pipe for a Christmas present,
or records—Bessie, bop, or Back.
I guess being colored doesn't make me not like
the same things other folks like who are other
    races.
So will my page be colored that I write?
Being me, it will not be white.
But it will be
a part of you, instructor.
You are white—
Yet a part of me, as I am a part of you.
that's American.
Sometimes perhaps you don't want to be a part
    of me.
Nor do I often want to be apart of you.
But we are, that's true!

As I learn from you
I guess you learn from me—
although you're older—and white—
and somewhat more free.

This is my page for English B.

Source: Langston Hughes, "Theme for English B" from *Collected Poems.* Copyright © 1994 by the estate of Langston Hughes. Reprinted by permission of Alfred A. Knopf, Inc.

HARLEM

Langston Hughes
1902–67

What happens to a dream deferred?

Does it dry up
like a raisin in the sun?
Or fester like a sore—
And then run?
Does it stink like rotten meat?
Or crust and sugar over—
like a syrupy sweet?

Maybe it just sags
like a heavy load.

Or does it explode?

Source: Langston Hughes, "Harlem" Copyright ©
1951 Langston Hughes. Reprinted from *The Panther
and the Lash* by permission of Alfred A. Knopf, Inc.

BIOGRAPHY

GOD BROUGHT ME SAFE

John Wesley
1703–1791

[Oct. 1743.]

Thur. 20—After preaching to a small, attentive congregation, I rode to Wednesbury. At
twelve I preached in a ground near the middle
of the town to a far larger congregation than
was expected, on "Jesus Christ, the same yes-
terday, and to-day, and for ever." I believe every
one present felt the power of God; and no creature offered to molest us, either going or coming; but the Lord fought for us, and we held our
peace.

I was writing at Francis Ward's in the afternoon when the cry arose that the mob had be-
set the house. We prayed that God would dis-
perse them, and it was so. One went this way,
and another that; so that, in half an hour, not a
man was left. I told our brethren, "Now is the
time for us to go"; but they pressed me ex-
ceedingly to stay; so, that I might not offend
them, I sat down, though I foresaw what would
follow. Before five the mob surrounded the
house again in greater numbers than ever. The
cry of one and all was, "Bring out the minister;
we will have the minister." I desired one to take
their captain by the hand and bring him into
the house. After a few sentences interchanged
between us the lion became a lamb. I desired
him to go and bring one or two more of the
most angry of his companions. He brought in
two, who were ready to swallow the ground
with rage; but in two minutes they were as calm
as he. I then bade them make way, that I might
go out among the people. As soon as I was in
the midst of them I called for a chair, and,
standing up, asked, "What do any of you want
with me?" Some said, "We want you to go with
us to the Justice." I replied, "That I will, with
all my heart." I then spoke a few words, which
God applied; so that they cried out with might
and main, "The gentlemen is an honest gentleman, and we will spill our blood in his defence." I asked, "Shall, we go to the Justice
to-night, or in the morning?" Most of them
cried, "To-night, to-night"; on which I went
before, and two or three hundred followed, the
rest returned whence they came.

The night came on before we had walked a
mile, together with heavy rain. However, on
we went to Bentley Hall, two miles from
Wednesbury. One or two ran before to tell Mr.
Lane they had brought Mr. Wesley before his
Worship. Mr. Lane replied, "What have I to do
with Mr. Wesley? Go and carry him back
again." By this time the main body came up,
and began knocking at the door. A servant told
them Mr. Lane was in bed. His son followed,
and asked what was the matter. One replied,
"Why an't please you, they sing psalms all day;
nay, and make folks rise at five in the morning.
And what would your Worship advise us to

do?" "To go home," said Mr. Lane, "and be quiet."

Here they were at a full stop, till one advised to go to Justice Persehouse at Walsall. All agreed to this; so we hastened on, and about seven came to his house. But Mr. P likewise sent word that he was in bed. Now they were at a stand again: but at last they all thought it the wisest course to make the best of their way home. About fifty of them undertook to convoy me. But we had not gone a hundred yards when the mob of Walsall came, pouring in like a flood, and bore down all before them. The Darlaston mob made what defense they could; but they were weary, as well as outnumbered; so that in a short time, many being knocked down, the rest ran away, and left me in their hands.

To attempt speaking was vain, for the noise on every side was like the roaring of the sea. So they dragged me along till we came to the town, where, seeing the door of a large house open, I attempted to go in; but a man, catching me by the hair, pulled me back into the middle of the mob. They made no more stop till they had carried me through the main street, from one end of the town to the other. I continued speaking all the time to those within hearing, feeling no pain or weariness. At the west end of the town, seeing a door half open, I made toward it, and would have gone in, but a gentleman in the shop would not suffer me, saying they would pull the house down to the ground. However, I stood at the door and asked, "Are you willing to hear me speak?" Many cried out, "No, no! knock his brains out; down with him; kill him at once." Others said, "Nay, but we will hear him first." I began asking, "What evil have I done? Which of you all have I wronged in word or deed?" and continued speaking for above a quarter of an hour, till my voice suddenly failed. Then the floods began to lift up their voice again, many crying out, "Bring him away! Bring him away!"

In the meantime my strength and my voice returned, and I broke out aloud into prayer. And now the man who had just before headed the mob turned and said, "Sir, I will spend my life for you: follow me, and not one soul here shall touch a hair of your head." Two or three of his fellows confirmed his words, and got close to me immediately. At the same time, the gentleman in the shop cried out, "For shame, for shame! Let him go." An honest butcher, who was a little farther off, said it was a shame they should do thus; and pulled back four or five, one after another, who were running on the most fiercely. The people then, as if it had been by common consent, fell to the right and left; while those three or four men took me between them, and carried me through them all. But on the bridge the mob rallied again: we therefore went on one side over the milldam, and thence through the meadows, till, a little before ten, God brought me safe to Wednesbury, having lost only one flap of my waistcoat and a little skin from one of my hands.

ESSAY

THE BENEFITS OF LUXURY, IN MAKING A PEOPLE MORE WISE AND HAPPY

Oliver Goldsmith
1730?–1774

From such a picture of nature in primeval simplicity, tell me, my much respected friend, are you in love with fatigue and solitude? Do you sigh for the severe frugality of the wandering Tartar, or regret being born amidst the luxury and dissimulation of the polite? Rather tell me, has not every kind of life vices peculiarly its own? Is it not a truth, that refined countries have more vices, but those not so terrible; barbarous nations few, and they of the most hideous complexion? Perfidy and fraud are the vices of civilized nations, credulity and violence those of the inhabitants of the desert. Does the luxury of the one produce half the evils of the inhumanity of the other? Certainly those philosophers who declaim against luxury have but little understood its benefits; they seem insensible, that to luxury we owe not only the greatest part of our knowledge, but even of our virtues.

It may sound fine in the mouth of a declaimer, when he talks of subduing our appetites, of teaching every sense to be content with a bare sufficiency, and of supplying only the wants of nature; but is there not more satisfaction in indulging those appetites, if with innocence and safety, than in restraining them? Am not I better pleased in enjoyment than in the sullen satisfaction of thinking that I can live without enjoyment? The more various our artificial necessities, the wider is our circle of pleasure; for all pleasure consists in obviating necessities as they rise: luxury, therefore as it increases our wants, increases our capacity for happiness.

Examine the history of any country remarkable for opulence and wisdom, you will find they would never have been wise had they not been first luxurious; you will find poets, philosophers, and even patriots, marching in luxury's train. The reason is obvious: we then only are curious after knowledge, when we find it connected with sensual happiness. The senses ever point out the way, and reflection comments upon the discovery. Inform a native of the desert of Kobi, of the exact measure of the parallax of the moon, he finds no satisfaction at all in the information; he wonders how any could take such pains, and lay out such treasures, in order to solve so useless a difficulty: but connect it with his happiness, by showing that it improves navigation, that by such an investigation he may have a warmer coat, a better gun, or a finer knife, and he is instantly in raptures at so great an improvement. In short, we only desire to know what we desire to possess; and whatever we may talk against it, luxury adds the spur to curiosity, and gives us a desire to becoming more wise.

But not our knowledge only, but our virtues are improved by luxury. Observe the brown savage of Thibet, to whom the fruits of the spreading pomegranate supply food, and its branches are habitation. Such a character has few vices, I grant, but those he has are of the most hideous nature: rapine and cruelty are scarcely crimes in his eye; neither pity nor tenderness, which ennoble every virtue, have any place in his heart; he hates his enemies, and kills those he subdues. On the other hand, the polite Chinese and civilized European seem even to love their enemies. I have just now seen an instance where the English have succoured those enemies, whom their own countrymen actually refused to relieve.

The greater the luxuries of every country, the more closely, politically speaking, is that country united. Luxury is the child of society alone; the luxurious man stands in need of a thousand different artists to furnish out his happiness; it is more likely, therefore, that he should be a good citizen who is connected by motives of self-interest with so many, than the abstemious man who is united to none.

In whatsoever light, therefore, we consider luxury, whether as employing a number of hands naturally too feeble for more laborious employment; as finding a variety of occupation for others who might be totally idle; or as furnishing our new inlets to happiness, without encroaching on mutual property; in whatever light we regard it, we shall have reason to stand up in its defence, and the sentiment of Confucius still remains unshaken: *that we should enjoy as many of the luxuries of life as are consistent with our own safety, and the prosperity of others; and that he who finds out a new pleasure is one of the most useful members of society.*

CHRONOLOGY OF SELECTED MAJOR PERIODS AND EXAMPLES FOR STUDY IN WESTERN LITERATURE

Prehistory–350 A.D.

Mesopotamia
  Gilgamesh Epic
  The Bible
Ancient Greece
  Homer: *The Iliad*
  Plato: *Dialogues*
  Aristotle: *Poetics*
Rome
  Virgil: *Aeneid*
  Horace: *The Art of Poetry*

c. 300–1400

The Early Middle Ages
  Beowulf
  Song of Roland
  Niberlungenlied
The Late Middle Ages
  Anon.: *The Lay of the Little Bird*
  Dante: *The Divine Comedy*
  Geoffrey Chaucer: *Canterbury Tales*

c. 1400–1525

The Early and High Renaissance
  Giovanni Boccaccio: *Decameron*
  Niccolò Machiavelli: *The Prince*

c. 1525–1750

The Late Renaissance and the Baroque Age
  Michel de Montaigne: *Essays*
  Christopher Marlowe: *The Tragical History of Doctor Faustus*
  Miguel de Cervantes Saavedra: *Don Quixote*

John Donne: *Of the Progress of the Soul*
Jonathan Swift: *A Modest Proposal*

c. 1700–1800

The Enlightenment
  Voltaire: *Candide*
  Samuel Johnson: *Idler Essays*
  Johann Gottfried von Herder: *Ideas for a Philosophy of the History of Mankind*

1800–1900

The Age of Industry
  Johann Wolfgang von Goethe: *Faust*
  Samuel Taylor Coleridge: *Rime of the Ancient Mariner*
  William Wordsworth: *Tintern Abbey*
  Lord Byron: *Don Juan*
  Fedor Mikhalovich Dostoevski: *The Peasant Marey*
  Herman Melville: *Benito Cereno*
  Guy de Maupassant: *Love*

c. 1900–

T. S. Eliot: *The Wasteland*
André Gide: *The Counterfeiters*
William Faulkner: *A Rose for Emily*
W. H. Auden: *Poems*
Langston Hughes: *Theme for English B; Harlem*
Flannery O'Connor: *Revelation*
Gayl Jones: *Corregidora*
Paula Gunn Allen: *Recuerdo*
Alice Walker: *The Color Purple*
Yasunari Kawabata: *Snow Country*
Alexander Solzhenitsyn: *One Day in the Life of Ivan Denisovich*

Afterword

Little needs to be said by way of summary to this text, except to draw attention to what has *not* been included. We have not dealt much with philosophy of art or literature; only in passing have we noted art and literary history. Above all, we have not even covered completely the technical information that was our focus. We have covered only the basic skeleton. Although we have attempted to remain as neutral as possible in presenting information about each of the disciplines, there is no denying that subjectivity is present. The method of treatment was arbitrary, as was the choice of information presented. You may find such a technical approach sterile and disturbing. As indicated earlier, however, these pages should be viewed only as an introduction. The real life, the enthusiasm, the enjoyment, and the meaning of the arts and literature depend on what happens next. If, through the information presented in these pages, you have found a new appreciation for a form that was previously an enigma, or have found a means by which your previous knowledge has been enlarged, then this book has achieved its goal.

Finally, it should be obvious, and it will become obvious, that not every definition of every term is uniformly agreed on by artists themselves. Words serve only as a convenience for us as we try in some way to cope with what we see and what we hear, how and why we react as we do to those experiences, and how and why we try to share them with others. It may not be possible to understand the *whats* and the *whys* of some works, such as totally abstract paintings or dance presentations. Sometimes the significance or the meaning must wait until we have passed the time barrier and become historians rather than journalists in our perception.

Glossary

A

ABA: in music, a three-part structure that consists of an opening section, a second section, and a return to the first section.

absolute music: music that is free from any reference to nonmusical ideas, such as a text or a program—for example, Mozart's Symphony No. 40 in G minor.

abstraction: a thing apart, that is, removed from real life.

accelerando: in music, a gradual increase in tempo.

accent: in music, a stress that occurs at regular intervals of time. In the visual arts, any device used to highlight or draw attention to a particular area, such as an accent color. See also *focal point*.

adagio: musical term meaning "slow and graceful."

additive: in sculpture, those works that are built. In color, the term refers to the mixing of hues of light.

aerial perspective: indication of distance in painting through use of light and atmosphere.

aesthetic distance: combination of mental and physical factors that provides the proper separation between a viewer and an artwork; it enables the viewer to achieve a desired response. See *detachment*.

affective: relating to feelings or emotions, as opposed to facts. See *cognitive.*

aleatory: deliberate incorporation of chance in the composition, whether using chance methods to determine one or more elements or allowing performers to utilize chance variations in performing the work.

allegretto: musical term denoting a lively tempo, but one slower than allegro.

allegro: musical term meaning brisk or lively.

alliteration: sound structure in which an initial sound is repeated for effect.

alto: in music, the lowest female voice.

andante: musical term meaning a medium, leisurely, walking tempo.

andantino: musical term meaning a tempo a little faster than andante.

appoggiatura: in music, an ornamental note or series of notes above and below a tone of a chord.

aquatint: intaglio printmaking process in which the plate is treated with a resin substance to create textured tonal areas.

arabesque: classical ballet pose in which the body is supported on one leg, and the other leg is extended behind with the knee straight.

arcade: series of arches placed side by side.

arch: in architecture, a structural system in which space is spanned by a curved member supported by two legs.

aria: in opera or oratorio, a highly dramatic melody for a single voice.

articulation: connection of the parts of an artwork.

art song: vocal musical composition in which the text is the principal focus. See *song cycle.*

assemblé: in ballet, a leap with one foot brushing the floor at the moment of the leap and both feet coming together in fifth position at the finish.

assonance: sound structure employing a similarity among vowels but not consonants.

atonality: avoidance or tendency to avoid tonal centers in musical composition.

B

balletomane: term used by ballet enthusiasts to refer to themselves. A combination of *ballet* and *mania.*

balloon construction: construction of wood using a skeletal framework. See *skeleton frame.*

baroque: seventeenth- and eighteenth-century style of art, architecture, and music that is highly ornamental.

barre: wooden railing used by dancers to maintain balance while practicing.

barrel vault (tunnel vault): series of arches placed back to back to enclose space.

battement jeté: ballet movement using a small brush kick with the toe sliding on the floor until the foot is fully extended about 2 inches off the floor.

bearing wall: construction in which the wall supports itself, the roof, and floors. See *monolithic construction.*

beats: in music, the equal parts into which a measure is divided.

binary form: musical form consisting of two sections.

biography: written account of a person's life.

biomorphic: representing life-forms, as opposed to geometric forms.

bridge: in music, transitional material between themes or sections of a composition.

C

cadence: in music, the specific harmonic arrangement that indicates the closing of a phrase.

camera pan: turning of the camera from one side to the other to follow the movement of a subject.

canon: musical composition in which each voice imitates the theme in counterpoint.

cantilever: architectural structural system in which an overhanging beam is supported only at one end.

capital: transition between the top of a column and the lintel.

chaîné: series of spinning turns in ballet utilizing a half turn of the body on each step.

chamber music: vocal or instrumental music suitable for performance in small rooms.

changement de pied: in ballet, a small jump in which the positions of the feet are reversed.

character oxfords: shoes worn by dancers that look like ordinary street shoes, but are actually specially constructed for dance.

chiaroscuro: light and shade. In painting, the use of highlight and shadow to give the appearance of three-dimensionality to two-dimensional forms. In theatre, the use of light to enhance the plasticity of the human body or the elements of scenery.

chord: three or more musical tones played at the same time.

choreography: composition of a dance work; the arrangement of patterns of movement in dance.

chromatic scale: musical scale consisting of half steps.

cinematic motif: in film, a visual image that is repeated either in identical form or in variation.

cinema verité: candid camera; a televisionlike technique of recording life and people as they are. The hand-held camera, natural sound, and minimal editing are characteristic.

classic: specifically referring to Greek art of the fifth century B.C.

classical: adhering to traditional standards. May refer to Greek and Roman art or any art in which simplicity, clarity of structure, and appeal to the intellect are fundamental.

coda: passage added to the end of a musical composition to produce a satisfactory close.

cognitive: facts and objectivity as opposed to emotions and subjectivity. See *affective*.

collography: printmaking process utilizing assorted objects glued to a board or plate.

composition: arrangement of line, form, mass, and color in a work of art.

conjunct melody: in music, a melody compromising notes close together in the scale.

consonance: the feeling of a comfortable relationship between elements of a composition, in pictures, sculpture, music, theatre, dance, or architecture. Consonance may be both physical and cultural in its ramifications.

conventions: customs or accepted underlying principles of an art, such as the willing suspension of disbelief in the theatre.

Corinthian: specific order of Greek column employing an elaborate leaf motif in the capital.

corps de ballet: chorus of a ballet ensemble.

counterpoint: in music, two or more independent melodies played in opposition to each other at the same time.

crescendo: an increase in loudness.

crosscutting: in film, alternation between two independent actions that are related thematically or by plot to give the impression of simultaneous occurrence.

curvilinear: formed or characterized by curved line.

cutting: the trimming and joining that occurs during the process of editing film.

cutting within the frame: changing the viewpoint of the camera within a shot by moving from a long or medium shot to a close-up, without cutting the film.

D

decrescendo: decrease in loudness.

demi-hauteur: ballet pose with the leg positioned at a 45-degree angle to the ground.

demi-plié: in ballet, a half bend of the knees in any of the five positions.

denouement: section of a play's structure in which events are brought to a conclusion.

detachment: intellectual as opposed to emotional involvement. The opposite of *empathy*.

diatonic minor: standard musical minor scale achieved by lowering by one half step the third and sixth of the diatonic or standard major scale.

disjunct melody: in music, melody characterized by skips or jumps in the scale. The opposite of *conjunct melody*.

dissonance: occurrence of inharmonious elements in music or the other arts. The opposite of *consonance*.

divertissement: dance, or a portion thereof, intended as a diversion from the idea content of the work.

documentary: in photography or film, the recording of actual events and relationships using real-life subjects as opposed to professional actors.

dome: architectural form based on the principles of the arch in which space is defined by a hemisphere used as a ceiling.

Doric: Greek order of column having no base and only a simple slab as a capital.

drypoint: intaglio process in which the metal plate is scratched with a sharp needlelike tool.

dynamics: range and relationship of elements such as volume, intensity, force, and action in an artwork.

E

eclecticism: style of design that combines examples of several differing styles in a single composition.

editing: composition of a film from various shots and sound tracks.

elevation: in dance, the height to which a dancer leaps.

empathy: emotional-physical involvement in events to which one is a witness but not a participant.

engraving: intaglio process in which sharp, definitive lines are cut into a metal plate.

en pointe: see *on point*.

entablature: upper section of a building; it is usually supported by columns, and includes a lintel.

entrechat: in ballet, a jump beginning from fifth position in which the dancer reverses the legs front and back one or more times before landing in fifth position. Similar to the *changement de pied.*

ephemeral: transitory, not lasting.

esprit d'escalier: French, meaning "spirit of the stairs." Remarks, thought of after the fact, that could have been *bon mots* had they been thought of at the right moment; witty remarks.

essay: short literary composition on a single subject, usually presenting the personal views of the author. Essays can be formal or informal.

etching: intaglio process in which lines are cut in the metal plate by an acid bath.

étude: a study; a lesson. A composition, usually instrumental, intended mainly for the practice of some point of technique.

F

farce: theatrical genre characterized by broad slapstick humor and implausible plots.

fenestration: exterior openings, such as windows and archways, in an architectural facade.

ferroconcrete: reinforced concrete that utilizes metal reinforcing embedded in the concrete.

fiction: literary work created from the author's imagination rather than from fact.

fluting: vertical ridges in a column.

focal point (focal area): major or minor area of visual attraction in picture, sculpture, dance, play, film, landscape design, or building.

foreground: area of a picture, usually at the bottom, that appears to be closest to the respondent.

form: shape, structure, configuration, or essence of something.

form cutting: in film, the framing in a successive shot of an object that has a shape similar to an image in the preceding shot.

forte: musical term meaning loud.

found object: object taken from life that is presented as an artwork.

fresco: method of painting in which pigment is mixed with wet plaster and applied as part of the wall surface.

fugue: originated from a Latin word meaning "flight." A conventional musical composition in which a theme is developed by counterpoint.

full round: sculptural works that explore full three-dimensionality and are meant to be viewed from any angle.

G

galliard: court dance done spiritedly in triple meter.

genre: category of artistic composition characterized by a particular style, form, or content.

geometric: based on patterns such as triangles, rectangles, circles, ellipses, and so on. The opposite of *biomorphic.*

Gestalt: a whole. The total of all elements in an entity.

glyptic: sculptural works emphasizing the qualities of the material from which they are created.

Gothic: style of architecture based on a pointed-arch structure and characterized by simplicity, verticality, elegance, and lightness.

gouache: watercolor medium in which gum is added to ground opaque colors mixed with water.

grande seconde: ballet pose with the leg in second position in the air.

grand jeté: in ballet, a leap from one foot to the other, usually with a running start.

grand plié: in ballet, a full bend of the knees with the heels raised and the knees opened wide toward the toes. May be done in any of the five positions.

grave: in music, a tempo marking meaning "slow."

groin vault: ceiling formation created by the intersection of two tunnel or barrel vaults.

H

harmony: relationship of like elements, such as musical notes, colors, and repetitional patterns. See *consonance* and *dissonance.*

homophony: musical texture characterized by chordal development of one melody. See *monophony* and *polyphony.*

hue: spectrum notation of color; a specific pure color with a measurable wavelength. There are primary hues, secondary hues, and tertiary hues.

I

icon: artwork whose subject matter includes idolatry, veneration, or some other religious content.

identification: see *empathy*

impasto: the painting technique of applying pigment so as to create a three-dimensional surface.

intaglio: printmaking process in which ink is transferred from the grooves of a metal plate to paper by extreme pressure.

intensity: the degree of purity of a hue. In music, theatre, and dance, that quality of dynamics denoting the amount of force used to create a sound or movement.

interval: difference in pitch between two tones.

Ionic: a Greek order of column that employs a scroll-like capital with a circular base.

iris: in film and photography, the adjustable circular control of the aperture of a lens.

isolation shot: in film, the isolation of the subject of interest in the center of the frame.

J

jeté: in ballet, a small jump from one foot to the other, beginning and ending with one foot raised.

jump cut: in film, the instantaneous cut from one scene to another or from one shot to another; often used for shock effect.

K

key: system of tones in music based on and named after a given tone—the tonic.

kouros: archaic Greek statue of a standing nude youth.

L

labanotation: system for writing down dance movements.

largo: in music, a tempo notation meaning large, broad, very slow, and stately movement.

legato: in music, a term indicating that passages are to be played with smoothness and without break between the tones.

lento: musical term indicating a slow tempo.

libretto: words, or text, of an opera or musical.

linear perspective: creation of the illusion of distance in a two-dimensional artwork through the convention of line and foreshortening—that is, the illusion that parallel lines come together in the distance.

linear sculpture: sculptural works emphasizing two-dimensional materials.

lintel: horizontal member of a post-and-lintel structure in architecture.

lithography: printmaking technique, based on the principle that oil and water do not mix, in which ink is applied to a piece of paper from a specially prepared stone.

M

magnitude: scope or universality of the theme in a play or film.

manipulation: sculptural technique in which materials such as clay are shaped by skilled use of the hands.

melodrama: theatrical genere characterized by stereotyped characters, implausible plots, and emphasis on spectacle.

melody: in music, a succession of single tones.

metaphor: figure of speech by which new implications are given to words.

mime: in dance or theatre, actions that imitate human or animal movements.

mise-en-scène: complete visual environment in the theatre, dance, and film, including setting, lighting, costumes, properties, and physical structure of the theatre.

modern dance: form of concert dancing relying on emotional use of the body, as opposed to formalized or conventional movement, and stressing human emotion and the human condition.

modulation: change of key or tonality in music.

monolithic construction: variation of *bearing-wall* construction in which the wall material is not jointed or pieced together.

monophony: musical texture employing a single melody line without harmonic support.

montage: in the visual arts, the process of making a single composition by combining parts of other pictures so the parts form a whole and yet remain distinct. In film, a rapid sequence of shots that bring together associated ideas or images.

motive (motif): in music, a short, recurrent melodic or rhythmic pattern. In the other arts, a recurrent element.

musique concrète: twentieth-century musical approach in which conventional and recorded sounds are altered electronically or otherwise and recorded on tape to produce new sounds.

N

neoclassicism: various artistic styles that borrow the devices or objectives of classic or classical art.

novel: prose narrative of considerable length which has a plot that unfolds by the actions, speech, and thoughts of the characters.

O

objective camera: camera position based on a third-person viewpoint.

objet d'art: French term meaning "object of art."

octave: in music, the distance between a specific pitch vibration and its double; for example, concert A equals 440 vibrations per second, one octave above that pitch equals 880, and one octave below equals 220.

on point: in ballet, a specific technique utilizing special shoes in which the dancer dances on the points of the toes.

opera bouffa: comic opera.

opus: single work of art.

overtones (overtone series): sounds produced by the division of a vibrating body into equal parts. See *sympathetic vibration.*

P

palette: in the visual arts, the composite use of color, including range and tonality.

pas: in ballet, a combination of steps forming one dance.

pas de deux: dance for two dancers, usually performed by a ballerina and her male partner.

pavane: stately court dance in ¾ time; usually follows a galliard.

pediment: typically triangular roof piece characteristic of the Greek and Roman style.

pendentives: curved triangular segments leading from the corners of a rectangular structure to the base of a dome.

perspective: representation of distance and three-dimensionality on a two-dimensional surface. See also *aerial perspective* and *linear perspective.*

photojournalism: photography of actual events that have sociological significance.

piano: musical term meaning "soft."

pirouette: in ballet, a full turn on the toe or ball of one foot.

plasticity: the capability of being molded or altered. In film, the ability to be cut and shaped. In painting, dance, and theatre, the accentuation of three-dimensionality of form through chiaroscuro.

platemark: ridged or embossed effect created by the pressure used in transferring ink to paper from a metal plate in the intaglio process.

poetry: literary work designed to convey a vivid and imagination sense experience through the use of condensed language selected for its sound and suggestive power and meaning, and employing specific technical devices such as meter, rhyme, and metaphor. There are three major types of poetry: narrative, dramatic, and lyric.

polyphony: see *counterpoint.*

port de bras: technique of moving the arms correctly in dance.

post-and-lintel: architectural structure in which horizontal pieces (lintels) are held up by vertical columns (posts); similar to post-and-beam structure, which usually utilizes wooden posts and beams held together by nails or pegs.

post-tensioned concrete: concrete using metal rods and wires under stress or tension to cause structural forces to flow in predetermined directions.

precast concrete: concrete cast in place using wooden forms around a steel framework.

presto: musical term signifying a rapid tempo.

prestressed concrete: see *post-tensioned concrete.*

program music: music that refers to nonmusical ideas through a descriptive title or text. The opposite of *absolute music.*

prototype: model on which something is based.

pyramidal structure: in theatre, film, and dance, the rising of action to a peak, which then tapers to a conclusion.

Q

quadrille: (1) an American square dance; (2) a European ballroom dance of the eighteenth and nineteenth centuries.

R

realism: artistic selection and use of elements from life; contrasts with naturalism, in which no artistic selection is utilized.

recitative: sung dialogue in opera, cantata, and oratorio.

rectilinear: in the visual arts, the formed use of straight lines and angles.

reinforced concrete: see *ferroconcrete.*

relevé: in ballet, the raising of the body to full height or the half height during the execution of a step or movement.

relief printing: process in printmaking by which the ink is transferred to the paper from raised areas on a printing block.

representational: objects that are recognizable from the real life.

requiem: mass for the dead.

rhyme: sound structure coupling words that sound alike.

rhythm: relationship, either of time or space, between recurring elements of a composition.

ribbed vault: structure in which arches are connected by diagonal as well as horizontal members.

ritardando: in music, a decrease in tempo.

rondo: form of musical composition employing a return to an initial theme after the presentation of each new theme.

ronds de jambe à terre: in ballet, a rapid semicircular movement of the foot in which the toe remains on the floor and the heel brushes the floor in first position as it completes the semicircle.

rubato: a style of musical performance in which liberty is taken by the performer with the rhythm of the piece.

S

saturation: in color, the purity of a hue in terms of whiteness; the whiter the hue, the less saturated it is.

scale: in music, a graduated series of ascending or descending musical tones. In architecture, the mass of the building in relation to the human body.

serigraphy: printmaking process in which ink is forced through a piece of stretched fabric, part of which has been blocked out—for example, silk-screening and stenciling.

short story: short fictional works of prose focusing on unity of characterization, theme, and effect.

skeleton frame: construction in which a skeletal framework supports the building. See *balloon construction* and *steel cage construction.*

song cycle: group of art songs combined around a similar text or theme.

sonority: in music, the characteristic of texture resulting from chordal spacing.

staccato: in music, the technique of playing so that individual notes are detached and separated from each other.

static: devoid of movement or other dynamic qualities.

steel cage construction: construction using a metal framework. See *skeleton frame.*

stereotype: standardized concept or image.

style: individual characteristics of a work of art that identify it with a particular artist, nationality, historical period, or school of artists.

stylization: reliance on conventions, distortions, or theatricality; the exaggeration of characteristics that are fundamentally verisimilar.

subjective camera: camera position that gives the audience the impression they are actual participants in the scene.

substitution: sculptural technique utilizing materials transformed from a plastic, molten, or fluid into a solid state.

subtractive: in sculpture, referring to works that are carved. In color, referring to the mixing of pigments as opposed to the mixing of colored light.

symbolism: suggestion through imagery of something that is invisible or intangible.

symmetry: balancing of elements in design by placing physically equal objects on either side of a centerline.

sympathetic vibration: physical phenomenon of one vibrating body being set in motion by a second vibrating body. See also *overtones.*

symphony: large musical ensemble; a symphony orchestra. Also, a musical composition for orchestra usually consisting of three or four movements.

syncopation: in a musical composition, the displacement of accent from the normally accented beat to the offbeat.

synthesizer (also called *Moog synthesizer*): electronic instrument that produces and combines musical sounds.

T

tempera: opaque watercolor medium, referring to ground pigments and their color binders such as gum, glue, or egg.

tempo: rate of speed at which a musical composition is performed. In theatre, film, or dance, the rate of speed of the overall performance.

terra-cotta: earth-brown clay used in ceramics and sculpture.

tessitura: general musical range of the voice in a particular composition.

texture: in art, the two-dimensional or three-dimensional quality of the surface of a work. In music, the melodic and harmonic characteristics of the composition.

theatricality: exaggeration and artificiality; the opposite of *verisimilitude.*

theme: general subject of an artwork, whether melodic or philosophical.

timbre: characteristic of a sound that results from the particular source of the sound. The difference between the sound of a violin and the sound of the human voice is a difference in timbre. Also called *tone color.*

toccata: composition usually for keyboard instrument intended to display technique.

tonality: in music, the specific key in which a composition is written. In the visual arts, the characteristics of value.

tondo: a circular painting.

tonic: in music, the root tone (*do*) of a key.

triad: chord consisting of three tones.

tunnel vault: see *barrel vault.*

tutu: many-layered bell-shaped crinoline skirt worn by a ballerina.

V

value (value scale): in the visual arts, the range of tonalities from white to black.

variation: repetition of a theme with minor or major changes.

verisimilitude: appearance of reality in any element of the arts.

virtuoso: referring to the display of impressive technique or skill by an artist.

vivace: musical term denoting a vivacious or lively tempo.

W

waltz: dance in ¾ time.

woodcut: relief printing executed from a design cut in the plank of the grain.

wood engraving: relief printing made from a design cut in the butt of the grain.

Bibliography

ABCARIAN, RICHARD, AND KLOTZ, MARVIN, eds., *Literature, the Human Experience*. New York: St. Martin's Press, 1986.

ANDERSON, DONALD M., *Elements of Design*. New York: Holt, Rinehart and Winston, 1961.

ARNHEIM, RUDOLPH, *Art and Visual Perception: A Psychology of the Creative Eye*. Berkeley: University of California Press, 1957.

———, *Film as Art*. Berkeley: University of California Press, 1967.

BACON, EDMUND N., *Design of Cities*. New York: Viking Press, 1967.

BAKER, BLANCHE M., *Theatre and Allied Arts*. New York: H. W. Wilson, 1952.

BATES, KENNETH F., *Basic Design: Principle and Practice*. New York: Funk and Wagnalls, 1975.

BAWDEN, LIZ-ANNE, ed., *The Oxford Companion to Film*. New York: Oxford University Press, 1976.

BEAM, P. C., *Language of Art*. New York: Wiley, 1958.

BLOOMER, CAROLYN M., *Principles of Visual Perception*. New York: Van Nostrand Reinhold, 1976.

BOBKER, LEE R., *Elements of Film*. New York: Harcourt Brace Jovanovich, 1969.

BORDWELL, DAVID, AND KRISTIN THOMPSON, *Film Art: An Introduction*. Reading, Mass.: Addison-Wesley, 1979.

BROCKETT, OSCAR, *The Theatre* (2d ed.). New York: Holt, Rinehart and Winston, 1969.

CANADAY, JOHN, *What Is Art?* New York: Knopf, 1980.

CHUJOY, ANATOLE, *Dance Encyclopedia*. New York: Simon & Schuster, 1967.

COLEMAN, RONALD, *Sculpture: A Basic Handbook for Students*. Dubuque, Iowa: William C. Brown, 1980.

COLLIER, GRAHAM, *Form, Space, and Vision*. Englewood Cliffs, N.J.: Prentice-Hall, 1972.

COOK, DAVID A., *A History of Narrative Film*. New York: Norton, 1981.

DAVIS, PHIL, *Photography*. Dubuque, Iowa: William C. Brown, 1979.

DEAN, ALEXANDER, AND LAWRENCE CARRA, *Fundamentals of Play Directing* (rev. ed.). New York: Holt, Rinehart and Winston, 1965.

ESSLIN, MARTIN, ed., *The Encyclopedia of World Theatre*. New York: Scribner's, 1977.

FAULKNER, RAY, AND EDWIN ZIEGFELD, *Art Today* (5th ed.). New York: Holt, Rinehart and Winston, 1969.

FULTON, ALBERT R., *Motion Pictures*. Norman: University of Oklahoma Press, 1960.

GESSNER, ROBERT, *The Moving Image: A Guide to Cinematic Literacy*. New York: Dutton, 1970.

GIANNETTI, LOUIS, *Understanding Movies* (2d ed.). Englewood Cliffs, N.J.: Prentice-Hall, 1976.

GILBERT, CECIL, *International Folk Dance at a Glance*. Minneapolis: Burgess, 1969.

GRAHAM, PETER, ed., *Dictionary of the Cinema*. London: Tantivy Press, 1964.

HALLIWELL, LESLIE, *The Filmgoer's Companion*. New York: Avon, 1978.

HATLEN, THEODORE, *Orientation to the Theatre* (3d ed.). Englewood Cliffs, N.J.: Prentice-Hall, 1981.

HEFFNER, HUBERT, *The Nature of Drama*. Boston: Houghton Mifflin, 1959.

HEYER, PAUL, *Architects on Architecture: New Directions in America*. New York: Walker and Company, 1966.

HICKOK, ROBERT, *Music Appreciation*. New York: Appleton-Century-Crofts, 1971.

HORNSTEIN, H., et al. *World Literature*. New York: Mentor, The New American Library, 1973.

JACOBS, LEWIS, ed., *Introduction to the Art of the Movies*. New York: The Noonday Press, 1960.

KASSLER, ELIZABETH B., *Modern Gardens and the Landscape*. New York: Museum of Modern Art, 1964.

KEPES, GYORGY, *Language of Vision*. Chicago: Paul Theobald and Company, 1951.

KERNODLE, GEORGE R., *Invitation to the Theatre*. New York: Harcourt Brace Jovanovich, 1967.

KNICKERBOCKER, K. L., AND RENINGER, H. WILLARD, *Interpreting Literature*. New York: Holt, Rinehart and Winston, 1969.

KNOBLER, NATHAN, *The Visual Dialogue*. New York: Holt, Rinehart and Winston, 1967.

MARTIN, JOHN, *The Dance*. New York: Tudor, 1946.

MILLER, HUGH, *Introduction to Music*. New York: Barnes and Noble, 1961.

MOORE, DOUGLAS, *Listening to Music*. New York: Norton, 1963.

MUNRO, THOMAS, *The Arts and Their Interrelationships*. New York: Liberal Arts Press, 1949.

NADEL, CONSTANCE, AND MYRON NADEL, *The Dance Experience*. New York: Praeger, 1970.

NEWMAN, WILLIAM S., *Understanding Music* (2d ed.). New York: Harper & Row, 1961.

OCVIRK, OTTO, ROBERT O. BONE, ROBERT E. STINSON, AND PHILIP R. WIGG, *Art Fundamentals* (4th ed.). Dubuque, Iowa: William C. Brown, 1981.

PARKER, OREN W., AND HARVEY K. SMITH, *Scenic Design and Stage Lighting* (2d ed.). New York: Holt, Rinehart and Winston, 1968.

PERKINS, V. F., *Film as Film: Understanding and Judging Movies*. New York: Penguin, 1972.

POLITOSKE, DANIEL, T., *Music*. (3d ed.). Englewood Cliffs, N.J.: Prentice-Hall, 1984.

PREBLE, DUANE, *We Create, Art Creates Us*. New York: Harper & Row, 1976.

_____, *Artforms*. New York: Harper & Row, 1978.

PURVES, FREDERICK, ed., *The Focal Encyclopedia of Photography*. London: Ford Press, 1965.

RASMUSSEN, STEEN EILER, *Experiencing Architecture*. New York: Wiley, 1959.

RENNER, PAUL, *Color, Order, and Harmony*. New York: Van Nostrand Reinhold, 1965.

SAYLOR, HENRY H., *Dictionary of Architecture*. New York: Wiley, 1963.

SCHNEIDER, ELISABETH, et al. *The Range of Literature*. New York: American Book Company, 1960.

SEIBERLING, FRANK, *Looking into Art*. New York: Holt, Rinehart and Winston, 1959.

SPORRE, DENNIS J., *The Arts*. Englewood Cliffs, N.J.: Prentice-Hall, 1984.

_____, *The Creative Impulse*. Englewood Cliffs, N.J.: Prentice Hall, 1987.

_____, *The Literary Spirit*. Englewood Cliffs, N.J.: Prentice Hall, 1988.

———, *Scene Design in the Threatre.* Englewood Cliffs, N.J.: Prentice Hall, 1990.

———, *Reality Through the Arts.* Englewood Cliffs, N.J.: Prentice Hall, 1991.

STEARNS, MARSHALL, AND JEAN MARSHALL, *Jazz Dance.* New York: Macmillan, 1968.

STEINBERG, COBBETT, *The Dance Anthology.* New York: Times Mirror, 1980.

STYAN, J. L., *The Dramatic Experience.* Cambridge: Cambridge University Press, 1965.

TRYTHALL, GILBERT, *Principles and Practice of Electronic Music.* New York: Grosset and Dunlap, 1973.

WIGMAN, MARY, *The Language of Dance.* Walter Sorrell, trans. Middleton, Conn.: Wesleyan University Press, 1963.

WITTLICH, GARY E., *Aspects of Twentieth-Century Music.* Englewood Cliffs, N.J.: Prentice-Hall, 1975.

Index